Other Books and Series by Jeff Bowen

Applications for Enrollment of Chickasaw Newborn Act of 1905
Volumes I thru VII

Cherokee Intermarried White 1906 Volume I thru X

Applications for Enrollment of Creek Newborn Act of 1905
Volumes I, II, III, IV, V & VI

Visit our website at **www.nativestudy.com** to learn more about these and other books and series by Jeff Bowen

APPLICATIONS FOR ENROLLMENT OF CREEK NEWBORN ACT OF 1905 VOLUME VII

TRANSCRIBED BY
JEFF BOWEN
NATIVE STUDY
Gallipolis, Ohio
USA

Other Books and Series by Jeff Bowen

1901-1907 Native American Census Seneca, Eastern Shawnee, Miami, Modoc, Ottawa, Peoria, Quapaw, and Wyandotte Indians (Under Seneca School, Indian Territory)

1932 Census of The Standing Rock Sioux Reservation with Births And Deaths 1924-1932

Census of The Blackfeet, Montana, 1897- 1901 Expanded Edition

Eastern Cherokee by Blood, 1906-1910, Volumes I thru XIII

Choctaw of Mississippi Indian Census 1929-1932 with Births and Deaths 1924-1931   Volume I
Choctaw of Mississippi Indian Census 1933, 1934 & 1937, Supplemental Rolls to 1934 & 1935 with Births and Deaths 1932-1938, and Marriages 1936-1938 Volume II

Eastern Cherokee Census Cherokee, North Carolina 1930-1939 Census 1930-1931 with Births And Deaths 1924-1931 Taken By Agent L. W. Page Volume I
Eastern Cherokee Census Cherokee, North Carolina 1930-1939 Census 1932-1933 with Births And Deaths 1930-1932 Taken By Agent R. L. Spalsbury   Volume II
Eastern Cherokee Census Cherokee, North Carolina 1930-1939 Census 1934-1937 with Births and Deaths 1925-1938 and Marriages 1936 & 1938 Taken by Agents R. L. Spalsbury And Harold W. Foght Volume III

Seminole of Florida Indian Census, 1930-1940 with Birth and Death Records, 1930-1938

Texas Cherokees 1820-1839 A Document For Litigation 1921

Choctaw By Blood Enrollment Cards 1898-1914 Volumes I thru XVII

Starr Roll 1894 (Cherokee Payment Rolls) Districts: Canadian, Cooweescoowee, and Delaware Volume One
Starr Roll 1894 (Cherokee Payment Rolls) Districts: Flint, Going Snake, and Illinois   Volume Two
Starr Roll 1894 (Cherokee Payment Rolls) Districts: Saline, Sequoyah, and Tahlequah; Including Orphan Roll Volume Three

Cherokee Intruder Cases Dockets of Hearings 1901-1909 Volumes I & II

Indian Wills, 1911-1921 Records of the Bureau of Indian Affairs Books One thru Seven;
Native American Wills & Probate Records 1911-1921

Other Books and Series by Jeff Bowen

Turtle Mountain Reservation Chippewa Indians 1932 Census with Births & Deaths, 1924-1932

Chickasaw By Blood Enrollment Cards 1898-1914 Volume I thru V

Cherokee Descendants East An Index to the Guion Miller Applications Volume I
Cherokee Descendants West An Index to the Guion Miller Applications Volume II (A-M)
Cherokee Descendants West An Index to the Guion Miller Applications Volume III (N-Z)

Applications for Enrollment of Seminole Newborn Freedmen, Act of 1905

Eastern Cherokee Census, Cherokee, North Carolina, 1915-1922, Taken by Agent James E. Henderson   Volume I (1915-1916)
Volume II (1917-1918)
Volume III (1919-1920)
Volume IV (1921-1922)

Complete Delaware Roll of 1898

Eastern Cherokee Census, Cherokee, North Carolina, 1923-1929, Taken by Agent James E. Henderson   Volume I (1923-1924)
Volume II (1925-1926)
Volume III (1927-1929)

Applications for Enrollment of Seminole Newborn Act of 1905 Volumes I & II

North Carolina Eastern Cherokee Indian Census 1898-1899, 1904, 1906, 1909-1912, 1914 Revised and Expanded Edition

1932 Hopi and Navajo Native American Census with Birth & Death Rolls (1925-1931) Volume 1 - Hopi
1932 Hopi and Navajo Native American Census with Birth & Death Rolls (1930-1932) Volume 2 - Navajo

Western Navajo Reservation Navajo, Hopi and Paiute 1933 Census with Birth & Death Rolls 1925-1933

Cherokee Citizenship Commission Dockets 1880-1884 and 1887-1889 Volumes I thru V

Copyright © 2012
by Jeff Bowen

ALL RIGHTS RESERVED
No part of this publication may be reproduced
or used in any form or manner whatsoever
without previous written permission from the
copyright holder or publisher.

Originally published:
Baltimore, Maryland
2012

Reprinted by:

Native Study LLC
Gallipolis, OH
www.nativestudy.com
2020

Library of Congress Control Number: 2020917992

ISBN: 978-1-64968-086-0

Made in the United States of America.

This series is dedicated to the descendants of the Creek newborn listed in these applications.

DEPARTMENT OF THE INTERIOR.

Commissioner to the Five Civilized Tribes.

NOTICE.

Opening of Land Office at Wewoka,
IN THE SEMINOLE NATION, INDIAN TERRITORY.

Notice is hereby given that on Monday, September 4, 1905, the Commissioner to the Five Civilized Tribes will establish a land office at Wewoka, in the Seminole Nation, Indian Territory, for the purpose of allowing citizens and freedmen of the Seminole Nation to select allotments of land for their minor children enrolled under the Act of Congress approved March 3, 1905 (33 Stat. L 1060), and for the further purpose of allowing citizens and freedmen of the Seminole Nation, whose allotments are incomplete, to select additional land in order to bring the value of their allotments up to the standard of $309.09, as nearly as may be practicable.

Each child whose enrollment in accordance with the Act of March 3, 1905, has been duly approved by the Secretary of the Interior, is entitled to receive an alllotment of forty acres without regard to the character or value of the land selected.

Selection of allotments for minor children must be made by their citizen or freedmen parents or by a duly appointed guardian, or curator, or by a duly appointed administrator.

TAMS BIXBY,
Commissioner.

Muskogee, Indian Territory,
July 29, 1905.

This particular notice makes mention of the Act of 1905. The Creek and Seminole were closely related tribes. Both tribes' notices were like similar in nature.

DEPARTMENT OF THE INTERIOR,
Commission to the Five Civilized Tribes.

Closing of Citizenship Rolls

OF THE MUSKOGEE OR CREEK NATION.

WHEREAS, on June 13, 1904, the Secretary of the Interior, under the authority in him vested by the provisions of the act of Congress approved March 3, 1901, (31 Stat., 1058) ordered that September 1, 1904, be and the same is hereby fixed as the time when the rolls of the Muskogee or Creek Nation shall be closed:

Notice is hereby given that the Commission to the Five Civilized Tribes will, at its office in Muskogee, Indian Territory, up to and inclusive of September 1, 1904, receive applications for the enrollment of citizens and freedmen of the Muskogee or Creek Nation, and that after that date the application of no person whomsoever for enrollment as a citizen or freedman of said nation will be received by the Commission.

Commission to the Five Civilized Tribes,
TAMS BIXBY, Chairman,
T. B. NEEDLES,
C. R. BRECKINRIDGE,
Commissioners.

Muskogee, Indian Territory,
June 25, 1904.

A notice like this was printed in newspapers and posted throughout Indian Territory.

INTRODUCTION

This series concerns Applications for Enrollment of Creek Newborn, National Archive film M-1301 (Act of 1905), as described in the National Archives publication *American Indians*. It falls under the heading Applications for Enrollment of the Commission to the Five Civilized Tribes, 1898-1914, M-1301 and is transcribed from microfilm rolls 414-419. This shows the application forms filled out by individuals applying for enrollment in the Five Civilized Tribes under the Dawes Commission. These applications contain additional information that wasn't abstracted to the census cards that you find in series M-1186. This particular roll (Creek by Birth) contains its own series of numbers separate from M-1186. To find each party's roll number you would have to reference M-1186. On July 25, 1898, there was an Indian Territory Division created in the Office of the Department of Interior. This division was created because of the increased work caused by what was called the Curtis Act, named after Senator Charles Curtis. Basically, this law stated that the tribal rolls needed to be descriptive and pointed out that each tribal roll was without description and had to be redone. At this point there was such a struggle among the Creeks to accept that the Government was going to change their way of life, again, that their leaders were refusing to cooperate in handing over their census information. The Commission had found that enrolling the Creeks was a difficult task not only because the Creek feared what was coming but also because their tribal structure was consistent with being a confederacy with forty-four different bands whose tribesmen lived in different towns of which each had a king that was supposed to keep track of their citizenry. The Commission reported that there was very little evidence of any census that existed and what there was had been kept carelessly. There were attempts and tribal conflicts along the way, but the Curtis Act would make it so they had to do it again no matter what effort from the past. In 1899, Agent Wesley Smith educated Washington to the fact that it was difficult to verify Creek eligibility. The acts passed by the Creeks themselves concerning enrollment since 1893 had been strewn amongst the archives of the Creek Council in Muskogee, I.T., and there was no provision ever approved for the printing of the those enrollments. There was confusion and difficulty let alone the fact that surnames were practically unknown among the Creek. But there was no confusion on March 9, 1905, when the Commission stated they would come to seven towns in the Creek Nation and accept applications that had to be made on a standardized blank form and contain a notarized affidavit from the mother and the attending doctor or midwife. A few by mail, but most of them were offered to a field party led by Commissioner Needles. The Commission took in applications for 2,410 children by the deadline of midnight, May 2, 1905.

This series contains applications and correspondence from 1,171 of those claimants. Realizing there were over 2,400 applicants originally, it is understood that not all were accepted. Also included are names of doctors, lawyers, mid-wives, and others who attended to the Creek Nation before and during this time in history.

Jeff Bowen
Gallipolis, Ohio
NativeStudy.com

Applications for Enrollment of Creek Newborn
Act of 1905 Volume VII

C 507

DEPARTMENT OF THE INTERIOR,
COMMISSION TO THE FIVE CIVILIZED TRIBES.
Holdenville, I. T., March 29, 1905.

In the matter of the application for the enrollment of Amos Lowry as a citizen of the Creek Nation.

LUCY LOWRY, being duly sworn, testified as follows:

Through Alex Posey Official Interpreter:

BY COMMISSION:
Q What is your name? A Lucy Lowry.
Q How old are you? A About 30.
Q What is your post office address? A Earlsboro, Oklahoma.
Q Are you a citizen of the Creek Nation? A Yes, sir.
Q To what town do you belong? A Tuckabatche.
Q Do you make application for the enrollment of your minor child, Amos Lowry, as a citizen of the Creek Nation? A Yes, sir.
Q Who is the child's father? A John Lowry.
Q Is he a citizen of the Creek Nation? A He is a Seminole.
Q Is he your lawful husband? A Yes, sir.
Q If it should be found that your child, Amos Lowry, is entitled to enrollment in either the Creek or Seminole Nations in which nation do you desire to have him enrolled? A In the Creek Nation.

---oooOOOooo---

I, D. C. Skaggs, on oath state that the above and foregoing is a full and true transcript of my stenographic notes as taken in said cause on said date.

DC Skaggs

Subscribed and sworn to before me this 20" day of July, 1905.

Edw C Griesel
Notary Public.

Applications for Enrollment of Creek Newborn
Act of 1905   Volume VII

Supplemental testimony taken.
DEPARTMENT OF THE INTERIOR.
COMMISSION TO THE FIVE CIVILIZED TRIBES.

IN RE APPLICATION FOR ENROLLMENT, as a citizen of the Creek Nation, of Amos Lowry, born on the 29 day of January, 1903

Name of Father: John Lowry   a citizen of the   Seminole   Nation.
Name of Mother: Lucy Lowry (nee Tiger)   a citizen of the   Creek   Nation.
Tuckabatche Town
                      Postoffice   Earlsboro, Okla.

AFFIDAVIT OF MOTHER.

UNITED STATES OF AMERICA, Indian Territory, }
    Western   DISTRICT.

Child is present

I, Lucy Lowry, on oath state that I am 30 years of age and a citizen by blood, of the Creek Nation; that I am the lawful wife of John Lowry, who is a citizen, by blood of the Seminole Nation; that a male child was born to me on 29 day of January, 1903, that said child has been named Amos Lowry, and was living March 4, 1905.

                                      her
                              Lucy x Lowry
Witnesses To Mark: mark
  { Alex Posey
    DC Skaggs

Subscribed and sworn to before me this 29 day of March, 1905.

                            Drennan C Skaggs
                            Notary Public.

AFFIDAVIT OF ATTENDING PHYSICIAN OR MID-WIFE.

UNITED STATES OF AMERICA, Indian Territory, }
    Western   DISTRICT.

                              my daughter
I, Josiah Tiger, a *(blank)*, on oath state that I attended on ^ Mrs. Lucy Lowry, wife of John Lowry on the 29 day of January, 1903; that there was born to her on said date a male child; that said child was living March 4, 1905, and is said to have been named Amos Lowry
                              his
                        Josiah x Tiger
                          mark

Applications for Enrollment of Creek Newborn
Act of 1905   Volume VII

Witnesses To Mark:
   { Alex Posey
     DC Skaggs

Subscribed and sworn to before me this 29 day of March, 1905.

                       Drennan C Skaggs
                       Notary Public.

NC. 507.

Muskogee, Indian Territory, July 18, 1905.

Commissioner to the Five Civilized Tribes,
      Seminole Enrollment Division,
           Muskogee, Indian Territory.

Gentlemen:

      March 31, 1905, application was made to the Commission to the Five Civilized Tribes for the enrollment of Amos Lowry, born January 29, 1903, as a citizen by blood of the Creek Nation. It is stated in said application that the father of said child is John Lowry, a citizen of the Seminole Nation, and that the mother is Lucy Lowry, an alleged citizen of the Creek Nation.

      You are requested to inform the Creek Enrollment Division as to whether application has been made for the enrollment of said Amos Lowry, as a citizen of the Seminole Nation, and if so, what disposition has been made of the same.

                       Respectfully,

                               Commissioner.

NC. 507.

Muskogee, Indian Territory, July 18, 1905.

Lucy Lowry,
      Earlsboro, Oklahoma Territory.

Dear Madam:

      In the matter of the application for the enrollment of your minor child, Amos Lowry, as a citizen of the Creek Nation, you are advised that this office requires further information in order to identify you as a citizen of said Nation.

Applications for Enrollment of Creek Newborn
Act of 1905   Volume VII

You are requested to furnish this office with your maiden name, the names of your parents, the Creek Indian Town to which you belong, and, if possible, the numbers which appear on your deeds to land in the Creek Nation, and any other information that will help to identify you as a citizen of the Creek Nation.

Respectfully,

Commissioner.

DEPARTMENT OF THE INTERIOR.
COMMISSION TO THE FIVE CIVILIZED TRIBES.

Muskogee, Indian Territory, July 19, 1905.

Chief Clerk,
    Creek Enrollment Division.

Dear Sir:

    Receipt is hereby acknowledged of your letter of July 14, 1905, (NC-507) stating that application was made to the Commission to the Five Civilized Tribes for the enrollment of Amos Lowry, born January 29, 1903, child of John Lowry, a citizen of the Seminole Nation, and Lucy Lowry, an alleged citizen of the Creek Nation, as a citizen by blood of the Creek Nation, and requesting to be informed as to whether an application was ever made for the enrollment of said Amos Lowry as a citizen of the Seminole Nation.

    In reply to your letter you are advised that it does not appear from an examination of the records of this office that any application was made to the Commission to the Five Civilized Tribes for the enrollment of said Amos Lowry as a citizen of the Seminole Nation.

Respectfully,

Tams Bixby Commissioner.

NC-507.

Muskogee, Indian Territory, August 8, 1905.

Lucy Lowry,
    Earlsboro, Oklahoma Territory.

Dear Madam:

Applications for Enrollment of Creek Newborn
Act of 1905   Volume VII

In the matter of the application for the enrollment of your minor son Amos Lowry as a citizen by blood of the Creek Nation this office is unable to identify you upon the final roll of citizens by blood of the Creek Nation from the evidence now on file.

In order that you may be identified you are requested to state the name under which you were finally enrolled, the names of your parents and other members of your family and your roll number as the same appears from your allotment certificate and deeds.

Please give this matter your prompt attention.

Respectfully,

Acting Commissioner.

Planters Trust Company
Capital $100,000

J.C. Chapman, President.
N.A. Gibson, Vice President.
W.S. Haston, Secretary.
C.D. Barnard, Treasurer.   Holdenville, I.T. Aug., 14, 1905.
R.M. McFarlin, Manager.
L.M. Miller, Interpreter.

Hon. Com. to Five Tribes.

Gentlemen:

Replying to yours[sic] N.C. 507 Will say the name under which I am alloted[sic] is Lucy Taylor, & my allotment is West 1/2 of SW 1/4 Sec. 16 and SE 1/4 of SE 1/4 Sec. 17. & homestead SW 1/4 of SW 1/4 Sec. 10 all in Township 6 North & Range 8 East. My father is Tarkosar Harjo & my mother was Lizzie Tiger (dec). The certified[sic] & Deeds are misplaced & cant[sic] give Roll No.

Yours &C[sic].

Lucy Taylor Lowery[sic].

Applications for Enrollment of Creek Newborn
Act of 1905   Volume VII

NC 507.

Muskogee, Indian Territory, November 12, 1906.

Chief Clerk,
    Seminole Enrollment Division,
        General Office,

Dear Sir:

    You are hereby advised that the name of Amos Lowry, born January 29, 1903, to John Lowry, an alleged citizen of the Seminole Nation, and Lucy Lowry, a citizen by blood of the Creek Nation, is contained in a schedule of New Born citizens by blood of the Creek Nation, approved by the Secretary of the Interior September 27, 1905, opposite Roll No. 507.

                Respectfully,

                              Commissioner.

BIRTH AFFIDAVIT.

DEPARTMENT OF THE INTERIOR.
COMMISSION TO THE FIVE CIVILIZED TRIBES.

IN RE APPLICATION FOR ENROLLMENT, as a citizen of the Creek Nation, of George Marks, born on the 11 day of August, 1902

Name of Father: John Marks	a citizen of the U.S. ~~Nation~~.
Name of Mother: Martha Marks	a citizen of the Creek Nation.
Eufaula Canadian Town.	

                      Postoffice   Holdenville, I.T.

AFFIDAVIT OF MOTHER.   Child present.

UNITED STATES OF AMERICA, Indian Territory,
      Western   **DISTRICT.**

    I, Martha Marks , on oath state that I am 28 years of age and a citizen by blood, of the Creek Nation; that I am the lawful wife of John Marks , who is a citizen, ~~by~~ *(blank)* of the United States Nation; that a male child was born to me on 11 day of August , 1902 , that said child has been named George Marks , and was living March 4, 1905.

                              Martha Marks

Applications for Enrollment of Creek Newborn
Act of 1905   Volume VII

Witnesses To Mark:
{

Subscribed and sworn to before me this 29 day of March, 1905.

Drennan C Skaggs
Notary Public.

AFFIDAVIT OF ATTENDING PHYSICIAN OR MID-WIFE.

UNITED STATES OF AMERICA, Indian Territory,
Western   DISTRICT.
}

assisted the physician who
I, Annie R Jackson, ~~a~~ *(blank)*, on oath state that I ^ attended on Mrs. Martha Marks, wife of John Marks ~~on the~~ sometime in ~~day of~~ August, 1902; that there was born to her on said date a male child; that said child was living March 4, 1905, and is said to have been named George Marks

Annie R Jackson

Witnesses To Mark:
{

Subscribed and sworn to before me this 29 day of March, 1905.

Drennan C Skaggs
Notary Public.

NC-509

DEPARTMENT OF THE INTERIOR,
COMMISSIONER TO THE FIVE CIVILIZED TRIBES.

Muskogee, Indian Territory, December 2, 1905.

In the matter of the application for the enrollment of Amos Yargee as a citizen by blood of the Creek Nation.

Cully Yargee, being duly sworn, testified as follows (through Jesse McDermott, Official Interpreter).

EXAMINATION BY THE COMMISSIONER:
Q What is your name? A Cully Yargee.
Q How old are you? A About 22.
Q What is your postoffice address? A Yeager.
Q Are you a citizen of the Creek Nation? A Yes sir.

Applications for Enrollment of Creek Newborn
Act of 1905   Volume VII

Q What is your father's name? A Tarmochee.
Q What is your mother's name? A Arnie Yargee.

The witness is identified as Cully Yargee on Creek Indian card, field No. 1682, opposite Roll No. 5394.

Q Have you a child named Amos Yargee? A Yes sir.
Q Living? A Yes sir.
Q When was he born? A The child was a little over two years old. I don't know when he was born, the names of his parents and whether or not he was living on March 4, 1905.
Q What is the name of the mother of this child? A Katie.
Q Is she your wife? A Yes sir.
Q What was her name before you married her? A Marsey.
Q What's the name of her father, do you remember? A Marsey; I don't know his other name.
Q Can you name any of his sisters? A Lumsey is her brother; Wisey his sister and Intie.

The mother of said child is identified as Katie Marsey, on Creek Indian card, Field No. 1552, opposite Roll No. 4986.

INDIAN TERRITORY, Western District.

I, J. Y. Miller, a stenographer to the Commissioner to the Five Civilized Tribes, do hereby certify that the above and foregoing is a true and complete translation of my notes as same appear in my stenographic report of this case.

JY Miller

Subscribed and sworn to before me
this the 5th day of December,
1905.   J McDermott
                                                        Notary Public.

BIRTH AFFIDAVIT.
DEPARTMENT OF THE INTERIOR.
COMMISSION TO THE FIVE CIVILIZED TRIBES.

IN RE APPLICATION FOR ENROLLMENT, as a citizen of the Creek Nation, of Amos Yargee, born on the 23 day of August, 1903

Name of Father: Cully Yargee   a citizen of the Creek   Nation.
Tuckabatche Town
Name of Mother: Katie Yargee (nee Marsey)   a citizen of the Creek   Nation.
Alabama Town
                        Postoffice   Holdenville, Ind. Ter.

Applications for Enrollment of Creek Newborn
Act of 1905   Volume VII

AFFIDAVIT OF MOTHER.   Child is present

UNITED STATES OF AMERICA, Indian Territory, }
       Western   DISTRICT.

I, Katy Yargee , on oath state that I am 25 years of age and a citizen by blood, of the Creek Nation; that I am the lawful wife of Cully Yargee , who is a citizen, by blood of the Creek Nation; that a male child was born to me on 23 day of August , 1903 , that said child has been named Amos Yargee , and was living March 4, 1905.

                                    her
                              Katy x Yargee
Witnesses To Mark: mark
 { Alex Posey
   DC Skaggs

Subscribed and sworn to before me this 29 day of March , 1905.

                              Drennan C Skaggs
                              Notary Public.

AFFIDAVIT OF ATTENDING PHYSICIAN OR MID-WIFE.

UNITED STATES OF AMERICA, Indian Territory, }
       Western   DISTRICT.

I, Anna Yargee , a midwife , on oath state that I attended on Mrs. Katy Yargee, wife of Cully Yargee on the 23 day of August , 1903 ; that there was born to her on said date a male child; that said child was living March 4, 1905, and is said to have been named Amos Yargee

                                    her
                              Anna x Yargee
Witnesses To Mark: mark
 { Alex Posey
   DC Skaggs

Subscribed and sworn to before me this 29 day of March, 1905.

                              Drennan C Skaggs
                              Notary Public.

Applications for Enrollment of Creek Newborn
Act of 1905   Volume VII

NC-509.

Muskogee, Indian Territory, August 5, 1905.

Katie Yorgee[sic],
    c/o Culley[sic] Yorgee,
        Holdenville, Indian Territory.

Dear Madam:

    In the matter of the application for the enrollment of your minor son Amos Yorgee as a citizen by blood of the Creek Nation this office is unable to identify you upon the final roll of citizens by blood of the Creek Nation.

    In order that you may be identified you are requested to immediately inform this office as to under which you were finally enrolled, the names of your parents, the Creek Indian town to which you belong and your roll number as the same appears upon your allotment certificate and deeds.

                      Respectfully,

                                  Commissioner.

(The letter below was apparently misplaced on the microfilm)

NBC 379

Muskogee, Indian Territory, January 2, 1907.

Mahoye Scott,
    Care of William Scott,
        Wetumka, Indian Territory.

Dear Madam:

    You are hereby advised that on December 18, 1906, the Secretary of the Interior approved the enrollment of your minor child, Lola Scott, as a citizen of the Creek Nation, and that the name of said child appears upon the roll of minor citizens by blood of the Creek Nation, enrolled Act of Congress approved April 26, 1906, as No. 324.

    This child is now entitled to allotment and application therefor should be made without delay at the Creek Land Office, Muskogee, Indian Territory.

                      Respectfully,

                                  Commissioner.

Applications for Enrollment of Creek Newborn
Act of 1905   Volume VII

NC. 510.

Muskogee, Indian Territory, July 14, 1905.

Commissioner to the Five Civilized Tribes,
    Cherokee Enrollment Division,
        Muskogee, Indian Territory.

Gentlemen:

    March 28, 1905, application was made to the Commission to the Five Civilized Tribes for the enrollment of Viola Anderson, born January 26, 1902, as a citizen by blood of the Creek Nation. It is stated in said application that the father of said child is Amos Anderson, a citizen of the Cherokee Nation, and that the mother is Jennie Anderson, identified as Jennie Miller, a citizen of the Creek Nation.

    You are requested to inform the Creek Enrollment Division as to whether application has been made for the enrollment of said Viola Anderson, as a citizen of the Cherokee Nation, and if so, what disposition has been made of the same.

    Respectfully,

    Commissioner.

REFER IN REPLY TO THE FOLLOWING:

DEPARTMENT OF THE INTERIOR,
COMMISSIONER TO THE FIVE CIVILIZED TRIBES.

Muskogee, Indian Territory, July 18, 1905.

Chief Clerk,
    Creek Enrollment Division,
        Muskogee, Indian Territory.

Dear Sir:

    Replying to your letter of July 14, 1905, (NC. 510) asking to be advised whether or not any application has ever been made for the enrollment, as a citizen of the Cherokee Nation, of Viola Anderson, a child of Amos Ander, a citizen of the Cherokee Nation, and Jennie Anderson, a citizen of the Creek Nation, you are advised that from an examination of the records of the Cherokee Enrollment Division it does not appear that any application has ever been made for the enrollment of said child as a citizen of that nation.

    Respectfully,

GHL   Tams Bixby   Commissioner.

Applications for Enrollment of Creek Newborn
Act of 1905 Volume VII

NC 510

Muskogee, Indian Territory, November 12, 1906.

Chief Clerk,
    Cherokee Enrollment Division,
        General Office.

Dear Sir:

    You are hereby advised that the name of Viola Anderson, born January 25, 1902, to Amos Anderson, an alleged citizen of the Cherokee Nation, and Jimmie[sic] Anderson, a citizen by blood of the Creek Nation, is contained in a schedule of New Born citizens of the Creek Nation, approved by the Secretary of the Interior September 27, 1905, opposite Roll No. 509.

                      Respectfully,

                                    Commissioner.

BIRTH AFFIDAVIT.

Department of the Interior,
COMMISSION TO THE FIVE CIVILIZED TRIBES.

    IN RE Application for Enrollment, as a citizen of the Creek Nation, of Viola Anderson , born on the 25 day of January , 1902

Name of Father: Amos Anderson   a citizen of the Cherokee   Nation.
Name of Father: Jennie Anderson (Miller?)   a citizen of the   Creek   Nation.

                      Post-office   Fort Gibson Ind Ter

AFFIDAVIT OF MOTHER.

UNITED STATES OF AMERICA,
    INDIAN TERRITORY,
    Western   District.

    I, Jennie Anderson, on oath state that I am 34 years of age and a citizen by blood , of the Creek Nation; that I am the lawful wife of Amos Anderson , who is a citizen, by Adoption of the Cherokee Nation; that a Female child was born to me on 25" day of January , 1902 , that said child has been named Viola Anderson, and is now living.

Applications for Enrollment of Creek Newborn
Act of 1905   Volume VII

Jinnie Anderson

WITNESSES TO MARK:

{

Subscribed and sworn to before me this 25" *day of* March , *1905.*

Wm D. McBride
NOTARY PUBLIC.

AFFIDAVIT OF ATTENDING PHYSICIAN OR MID-WIFE.

UNITED STATES OF AMERICA,
    INDIAN TERRITORY,
            District.

I, Sarah Varion , a midwife , on oath state that I attended on Mrs. Jennie Anderson , wife of Amos Anderson on the 25 day of January , 1902 ; that there was born to her on said date a Female child; that said child is now living and is said to have been named Viola Anderson

her
Sarah Varion x
mark

WITNESSES TO MARK:
{ Veldoni McBride
  HW Miller

Subscribed and sworn to before me this 25" *day of* March , *1905.*

Wm D. McBride
NOTARY PUBLIC.

NC-511

Muskogee, Indian Territory, August 8, 1905.

Mary Culler,
    c/o Thomas Culler,
        Yeager, Indian Territory.

Dear Madam:

It appear from your affidavit on file with the records of this office in the matter of the enrollment of your minor daughter Millie Culler that said child was born February 27, 1904, and from the joint affidavit of Hepsey McGirt and Coejagie Shipley that said child was born February 27, 1905.

Applications for Enrollment of Creek Newborn
Act of 1905   Volume VII

For the purpose of correcting this discrepancy as to the date of birth there is inclosed herewith a blank for proof of birth which has been partially filled out. You are requested to have the same executed taking care this time to insert the correct date of the birth of said child.

It also appears that on March 29, 1905 Thomas Culler appeared before the Commission to the Five Civilized Tribes and made application for the enrollment of his minor daughter Leah Culler, submitting his affidavit relative to the birth of said child, from which it appears that she was born on February 27, 1904. For the purpose of making proper proof of birth of this child there is inclosed herewith a blank for proof of birth. The affidavit of the mother of said child and the midwife who was in attendance at her birth should be supplied on said blank.

When the affidavits have been properly executed return them to this office in the inclosed envelope.

        Respectfully,

                Acting Commissioner.

CTD-32
Env.

THE YEAGER RECORD.
By W. R. CLAWSON.

        Yeager 12/27 05

The father & mother of Leah Culler desired me to inform you that Leah Culler was the name of their child. They state they have no child by the name of Millie.

        Very truly

          W R Clawson
          Notary Public

REFER IN REPLY TO THE FOLLOWING:
NC-511

DEPARTMENT OF THE INTERIOR,
COMMISSIONER TO THE FIVE CIVILIZED TRIBES.

        Muskogee, Indian Territory, December 13, 1905.

Mary Culler,
  Care of Thomas Culler,
    Yeager, Indian Territory.

Applications for Enrollment of Creek Newborn
Act of 1905   Volume VII

Dear Madam:

It appears from your affidavit on file with the records in this Office in the matter of the application for the enrollment of your minor daughter, Millie Culler, as a citizen by blood of the Creek Nation, that said child was born February 27, 1904, and from the joint affidavit of Hepsey McGirt and Coejagie Shipley that said child was born February 27, 1905.

For the purpose of correcting this discrepancy, there is herewith enclosed a blank form of birth affidavit, and you are requested to execute same, taking care to insert the correct date of the birth of said child and giving correctly all the other information. You should see that the notary public dates, signs and seals your affidavit and that of the midwife.

This matter should receive your prompt attention.

Respectfully,

Tams Bixby   Commissioner

REFER IN REPLY TO THE FOLLOWING:
NC-511

**DEPARTMENT OF THE INTERIOR,
COMMISSIONER TO THE FIVE CIVILIZED TRIBES.**

Muskogee, Indian Territory, December 13, 1905.

Mary Culler,
    Care of Thomas Culler,
        Yeager, Indian Territory.

Dear Madam:

It appears that on March 29, 1905, Thomas Culler appeared before the Commission to the Five Civilized Tribes and made application for the enrollment of his minor daughter, Leah Culler, as a citizen by blood of the Creek Nation, submitting his affidavit relative to the birth of said child, from which it appears that she was born February 27, 1904.

For the purpose of making proper proof of the birth of this child, there is herewith enclosed blank form of birth affidavit. The affidavit of the mother of said child and of the midwife who was in attendance at its birth should be supplied on this blank.

You are further requested to advise this Office whether or not Millie Culler and Leah Culler are one and the same child; and if so, whether the correct name of said child is Millie Culler or Leah Culler. This matter should receive your prompt attention.

Applications for Enrollment of Creek Newborn
Act of 1905 Volume VII

Respectfully,

Tams Bixby   Commissioner.

1 B A

DEPARTMENT OF THE INTERIOR.
COMMISSION TO THE FIVE CIVILIZED TRIBES.

IN RE APPLICATION FOR ENROLLMENT, as a citizen of the Creek Nation, of Millie Culler, born on the 27 day of February, 1904

Name of Father: Tom Culler	a citizen of the Creek	Nation.
Name of Mother: Mary Culler	a citizen of the Creek	Nation.

Postoffice   Yeager I.T.

AFFIDAVIT OF MOTHER.

UNITED STATES OF AMERICA, Indian Territory, }
  Western   DISTRICT.   }

I, Mary Culler, on oath state that I am Forty years of age and a citizen by blood, of the Creek Nation; that I am the lawful wife of Tom Culler, who is a citizen, by blood of the Creek Nation; that a female child was born to me on 27 day of February, 1904, that said child has been named Millie Culler, and was living March 4, 1905.

Mary Culler

Witnesses To Mark:
{

Subscribed and sworn to before me this Fifth day of April, 1905.

My Com Ex June 13 1908   W.R. Clawson
                                      Notary Public.

AFFIDAVIT OF ATTENDING PHYSICIAN OR MID-WIFE.

UNITED STATES OF AMERICA, Indian Territory, }
  Western   DISTRICT.   }

We I, Hepsey McGirt and Coejagie Shipley, a midwife, on oath state that we attended on Mrs. Mary Culler, wife of Tom Culler on the 27 day of February, 1905; that there was born to her on said date a female child; that said child was living March 4, 1905, and is said to have been named Millie Culler

Applications for Enrollment of Creek Newborn
Act of 1905   Volume VII

Witnesses To Mark:	her Hepsey x McGirt mark
{ George Yargee { WR Clawson	her Coejagie x Shipley mark

Subscribed and sworn to before me this 5 day of April, 1905.

My Com Ex June 13 1908   W.R. Clawson
                                                                    Notary Public.

BIRTH AFFIDAVIT.

DEPARTMENT OF THE INTERIOR.
COMMISSION TO THE FIVE CIVILIZED TRIBES.

IN RE APPLICATION FOR ENROLLMENT, as a citizen of the Creek Nation, of Leah Culler, born on the 27 day of February, 1904

Name of Father: Thomas Culler   a citizen of the   Creek   Nation.
Tuckabatche Town
Name of Mother: Millie Culler   a citizen of the   Creek   Nation.
Tuckabatche Town

Postoffice   Yeager, Ind. Ter.

AFFIDAVIT OF MOTHER.

UNITED STATES OF AMERICA, Indian Territory, }   Child is not present
        Western   DISTRICT.

I, Thomas Culler, on oath state that I am about 60 years of age and a citizen by blood, of the Creek Nation; that I am the lawful ~~wife~~ Husband of Millie Culler, who is a citizen, by blood of the Creek Nation; that a female child was born to me on 27 day of February, 1904, that said child has been named Leah Culler, and was living March 4, 1905. That the mother of the child is unable to appear personally to make application on account of illness.

                                                              his
                                                    Thomas x Culler
Witnesses To Mark: mark
{ Alex Posey
{ DC Skaggs

Subscribed and sworn to before me this 29 day of March, 1905.

                                                    Drennan C Skaggs
                                                         Notary Public.

Applications for Enrollment of Creek Newborn
Act of 1905   Volume VII

DEPARTMENT OF THE INTERIOR.
COMMISSION TO THE FIVE CIVILIZED TRIBES.

IN RE APPLICATION FOR ENROLLMENT, as a citizen of the Creek Nation, of Leah Culler, born on the 27 day of February, 1904

Name of Father: Thomas Culler   a citizen of the   Creek   Nation.
Name of Mother: Mary Culler   a citizen of the   Creek   Nation.

Postoffice   Yeager I.T.

AFFIDAVIT OF MOTHER.

UNITED STATES OF AMERICA, Indian Territory,
Western Jud   DISTRICT.

I, Mary Culler, on oath state that I am about 35 yrs years of age and a citizen by blood, of the Creek Nation; that I am the lawful wife of Thomas Culler, who is a citizen, by blood of the Creek Nation; that a female child was born to me on 27th day of February, 1904, that said child has been named Leah Culler, and is now living.

                     Mary Culler
Witnesses To Mark:

Subscribed and sworn to before me this 27th day of Dec., 1905.

My Com Ex June 13 1908   W.R. Clawson
                                 Notary Public.

AFFIDAVIT OF ATTENDING PHYSICIAN OR MID-WIFE.

UNITED STATES OF AMERICA, Indian Territory,
Western Jud   DISTRICT.

We I, Hepsey McGirt and Coejagie Shipley, a midwive[sic], on oath state that we attended on Mrs. Mary Culler, wife of Thom Culler on the 27 day of February, 1905; that there was born to her on said date a female child; that said child is now living and is said to have been named Leah Culler

                                       her
                     Hepsey McGirt   x
                                       mark

Applications for Enrollment of Creek Newborn
Act of 1905   Volume VII

Witnesses To Mark: her
{ WR Clawson   Coejagie Shipley   x
  L.L. Clawson   mark

Subscribed and sworn to before me this 27 day of December, 1905.

My Com Ex June 13 1908   W.R. Clawson
                                              Notary Public.

BA- 112, 209 & 210.

DEPARTMENT OF THE INTERIOR,
COMMISSION TO THE FIVE CIVILIZED TRIBES.
MUSKOGEE, INDIAN TERRITORY, March 28, 1905.

-ooOoo-

In the matter of the application for the enrollment of application for the enrolment of David, Minnie May and Clarinda Doyle, as citizens by blood of the Creek Nation.

WALLACE DOYLE, being duly sworn, testified as follows:

EXAMINATION BY COMMISSION:
Q What is your name? A Wallace Doyle.
Q How old are you? A 29.
Q What is your postoffice address? A Hitchita.
Q Have you any children? A Yes.
Q Name them? A David, Clarinda, Minnie May and Susie.
Q Who is the mother of these children? A Maude Doyle.
Q Is she a citizen of the Creek Nation? A No.
Q She is a non-citizen, is she? A Yes, sir.
Q When was David Doyle born? A I do not remember now.
Q Is he living? A No.
Q When did he die? A I do not remember just when he died.
Q How old was he when he died? A About four months old.
Q Can't you think what year he was born in? A No.--I believe it was '99
Q What month? A September 15th, I believe.
Q When did he die----you say he lived four months? A January 2nd.
Q The next year, 1900? A Yes.
Q When was Minnie may Doyle born? A She [sic] born 1903.
Q What month? A May.
Q What day? A I do not remember.
Q Is she living? A Yes.
Q Do you know how old she is not? A She will be two years old in May.
Q Who was the mid-wife in that case? A Mrs. Haley.

Applications for Enrollment of Creek Newborn
Act of 1905   Volume VII

Q Are you sure about that? A Let me see---
Q Who was Samantha Steen? A She is the same woman.
Q The same woman but by a different name? A Yes.
Q When was Clarinda Doyle born? A 1901, I think.
Q Do you know the month? A July 17th.
Q Is that child living? A Yes.
Q How old will that child be next July? A Next July she will be four years old.
Q Did you have the same mid-wife in that case that you had in Minnie May's? A We had Kate Dean.
Q Was Mrs. Haley or Samantha Steen there? A Yes.
Q When was Susie born? A January 22nd this year.
Q Is that child living? A Yes.

The records of the Commission examined and the name of Wallace Doyle is identified on Creek Indian Card, Field Number 1894, and his name is contained in the partial list of citizens by blood, approved by the Secretary of the Interior March 28, 1902, Roll Number 5971.

Zera Ellen Parrish, being sworn on her oath states that as a stenographer to the Commission to the Five Civilized Tribes she reported the above case and that this is a full, true and correct transcript of her stenographic notes in same.   Zera Ellen Parrish

Subscribed and sworn to before   Edw C Griesel
me this 28th day of March, 1905.   Notary Public.

BIRTH AFFIDAVIT.

DEPARTMENT OF THE INTERIOR.
COMMISSION TO THE FIVE CIVILIZED TRIBES.

IN RE APPLICATION FOR ENROLLMENT, as a citizen of the Creek or Muskogee Nation, of Susie Lee Doyle, born on the 23 day of January , 1905

Name of Father: Wallace Doyle   a citizen of the   Creek   Nation.
Name of Mother: Maud S Doyle   a citizen of the   U. S.   Nation.

Postoffice   Hitchita I.T.

Applications for Enrollment of Creek Newborn
Act of 1905   Volume VII

AFFIDAVIT OF MOTHER.

UNITED STATES OF AMERICA, Indian Territory,
   Western   DISTRICT.

I, Maud S. Doyle , on oath state that I am 21 years of age and a citizen ~~by~~ *(blank)* , of the United States ~~Nation~~; that I am the lawful wife of Wallace Doyle , who is a citizen, by Blood of the Creek Nation; that a Female child was born to me on 23 day of January , 1905, that said child has been named Susie Lee Doyle , and was living March 4, 1905.

Maud S Doyle

Witnesses To Mark:
{

Subscribed and sworn to before me this 24 day of March , 1905.

Joseph C. Morton
Notary Public.

My Commission Expires Feb 29-1908

AFFIDAVIT OF ATTENDING PHYSICIAN OR MID-WIFE.

UNITED STATES OF AMERICA, Indian Territory,
   Western   DISTRICT.

I, R. L. Haley a mid-wife , on oath state that I attended on Mrs. Maud S Doyle, wife of Wallace Doyle on the 23 day of January , 1905 ; that there was born to her on said date a Female child; that said child was living March 4, 1905, and is said to have been named Susie Lee Doyle

R L Haley

Witnesses To Mark:
{

Subscribed and sworn to before me this 24 day of March , 1905.

Joseph C. Morton
Notary Public.

My Commission Expires Feb 29-1908

BIRTH AFFIDAVIT.

Department of the Interior,
COMMISSION TO THE FIVE CIVILIZED TRIBES.

IN RE Application for Enrollment, as a citizen of the Creek Nation, of Minnie May Doyle , born on the 5th. day of April , 1903

Applications for Enrollment of Creek Newborn
Act of 1905   Volume VII

Name of Father: Wallace Doyle   a citizen of the   Creek   Nation.
Name of Father: Maud Doyle   a citizen of the United States ~~Nation~~.

Post-office   Hichita[sic], I.T.

AFFIDAVIT OF MOTHER.

UNITED STATES OF AMERICA,
   INDIAN TERRITORY,
  Western   District.

    I, Maud Doyle , on oath state that I am 21 years of age and a citizen by marriage , of the Creek Nation; that I am the lawful wife of Wallace Dolye[sic] , who is a citizen, by blood of the Creek Nation; that a female child was born to me on 5th. day of April , 1903 , that said child has been named Minnie May Doyle, and is now living.

                               her
                        Maud x Doyle
WITNESSES TO MARK: mark
  { *(Name Illegible)*
    A. J. Lacy

Subscribed and sworn to before me this 30 day of August , 1904.

                        David A Lee
                          NOTARY PUBLIC.
My Com Exp July 7 1906

AFFIDAVIT OF ATTENDING PHYSICIAN OR MID-WIFE.

UNITED STATES OF AMERICA,
   INDIAN TERRITORY,
  Western   District.

    I, Samantha Steen , a midwife , on oath state that I attended on Mrs. Maud Doyle , wife of Wallace Doyle on the 5th day of April , 1903 ; that there was born to her on said date a female child; that said child is now living and is said to have been named   Minnie May Doyle

                        Samantha Steen
WITNESSES TO MARK:
  {

Subscribed and sworn to before me this 30 day of August , 1904.

                        David A Lee
My Com Exp July 7 1906   **NOTARY PUBLIC.**

Applications for Enrollment of Creek Newborn
Act of 1905 Volume VII

BIRTH AFFIDAVIT.

DEPARTMENT OF THE INTERIOR.
COMMISSION TO THE FIVE CIVILIZED TRIBES.

IN RE APPLICATION FOR ENROLLMENT, as a citizen of the Creek Nation, of Clarinda Doyle, born on the 17 day of July, 1901

Name of Father:	Wallace Doyle	a citizen of the	Creek	Nation.
Name of Mother:	Maud Doyle	a citizen of the	U. S.	Nation.

Postoffice   Checotah, I.T.

AFFIDAVIT OF MOTHER.

UNITED STATES OF AMERICA, Indian Territory,
Western   DISTRICT.

I, Maud Doyle, on oath state that I am 21 years of age and a citizen ~~by~~ ~~(illegible)~~, of the United States ~~Nation~~; that I am the lawful wife of Wallace Doyle, who is a citizen, by blood of the Creek Nation; that a female child was born to me on 17 day of July, 1901, that said child has been named Clarinda Doyle, and was living March 4, 1905.

Maud S Doyle

Witnesses To Mark:
{ Wilford E Wood
{ Charles J Shields

Subscribed and sworn to before me this 24 day of Oct, 1905.

W. C. McAdoo
Notary Public.

My Com Exp Apr. 23-1907

AFFIDAVIT OF ATTENDING PHYSICIAN OR MID-WIFE.

UNITED STATES OF AMERICA, Indian Territory,
Western   DISTRICT.

I, Samantha Steen, a mid-wife, on oath state that I attended on Mrs. Maud Doyle, wife of Wallace Doyle on the 17 day of July, 1901 ; that there was born to her

23

Applications for Enrollment of Creek Newborn
Act of 1905   Volume VII

on said date a female child; that said child was living March 4, 1905, and is said to have been named Clarinda Doyle

         Samantha Steen

Witnesses To Mark:
{ Wilford E Wood
{ Charles J Shields

  Subscribed and sworn to before me this 24 day of Oct , 1905.

My Com Exp Apr. 23-1907   W. C. McAdoo
           Notary Public.

BIRTH AFFIDAVIT.

Department of the Interior,
COMMISSION TO THE FIVE CIVILIZED TRIBES.

IN RE Application for Enrollment, as a citizen of the Creek Nation, of Clarinda Doyle , born on the 17th day of July , 1901

Name of Father: Wallace Doyle a citizen of the   Creek   Nation.
Name of Father: Maud Doyle   a citizen of the United States ~~Nation~~.

      Post-office   Hichita[sic], I.T.

AFFIDAVIT OF MOTHER.

UNITED STATES OF AMERICA, ⎫
 INDIAN TERRITORY,   ⎬
  Western District. ⎭

  I, Maud Doyle , on oath state that I am 21 years of age and a citizen by marriage , of the Creek Nation; that I am the lawful wife of Wallace Doyle , who is a citizen, by blood of the Creek Nation; that a female child was born to me on 17th. day of July. , 1901 , that said child has been named Clarinda Doyle, and is now living.
            her
         Maud x Doyle
WITNESSES TO MARK: mark
{ *(Name Illegible)*
{ A. J. Lacy

  Subscribed and sworn to before me this 30 *day of* August , *190*4.

         David A Lee
My Com Exp July 7 1906   NOTARY PUBLIC.

Applications for Enrollment of Creek Newborn
Act of 1905 Volume VII

AFFIDAVIT OF ATTENDING PHYSICIAN OR MID-WIFE.

UNITED STATES OF AMERICA,
INDIAN TERRITORY,
Western District.

I, Samantha Steen , a midwife , on oath state that I attended on Mrs. Maud Doyle , wife of Wallace Doyle on the 17th. day of July. , 1901 ; that there was born to her on said date a female child; that said child is now living and is said to have been named Clarinda Doyle

Samantha Steen

WITNESSES TO MARK:

Subscribed and sworn to before me this 30 day of August , 1904.

David A Lee
NOTARY PUBLIC.

My Com Exp July 7 1906

BIRTH AFFIDAVIT.

DEPARTMENT OF THE INTERIOR.
COMMISSION TO THE FIVE CIVILIZED TRIBES.

IN RE APPLICATION FOR ENROLLMENT, as a citizen of the Creek Nation, of Minnie May Doyle, born on the 5 day of August , 1903

| Name of Father: | Wallace Doyle | a citizen of the | Creek | Nation. |
| Name of Mother: | Maud Doyle | a citizen of the | U. S. | Nation. |

Postoffice   Checotah, I.T.

AFFIDAVIT OF MOTHER.

UNITED STATES OF AMERICA, Indian Territory,
Western DISTRICT.

I, Maud Doyle , on oath state that I am 21 years of age and a citizen ~~by (illegible)~~ , of the United States ~~Nation~~; that I am the lawful wife of Wallace Doyle , who is a citizen, by blood of the Creek Nation; that a female child was born to me on 5 day of April , 1903, that said child has been named Minnie May Doyle , and was living March 4, 1905.

Maud S Doyle

Witnesses To Mark:
 Wilford E Wood
 Charles J Shields

25

Applications for Enrollment of Creek Newborn
Act of 1905   Volume VII

Subscribed and sworn to before me this 24 day of Oct , 1905.

                                    W. C. McAdoo
                                    Notary Public.

My Com Exp Apr. 23-1907

AFFIDAVIT OF ATTENDING PHYSICIAN OR MID-WIFE.

UNITED STATES OF AMERICA, Indian Territory, }
    Western   DISTRICT.

    I, Samantha Steen , a mid-wife , on oath state that I attended on Mrs. Maud Doyle, wife of Wallace Doyle on the 5 day of April , 1903 ; that there was born to her on said date a female child; that said child was living March 4, 1905, and is said to have been named Minnie May Doyle

                                    Samantha Steen

Witnesses To Mark:
  { Wilford E Wood
    Charles J Shields

Subscribed and sworn to before me this 24 day of Oct , 1905.

                                    W. C. McAdoo
                                    Notary Public.

My Com Exp Apr. 23-1907

NC-512.

                        Muskogee, Indian Territory August 8, 1905.

Maud S. Doyle
    c/o Wallace Doyle,
        Hitchita, Indian Territory.

Dear Madam:

    In the matter of the application for the enrollment of your minor daughter Susie L. Doyle as a citizen by blood of the Creek Nation it will be necessary, before the rights of said child as such citizen can be finally determined, for you to file with this office either the original or a certified copy of the marriage license and certificate showing marriage between you and Wallace Doyle the father of said child.

                              Respectfully,

                              Acting Commissioner.

Applications for Enrollment of Creek Newborn
Act of 1905   Volume VII

NC 512

Muskogee, Indian Territory, October 21, 1905.

Wallace Doyle,
    Hitchita, Indian Territory.

Dear Sir:

In accordance with your verbal request of this date, there is herewith returned to you your marriage license and certificate of marriage filed by you in the case of Susie Lee Doyle et al., applicants for enrollment as citizens by blood of the Creek Nation.

Respectfully,

Commissioner

AG-50

CERTIFICATE OF RECORD.

United States of America
Indian Territory   SS
Northern District

I, James A. Winston, clerk of the United States Court in the Northern District, Indian Territory, do hereby certify that the instrument hereto attached was filed for record in my office the 16 day of May 1898, at M and duly recorded in Book F, Marriage Record, page 489

Witness my hand and seal of said Court at Muscogee[sic] in said Territory this 17 day of May A D 1898

J A Winston Clerk

FILED

    May 15, 1898
    James A. Winston
        Clerk

I, Anna Garrigues, state on oath that the above and foregoing is a true and correct copy of the original.

Anna Garrigues

Applications for Enrollment of Creek Newborn
Act of 1905 Volume VII

Subscribed and sworn to before me this 21 day of October 1905

My Commission
Ex July 25" 1907

J McDermott
Notary Public.

MARRIAGE LICENSE

United States of America
Indian Territory   ss
Northern District

No. 1137

To any person authorized by law to solemnize marriage

Greeting

You are hereby commanded to solemnize the rite and publish the Banns of Matrimony between Mr. Wallace Doyle of Checotah in the Indian Territory, aged 22 years and Miss Maude Hailey of Checotah in the Indian Territory, aged 15 years, according to law, and do you officially sign and return this license to the parties therein named.

Witness my hand and official seal at Muscogee[sic], Indian Territory, this 12 day of May A.D. 1898

N.S. Young deputy

J.A. Winston
Clerk of the U.S. Court

(Seal)

CERTIFICATE OF MARRIAGE.

United States of America
Indian Territory   ss
Northern District

I, Young Poleman, a minister of the gospel do hereby certify that on the 14 day of May AD 1898 I did duly and according to law a commanded in the foregoing license, solemnize the rite and publish the Banns of Matrimony between the parties therein named.

Witness my hand this 14 day of May AD 1898

My credentials are recorded in the office of the clerk of the United States Court, Indian Territory, Northern District

Book A page 31
Central Division

Young Poleman
A minister of the Gospel

Applications for Enrollment of Creek Newborn
Act of 1905   Volume VII

D & BA. 11.

DEPARTMENT OF THE INTERIOR,
COMMISSION TO THE FIVE CIVILIZED TRIBES.
Yeager, I. T., December 9, 1904.

In the matter of the application for the enrollment of William McKane as a citizen by blood of the Creek Nation.

EPSEY McKANE, being duly sworn, testified as follows:

Through Alex Posey Official Interpreter:

BY COMMISSION:
Q What is your name? A Epsey McKane.
Q How old are you? A I do not know.

Witness appears to be about twenty-five years of age.

Q What is your post office address? A Yeager.
Q Are you a citizen of the Creek Nation? A Yes, sir.
Q To what town do you belong? A Tuckabatche.
Q Have you a child named William McKane? A Yes, sir, this is the boy. (indicating a small boy)
Q How old is William? A I think he is four years old.
Q Who is his father? A John McKane.
Q When was William born? A In July 19-- I don't know what year.
Q Are you positive that the child is four years old? A Yes, sir.
Q Who attended on you at the time this child was born? A There was no one present when the child was born?[sic]
Q Was your husband present? A Yes, sir.
Q Did you and your husband execute an affidavit relative to the birth of William?
A We executed an affidavit at Wewoka and sent it to the Commission.
Q When was that? A I think we executed the affidavit in May. The child at that time was not walking. I do not know what year it was.
Q Are the dates as given in that affidavit correct? A Yes, sir.
Q Do you remember the circumstances of the opening of the Creek Land Office?
A Yes, sir.
Q Was William born before the land office opened? A The child was not born at the time the land office opened. He was born afterward.
Q How long after? A The year after the opening of the land office.

The child is present and appears to be at least four years of age.

---oooOOOooo---

Applications for Enrollment of Creek Newborn
Act of 1905   Volume VII

I, D. C. Skaggs, on oath state that the above and foregoing is a full and true transcript of my stenographic notes as taken in said cause on said date.

D.C. Skaggs

Subscribed and sworn to before me this 20 day of December, 1904.

Edw C Griesel
Notary Public.

N.C. 513.

DEPARTMENT OF THE INTERIOR,
COMMISSIONER TO THE FIVE CIVILIZED TRIBES.
Muskogee, Indian Territory, February 9, 1906.

In the matter of the application for the enrollment of George McKan[sic] as a citizen of the Creek Nation.

Mitchell Compier being duly sworn, testified as follows through Alex Posey official interpreter.

Q What is your name? A Mitchell Compier.
Q What is your age? A Twenty five years, about.
Q What is your post office address? A Yeager.
Q Do you know John and Hepsey McGee? A Yes, sir.
Q Are they both living? A John is dead.
Q Were these people ever known by any other name than McGee? [sic] They are some times but not often called McGee but their correct name is McKan[sic].
Q Do you know how they are enrolled? A Enrolled as McKan I think.
Q What kin are you to John McKan? A He is my uncle.

On Creek Indian care No. 1628 the witness is listed along with his said uncle, John McKan, and Hepsey McKan. Said John and Hepsey McKan are on the final roll opposite Nos. 5238 and 5239, respectively.

Q What was Hepsey's name before she married? A Just Hepsey. She might have had a surname but I never heard it.
Q Have they another child enrolled here before this new born child, George McKan?
A Yes, they have one, William McKan.

Said William McKan, son of said John and Hepsey McKan, is enrolled opposite Creek Indian No. 9978.

Q Do you know their new born child George McKan? A Yes, sir.
Q Its correct name is McKan and not McGee? A Yes, sir.
Q Is it living? A Yes, sir.

Applications for Enrollment of Creek Newborn
Act of 1905   Volume VII

Q Do you know how old it is? A I don't know the age of the child.
Q We have here an affidavit executed by Hepsey under the name of McGee in which she says there was no midwife or physician in attendance at the birth of said child physician present at the birth of the child: It will be necessary that we have a new affidavit from said Hepsey, giving her correct name and the name of the child as McKan, if that is the correct name, and instead of the midwife we will have to have the affidavit of two disinterested witnesses.

I, Anna Garrigues, on oath state that the above and foregoing is a true and correct copy of my stenographic notes taken in said case on said date.

Anna Garrigues

Subscribed and sworn to before
me this 10 day of February 1906.

J McDermott
Notary Public.

Indian Territory)
)
Western District) SS

We, the undersigned, on oath state that we are personally acquainted with Hepsey McKan wife of John McKan that on or about the 22 day of June, 1903, a male child was born to them and has been named George McKan; and that said child was living March 4, 1905.
We further state that we have no interest in this case.

his
Robert x Shuder
mark

Lilla Harjo

Witnesses to mark:

W R Clawson

Mitchel Compier

Subscribed and sworn to before me this 15th day of Feb 1906.

WR Clawson

Applications for Enrollment of Creek Newborn
Act of 1905   Volume VII

BIRTH AFFIDAVIT.

DEPARTMENT OF THE INTERIOR.
COMMISSION TO THE FIVE CIVILIZED TRIBES.

IN RE APPLICATION FOR ENROLLMENT, as a citizen of the Creek Nation, of George McGee, born on the 22 day of June, 1903

Name of Father: John McGee	a citizen of the	Creek	Nation. Tuckabatche Town
Name of Mother: Hepsey McGee (nee Harjo)	a citizen of the	Creek	Nation. Tuckabatche Town

Postoffice   Holdenville, Ind. Ter.

AFFIDAVIT OF MOTHER.

UNITED STATES OF AMERICA, Indian Territory,	Child is present
Western	DISTRICT.

I, Hepsey McGee, on oath state that I am about 26 years of age and a citizen by blood, of the Creek Nation; that I am the lawful wife of John McGee, who is a citizen, by blood of the Creek Nation; that a male child was born to me on 22 day of June, 1903, that said child has been named George McGee, and was living March 4, 1905. That no one attended on me as midwife or physician at the birth of the child. me as midwife or physician at the birth of the child.

                                  her
                          Hepsey x McGee
Witnesses To Mark: mark
  { Alex Posey
  { DC Skaggs

Subscribed and sworn to before me this 29 day of March, 1905.

                          Drennan C Skaggs
                              Notary Public.

BIRTH AFFIDAVIT.

DEPARTMENT OF THE INTERIOR.
COMMISSION TO THE FIVE CIVILIZED TRIBES.

IN RE APPLICATION FOR ENROLLMENT, as a citizen of the Creek Nation, of George McKan, born on the 22 day of June, 1903

Applications for Enrollment of Creek Newborn
Act of 1905   Volume VII

Name of Father: John McKan   a citizen of the   Creek   Nation.
Name of Mother: Hepsey McKan   a citizen of the   Creek   Nation.

                              Postoffice   Holdenville, Ind. Ter.

AFFIDAVIT OF MOTHER.

UNITED STATES OF AMERICA, Indian Territory, }   Child is present
　　Western　　　　　　　　**DISTRICT.**

    I, Hepsey McKan, on oath state that I am about 26 years of age and a citizen by blood, of the Creek Nation; that I am the lawful wife of John McKan, deceased, who ~~is~~ was a citizen, by blood of the Creek Nation; that a male child was born to me on 22 day of June, 1903, that said child has been named George McKan, and was living March 4, 1905.

                                                               her
Witnesses To Mark: Hepsey x McGee
{ WR Clawson   mark
{ Mitchell Compier

    Subscribed and sworn to before me this 15th day of February, 1906.

                                              WR Clawson
My Commission Expires June 18th, 1908.   Notary Public.

COMMISSIONERS:
TAMS BIXBY,
THOMAS B. NEEDLES,
C.R. BRECKINBRIDGE,
W.E. STANLEY

DEPARTMENT OF THE INTERIOR,
COMMISSIONER TO THE FIVE CIVILIZED TRIBES.

REFER IN REPLY TO THE FOLLOWING:

B. A. 111

ALLISON L. AYLESWORTH,
    SECRETARY

ADDRESS ONLY THE
COMMISSION TO THE FIVE CIVILIZED TRIBES.
                          Muskogee, Indian Territory, November 19, 1903.

Hepsey McKane,
        Wewoka, Indian Territory.

Dear Madam:

    There is on file with the Commission an affidavit executed by you relative to the birth of your minor child, William McKane, who, it is claimed, is entitled to enrollment as a citizen of the Creek Nation. It is desired that further evidence be submitted in the case.

Applications for Enrollment of Creek Newborn
Act of 1905 Volume VII

You are therefore required to appear before the Commission at its office in Muskogee, Indian Territory, with two witnesses who know the date of the birth of said child, for the purpose of being examined under oath.

Respectfully,

Tams Bixby Chairman.

REFER IN REPLY TO THE FOLLOWING:

NC-513.

DEPARTMENT OF THE INTERIOR,
COMMISSIONER TO THE FIVE CIVILIZED TRIBES.

Muskogee, Indian Territory, August 8, 1905.

Hepsey McGee,
   C/O John McGee,
      Holdenville, Indian Territory.

Dear Madam:

On March 29, 1905 you appeared before the Commission to the Five Civilized Tribes and made application for the enrollment of your minor son George McGee, born June 22, 1903, as a citizen by blood of the Creek Nation, and at that time submitted your affidavit as to the birth of said child, from which it appears that there was no physician or midwife attended you at the birth of said child.

You are advised that it will be necessary for you to furnish, in lieu of the affidavit of the attending physician or midwife at the birth of said child, the affidavits of two disinterested persons relative to the birth of said child; said affidavits to set forth said child's name, the date of his birth, the names of his parents and whether or not he was living March 4, 1905.

In order that you may be identified upon the final roll of citizens by blood of the Creek Nation you are requested to state the name under which you were finally enrolled, the names of your parents and other members of your family and your final roll number as the same appears upon your allotment certificate and deeds.

This matter should have your prompt attention.

Respectfully,

Wm O. Beall
Acting Commissioner.

Applications for Enrollment of Creek Newborn
Act of 1905   Volume VII

NC-513

Muskogee, Indian Territory, December 13, 1905.

Hepsey McGee,
    Care of John McGee,
        Holdenville, Indian Territory.

Dear Madam:

    March 29, 1905, you appeared before the Commission to the Five Civilized Tribes and made application for the enrollment of your minor son, George McGee, born June 22, 1903, as a citizen by blood of the Creek Nation, and at that time submitted your affidavit as to the birth of said child, from which it appears that there was no physician or midwife in attendance on you at the birth of said child.

    You are again advised that it will be necessary for you to furnish this Office, in lieu of the affidavit of an attending physician or midwife, the affidavits of two disinterested persons relative to said child's birth, and a blank for this purpose is herewith enclosed.

    In order that you may be identified upon the final roll of citizens by blood of the Creek Nation, you are requested to write this Office at an early date, giving your maiden name, the names of your parents and other members of your family, the Creek Indian Town to which you belong, and, if possible, your name and roll number as same appears on your allotment certificate or deeds to land in the Creek Nation.

    This matter should receive your prompt attention.

        Respectfully,

                Commissioner.

Dis

HGH

REFER IN REPLY TO THE FOLLOWING:

**DEPARTMENT OF THE INTERIOR,
COMMISSIONER TO THE FIVE CIVILIZED TRIBES.**

Muskogee, Indian Territory, October 23, 1906.

Hepsey McKan,
    c/o John McKan,
        Holdenville, Indian Territory.

Dear Madam:

Applications for Enrollment of Creek Newborn
Act of 1905 Volume VII

You are hereby advised that the name of your minor child, George McKan, is contained in the partial list of citizens by blood of the Creek Nation, approved by the Secretary of the Interior October 15, 1906, and that a selection of land in the Creek Nation may now be made for him at the Creek Land Office in Muskogee, Indian Territory.
This matter should receive your prompt attention.

                              Respectfully,

                        Tams Bixby   Commissioner.

BIRTH AFFIDAVIT.

DEPARTMENT OF THE INTERIOR.
COMMISSION TO THE FIVE CIVILIZED TRIBES.

IN RE APPLICATION FOR ENROLLMENT, as a citizen of the Creek Nation, of Charlie Antion Adelhelm , born on the 1 day of March, 1905

Name of Father: William Adelhelm   a citizen of the United States Nation.
Name of Mother: Jennie Adelhelm (nee McGaslin) a citizen of the Creek Nation. Tulsa L.R. Town
                        Postoffice   Holdenville, Ind. Ter.

AFFIDAVIT OF MOTHER.
                                  Child present

UNITED STATES OF AMERICA, Indian Territory,
    Western   **DISTRICT.**

    I, Jennie Adelhelm , on oath state that I am about 37 years of age and a citizen by blood , of the Creek Nation; that I am the lawful wife of William Adelhelm , who is a citizen, by *(blank)* of the United States ~~Nation~~; that a male child was born to me on 1 day of March , 1905 , that said child has been named Charlie Antion Adelhelm , and was living March 4, 1905.
                                Jennie Adelhelm

Witnesses To Mark:
{

    Subscribed and sworn to before me this 29 day of March, 1905.

                          Drennan C Skaggs
                          Notary Public.

Applications for Enrollment of Creek Newborn
Act of 1905   Volume VII

AFFIDAVIT OF ATTENDING PHYSICIAN OR MID-WIFE.

UNITED STATES OF AMERICA, Indian Territory,
Western   DISTRICT.

I, Jno. W. Lowe , a physician , on oath state that I attended on Mrs. Jennie Adelhelm , wife of William Adelhelm on the 1 day of March , 1905 ; that there was born to her on said date a male child; that said child was living March 4, 1905, and is said to have been named Charlie Antion Adelhelm

Jno W. Lowe M.D.

Witnesses To Mark:
{

Subscribed and sworn to before me this 29 day of March, 1905.

Drennan C Skaggs
Notary Public.

BIRTH AFFIDAVIT.
DEPARTMENT OF THE INTERIOR.
COMMISSION TO THE FIVE CIVILIZED TRIBES.

IN RE APPLICATION FOR ENROLLMENT, as a citizen of the Creek Nation, of Chester Adelhelm , born on the 16 day of March, 1 two years ago

Name of Father: William Adelhelm   a citizen of the United States Nation.
Name of Mother: Jennie Adelhelm   a citizen of the   Creek   Nation.
L.R. Tulsa Town
                        Postoffice   Holdenville, I.T.

AFFIDAVIT OF MOTHER.
Child present

UNITED STATES OF AMERICA, Indian Territory,
Western   DISTRICT.

I, Jennie Adelhelm , on oath state that I am about 38 years of age and a citizen by blood , of the Creek Nation; that I am the lawful wife of William Adelhelm , who is a citizen, by *(blank)* of the United States ~~Nation~~; that a male child was born to me on 16 day of March , about 2 years ago 19*(blank)* , that said child has been named Chester Adelhelm , and was living March 4, 1905.

Jennie Adelhelm

Witnesses To Mark:
{

Applications for Enrollment of Creek Newborn
Act of 1905   Volume VII

Subscribed and sworn to before me this 29 day of March, 1905.

Drennan C Skaggs
Notary Public.

AFFIDAVIT OF ATTENDING PHYSICIAN OR MID-WIFE.

UNITED STATES OF AMERICA, Indian Territory, }
    Western   DISTRICT.

    I, Tillie Renfro , a mid-wife , on oath state that I attended on Mrs. Jennie Adelhelm , wife of William Adelhelm on the 16 day of March , 1903 ; that there was born to her on said date a male child; that said child was living March 4, 1905, and is said to have been named Chester Adelhelm

Tillie Renfro

Witnesses To Mark:
{

Subscribed and sworn to before me this 29 day of March, 1905.

Drennan C Skaggs
Notary Public.

NC-515.

Muskogee, Indian Territory, August 8, 1905.

May E. Posey,
    Wagoner, Indian Territory.

Dear Madam:

    In the matter of the application for the enrollment of your minor son William Edward Posey as a citizen by blood of the Creek Nation it will be necessary for you to file with this office either the original or a certified copy of the marriage license and certificate showing the marriage between you and Henry A. Posey the father of said child.

Respectfully,

Acting Commissioner.

Applications for Enrollment of Creek Newborn
Act of 1905   Volume VII

MARRIAGE LICENSE

United States of America
   Indian Territory   ss.   No. 393.
   Northern District

                                                                  (Copy)

To Any Person Authorized by Law To Solemnize Marriage--Greeting

     You are hereby commanded to solemnize the Rite and publish the Banns of Matrimony between Mr. Henry Posey of Wagoner, in the Indian Territory, aged 25 years, and Miss Mary Stuckey of Wagoner, in the Indian Territory, aged 18 years, according to law, and do you officially sign and return this License to the parties therein named.

     WITNESS my hand and official seal at Wagoner, Indian Territory, this 22nd day of April, A. D. 1902.

                                    (signed)   CHAS. A. DAVIDSON
                                                                Clerk of the U.S. Court.
By R. C. Hunter,   Deputy.

CERTIFICATE OF MARRIAGE.

United States of America
   Indian Territory   ss.
   Northern District

     I, W. H. Shank, a Minister of the Gospel, do hereby certify, that on the 20th day of April, A.D. 1902, I did duly and according to law as commanded in the foregoing License, solemnize the Rite and apublish[sic] the Banns of Matrimony between the parties therein named.
     WITNESS my hand this 26 day of April, A. D. 1902.
My credentials are recorded in the office of the Clerk of the United States Court, Indian Territory, Northern District, Book B, Page 25.

                              (signed)   Wm. H. SHANK
                                                         A Minister of the Gospel.
                               Witness N. A. Hale

Endorsed on back:
CERTIFICATE OF RECORD.

United State of America
   Indian Territory   )ss
   Northern District

Applications for Enrollment of Creek Newborn
Act of 1905 Volume VII

  I, Charles A. Davidson, Clerk of the United States Court in the Northern District, Indian Territory, do hereby certify that the instrument hereto attached was filed for record in my office the 6 day of May 1902, at 8 A M., and duly recorded in Book M, Marriage Record, Page 439.

  WITNESS my hand and seal of said Court at Wagoner, in said Territory this 6 day of May, A.D. 1902.

  Seal   (Signed) Chas A. Davidson   Clerk.

Posey
&
Stuckey

Northern Dist. Ind. Ter.
 FILED
 May 2 1902
Chas A. Davidson,
 Clerk, U.S. Courts.

I, Henry G. Hains on oath hereby certify that the above and foregoing is a true and correct copy of said marriage license and certificate as appears from the records of this office.

                 Henry G. Hains

Subscribed and sworn to before me this 18th day of August, 1905

                 Edw C Griesel
                 Notary Public

BIRTH AFFIDAVIT.

DEPARTMENT OF THE INTERIOR.
COMMISSION TO THE FIVE CIVILIZED TRIBES.

(Child present)

 IN RE APPLICATION FOR ENROLLMENT, as a citizen of the Creek or Muskogee Nation, of William Edward Posey , born on the 22 day of February, 1903
            deceased
Name of Father: Henry A. Posey   ^   a citizen of the Creek or Muskogee Nation.
Name of Mother: Mary E. Posey   now a citizen of the Creek or Muskogee Nation.
but a citizen of the United States
           Postoffice   Wagoner, Ind. Ter.

Applications for Enrollment of Creek Newborn
Act of 1905   Volume VII

AFFIDAVIT OF MOTHER.

UNITED STATES OF AMERICA, Indian Territory, }
  Western   DISTRICT.

   I, Mary E. Posey , on oath state that I am twenty years of age and a citizen of the United States , of the ----- Nation; that I am the lawful wife of Henry A. Posey , who is a citizen, by blood of the Creek or Muskogee   Nation; that a ~~female~~ male child was born to me on 22 day of February , 1903 , that said child has been named William Edward Posey , and was living March 4, 1905.

                                    Mary E Posey

Witnesses To Mark:
  {

   Subscribed and sworn to before me this 22 day of March , 1905.

                                    Edward L. Moore
                                    Notary Public.

AFFIDAVIT OF ATTENDING PHYSICIAN OR MID-WIFE.

UNITED STATES OF AMERICA, Indian Territory, }
  Western   DISTRICT.

   I, G. W. Jobe , a physician , on oath state that I attended on Mrs. Mary E. Posey , wife of Henry A. Posey on the 22 day of February , 1903 ; that there was born to her on said date a male child; that said child was living March 4, 1905, and is said to have been named William Edward Posey

                                    G.W. Jobe, M.D.

Witnesses To Mark:
  {

   Subscribed and sworn to before me this 22 day of March , 1905.

                                    Edward L. Moore
                                    Notary Public.

NB-516.

                    Muskogee, Indian Territory, August 8, 1905.

Elizabeth Bewley,
   Red Fork, Indian Territory.

Applications for Enrollment of Creek Newborn
Act of 1905   Volume VII

Dear Madam:

In the matter of the application for the enrollment of your minor son Eugene L. Bewley as a citizen by blood of the Creek Nation this office is unable to identify you upon the final roll of citizens by blood of the Creek Nation. It is necessary that you be so identified before the rights of your said child can be finally determined.

You are, therefore, requested to state the name under which you are finally enrolled, the names of your parents and other members of your family, the Creek Indian town to which you belong and your final roll number as the same appears upon your allotment certificate and deeds.

Respectfully,

Acting Commissioner.

(The letter below typed as given)

Red Fork, Ind. Ter. 8/9/1905.

Mr. W. O. Beall,
Acting Commissioner,
   Muskogee, Ind. Ter.

Dear Sir:- Replying to your communication #NB-516, of 8th inst, beg state that I was finally enrolled under the name of Elizabeth Yargee my Farthers name was George Washington Yargee, and my sirters name is Allice Jack, (formerly Allice Yargee) on the 14th day of May A.D. 1903 I was married to Lawrence W. Bewley and on the 11th day of January A.D. 1904. My son Eugene L. Bewley was born. My final roll number was 2789. I belong [sic] the Locapoka creek Indian Town.
Hoping this information will be sufficient I am very truly yours,

(Signed) Elizabeth Yargee Bewley

Muskogee, Indian Territory, August 14, 1905.

Elizabeth Yargee Bewley,
   Red Fork, Indian Territory.

Dear Madam:

Receipt is acknowledged of your letter of August 9, 1905 identifying yourself as a citizen of the Creek Nation. Same has been filed in the matter of the application for the enrollment of your child and when finally approved by the Secretary of the Interior, you will be notified to come in and file for said child.

Respectfully,

Acting Commissioner.

Applications for Enrollment of Creek Newborn
Act of 1905 Volume VII

BIRTH AFFIDAVIT.
DEPARTMENT OF THE INTERIOR,
COMMISSIONER TO THE FIVE CIVILIZED TRIBES.

IN RE APPLICATION FOR ENROLLMENT, as a citizen of the Creek Nation, of Eugene L. Bewley, born on the 11 day of January, 1904

Name of Father: Lawrence W. Bewley   a citizen of the   U.S.   Nation.
Name of Mother: Elizabeth Bewley   a citizen of the   Creek   Nation.

Postoffice   Red Fork, IT

AFFIDAVIT OF MOTHER.

UNITED STATES OF AMERICA, Indian Territory,
Western   District.

I, Elizabeth Bewley, on oath state that I am 22 years of age and a citizen by Blood, of the Creek Nation; that I am the lawful wife of Lawrence W. Bewley, who is a citizen, by Blood of the U. S Nation; that a Male child was born to me on 11 day of January, 1904, that said child has been named Eugene L. Bewley, and was living March 4, 1905.

Elizabeth Bewley

WITNESSES TO MARK:

Subscribed and sworn to before me this 28 day of March , 1905.

Robert E Lynch

Com Ex 7/3/1906   Notary Public.

AFFIDAVIT OF ATTENDING PHYSICIAN OR MID-WIFE.

UNITED STATES OF AMERICA, Indian Territory,
Western   District.

I, William H. Manes, a Physician, on oath state that I attended on Mrs. Elizabeth Bewley, wife of Lawrence W. Bewley on the 11 day of January, 1904 ; that there was born to her on said date a male child; that said child was living March 4, 1905, and is said to have been named Eugene L. Bewley

William H. Manes MD

WITNESSES TO MARK:

Applications for Enrollment of Creek Newborn
Act of 1905   Volume VII

Subscribed and sworn to before me this   28   day of   March   , 1905.

                        Robert E Lynch
Com Ex 7/3/1906   Notary Public.

Child present MAR 29 1905   Gr.
BIRTH AFFIDAVIT.

DEPARTMENT OF THE INTERIOR,
COMMISSIONER TO THE FIVE CIVILIZED TRIBES.

IN RE APPLICATION FOR ENROLLMENT, as a citizen of the Creek Nation, of   Robert Henry Wilson , born on the 7" day of August , 1904

Name of Father: H.C. Wilson	a citizen of the	U.S.	Nation.
Name of Mother: Lucy Wilson	a citizen of the	Creek	Nation.

                 Postoffice   Melvin, I.T.
                           (Cherokee Nation)

AFFIDAVIT OF MOTHER.

UNITED STATES OF AMERICA, Indian Territory, }
    Western   District. }

I, Lucy Wilson , on oath state that I am   20   years of age and a citizen by   Blood , of the   Creek   Nation; that I am the lawful wife of   H.C. Wilson , who is a citizen, by   Blood   of the   U.S.   Nation; that a   Male   child was born to me on   7"   day of August , 1904 , that said child has been named   Robert Henry Wilson , and was living March 4, 1905.

                                    Lucy Wilson

Witness to Mark:

                }

Subscribed and sworn to before me this   29   day of   March   , 1905.

                               Edw C Griesel
                                    Notary Public.

Applications for Enrollment of Creek Newborn
Act of 1905   Volume VII

AFFIDAVIT OF ATTENDING PHYSICIAN OR MID-WIFE.

UNITED STATES OF AMERICA, Indian Territory,
Western District.

I, Mrs. Mattie Stout , a Midwife , on oath state that I attended on Mrs. Lucy Wilson , wife of Robert Henry Wilson[sic] on the 7" day of August , 1904 ; that there was born to her on said date a male child; that said child was living March 4, 1905, and is said to have been named *(blank)*

Mrs. Mattie Stout

Witness to Mark:

Subscribed and sworn to before me this 29 day of March , 1905.

Edw C Griesel
Notary Public.

NC-517.

Muskogee, Indian Territory, August 8, 1905.

Lucy Wilson,
    c/o H.C. Wilson,
        Melvin, Indian Territory.

Dear Madam:

    In the matter of the application for the enrollment of your minor son Robert Henry Wilson as a citizen by blood of the Creek Nation it will be necessary for you to furnish this office with proper proof of birth of said child and a blank for that purpose, which has been properly filled out, is inclosed herewith. The name of your said child is omitted from the affidavit of the attending midwife in the proof of birth now on file.

    When the affidavits inclosed have been sworn to return them to this office in the inclosed envelope.

Respectfully,

Acting Commissioner.

CTD-33
Env.

Applications for Enrollment of Creek Newborn
Act of 1905   Volume VII

BIRTH AFFIDAVIT.

DEPARTMENT OF THE INTERIOR.
COMMISSION TO THE FIVE CIVILIZED TRIBES.

IN RE APPLICATION FOR ENROLLMENT, as a citizen of the Creek Nation, of Robert Henry Wilson, born on the 7th day of August, 1904

Name of Father: H. C. Wilson   a citizen of the United States Nation.
Name of Mother: Lucy Wilson   a citizen of the   Creek   Nation.

Postoffice   Melvin, Indian Territory I.T.

AFFIDAVIT OF MOTHER.

UNITED STATES OF AMERICA, Indian Territory,
   Western   DISTRICT.

I, Lucy Wilson, on oath state that I am 20 years of age and a citizen by blood, of the Creek Nation; that I am the lawful wife of H.C. Wilson, who is a citizen, by *(blank)* of the United States Nation; that a male child was born to me on 7th day of August, 1904, that said child has been named Robert Henry Wilson, and was living March 4, 1905.

Lucy Wilson

Witnesses To Mark:
 { R.F. King
 { H.S. Duncan

Subscribed and sworn to before me this 14 day of Aug, 1905.

My Com E 12/30/06   D M. Butler
                                   Notary Public.

AFFIDAVIT OF ATTENDING PHYSICIAN OR MID-WIFE.

UNITED STATES OF AMERICA, Indian Territory,
   Western   DISTRICT.

I, Mrs. Mattie Stout, a mid-wife, on oath state that I attended on Mrs. Lucy Wilson, wife of H. C. Wilson on the 7th day of August, 1904; that there was born to her on said date a male child; that said child was living March 4, 1905, and is said to have been named Robert Henry Wilson

Mrs. Mattie Stout

Witnesses To Mark:
 { H R. Cline
 { *(Name Illegible)*

Applications for Enrollment of Creek Newborn
Act of 1905   Volume VII

Subscribed and sworn to before me this 18th day of August, 1905.

                                      Walter J *(Illegible)*
                                      Notary Public.

My Com expires Oct. 11-1906.

AFFIDAVIT OF DISINTERESTED WITNESSES.

UNITED STATES OF AMERICA,
INDIAN TERRITORY,   SS
Western DISTRICT.

    We, the undersigned, on oath state that we are personally acquainted with Suckey Fish, wife of Jinsey Fish ; that on or about the 13" day of October - 1904; that the said child has been named Lizzie Fish, and ~~was living March 4, 1905~~. died in the Spring of 1906.

                                  her
                              Liza x Barnett
                                 mark
                                 her
                             Austin x Barnett
                                 mark

WITNESSES:

H G. Hains

Lona Merrick

                            23"
Subscribed and sworn to before me this ~~15~~ day of October, 1906.

                                   H G Hains
                                   Notary Public.

BIRTH AFFIDAVIT.
DEPARTMENT OF THE INTERIOR.
COMMISSION TO THE FIVE CIVILIZED TRIBES.

    IN RE APPLICATION FOR ENROLLMENT, as a citizen of the CREEK Nation, of Lizzie Fish, born on the 13 day of Oct , 1904

Name of Father: Jimsey Fish   a citizen of the   Creek   Nation.
Name of Mother: Sucky "   a citizen of the   "   Nation.

Applications for Enrollment of Creek Newborn
Act of 1905 Volume VII

Postoffice   Melette[sic]

(Child present)

AFFIDAVIT OF MOTHER.

UNITED STATES OF AMERICA, Indian Territory,
WESTERN   DISTRICT.

I, Suckey Fish , on oath state that I am 23 years of age and a citizen by blood , of the Creek Nation; that I am the lawful wife of Jimsey Fish , who is a citizen, by blood of the Creek Nation; that a female child was born to me on 13 day of October , 1904 , that said child has been named Lizzie Fish , and was living March 4, 1905.

Witnesses To Mark:
{ J McDermott
{ EC Griesel

Her
Sucky x Fish
mark

Subscribed and sworn to before me this 30" day of March , 1905.

Edw C Griesel
Notary Public.

AFFIDAVIT OF ATTENDING PHYSICIAN OR MID-WIFE.

UNITED STATES OF AMERICA, Indian Territory,
WESTERN   DISTRICT.

I, Jinsey Fish , a ----- , on oath state that I attended on Mrs. Suckey Fish , wife of myself on the 13" day of Cct , 1904 ; that there was born to her on said date a female child; that said child was living March 4, 1905, and is said to have been named Lizzie Fish

Witnesses To Mark:
{ J McDermott
{ EC Griesel

His
Jimsey x Fish
mark

Subscribed and sworn to before me this 30" day of March, 1905.

Edw C Griesel
Notary Public.

Applications for Enrollment of Creek Newborn
Act of 1905   Volume VII

BIRTH AFFIDAVIT.

DEPARTMENT OF THE INTERIOR.
COMMISSION TO THE FIVE CIVILIZED TRIBES.

IN RE APPLICATION FOR ENROLLMENT, as a citizen of the CREEK Nation, of Susie Fish, born on the -- day of Oct , 1903

Name of Father:	Jimsey Fish	a citizen of the	Creek	Nation.
Name of Mother:	Sucky "	a citizen of the	"	Nation.

Postoffice   Melette[sic]

AFFIDAVIT OF MOTHER.

UNITED STATES OF AMERICA, Indian Territory,
    WESTERN   DISTRICT.

I, Sucky Fish , on oath state that I am 23   years of age and a citizen by blood , of the Creek Nation; that I am the lawful wife of Jimsey Fish , who is a citizen, by blood of the Creek Nation; that a female child was born to me on ---- day of Oct , 1904 , that said child has been named Susie Fish , and is now living. died about 10 months after birth

                                        Her
Witnesses To Mark: Sucky x Fish
    { J McDermott   mark
    { EC Griesel

    Subscribed and sworn to before me this 30" day of March , 1905.

                                        Edw C Griesel
                                          Notary Public.

AFFIDAVIT OF ATTENDING PHYSICIAN OR MID-WIFE.

UNITED STATES OF AMERICA, Indian Territory,
    WESTERN   DISTRICT.

    I, Jinsey Fish , a midw , on oath state that I attended on Mrs. Sucky Fish , wife of myself on the ---- day of Oct , 1903 ; that there was born to her on said date a female child; that said child is now living and is said to have been named Susie Fish & died about 10 months after birth

                                        His
Witnesses To Mark: Jimsey x Fish
    { J McDermott   mark
    { EC Griesel

Applications for Enrollment of Creek Newborn
Act of 1905 Volume VII

Subscribed and sworn to before me this 30" day of March, 1905.

        Edw C Griesel
         Notary Public.

NC 518   JLD
DEPARTMENT OF THE INTERIOR,
COMMISSIONER TO THE FIVE CIVILIZED TRIBES.

In the matter of the application for the enrollment of Susie Fish, deceased, as a citizen by blood of the Creek Nation.

....

STATEMENT AND ORDER.

The record in this case shows that on March 30, 1905, application was made, in affidavit form, for the enrollment of Susie Fish, deceased, as a citizen by blood of the Creek Nation, under the provisions of the act of Congress approved March 3, 1905.

It appears from the affidavit filed in this matter that said Susie Fish, deceased, was born in October 1903, and died about 10 months after birth..

The Act of Congress approved March 3, 1905, (33 Stats., 1048), provides:

"That the Commission to the Five Civilized Tribes is authorized for sixty days after the date of the approval of this act to receive and consider applications for enrollment, of children, born subsequent to May twenty-fifth, nineteen hundred and one, and prior to March fourth, nineteen hundred and five, and living on said latter date, to citizens of the Creek tribe of Indians whose enrollment has been approved by the Secretary of the Interior prior to the approval of this act; and to enroll and make allotments to such children."

It is, therefore, ordered that the application for the enrollment of said Susie Fish, deceased, as a citizen by blood of the Creek Nation, be, and the same is, hereby dismissed.

        Tams Bixby Commissioner.
Muskogee, Indian Territory.
 JAN 4 – 1907

NC-518.

            Muskogee, Indian Territory, August 8, 1905.

Jimsey Fish,
  Melette[sic], Indian Territory.

Dear Sir:

Applications for Enrollment of Creek Newborn
Act of 1905   Volume VII

In the matter of the application for the enrollment of your minor child Lizzie Fish, born October 13, 1904, as a citizen by blood of the Creek Nation it will be necessary for you to furnish this office with the affidavits of two disinterested persons relative to the birth of said child; said affidavits to set forth said child's name, the date of her birth, the names of her parents and whether or not she was living on March 4, 1905.

This matter should have prompt attention.

Respectfully,

Acting Commissioner.

NC-518

Muskogee, Indian Territory, December 13, 1905.

Sucky Fish,
    Care of Jimsey Fish,
        Mellette, Indian Territory.

Dear Madam:

In the matter of the application for the enrollment of your minor child, Lizzie Fish, born October 13, 1904, as a citizen by blood of the Creek Nation, it will be necessary for you to furnish this Office with the affidavits of two disinterested persons relative to the birth of said child. A blank for that purpose is herewith enclosed.

Respectfully,

Commissioner.

Dis

JWH

N C 518

Muskogee, Indian Territory, March 1, 1907.

Sucky Fish,
    % Jimsey Fish,
        Melette[sic], Indian Territory.

Dear Madam :--

You are hereby advised that on February 15, 1907, the Secretary of the Interior approved the enrollment of your minor child, Lizzie Fish, as a citizen by blood of the Creek Nation, and that the name of said child appears upon the roll of New Born citizens

Applications for Enrollment of Creek Newborn
Act of 1905   Volume VII

by blood of the Creek Nation, enrolled under the Act of Congress approved March 3, 1905, as number 1154.

This child is now entitled to allotment and application therefor should be made without delay at the Creek Land Office, Muskogee, Indian Territory.

Respectfully,

Commissioner.

BIRTH AFFIDAVIT.

DEPARTMENT OF THE INTERIOR.
COMMISSION TO THE FIVE CIVILIZED TRIBES.

IN RE APPLICATION FOR ENROLLMENT, as a citizen of the CREEK Nation, of Mary E. Barber, born on the 13" day of Feb., 1904

Name of Father: Robert T. Barber	a citizen of the	Creek	Nation.
Name of Mother: Carnie "	a citizen of the	U.S.	Nation.

Postoffice   Red Fork

AFFIDAVIT OF ~~MOTHER~~. Father

UNITED STATES OF AMERICA, Indian Territory,
WESTERN   DISTRICT.

I, Robert T. Barber, on oath state that I am 21 years of age and a citizen by blood, of the Creek Nation; that I am the lawful ~~wife~~ husband of Carrie Barber, who is a citizen, by ----- of the U.S. Nation; that a female child was born to me on 13" day of Feby, 1904, that said child has been named Mary E. Barber, and is now living.

Robert T Barber

Witnesses To Mark:

Subscribed and sworn to before me this 30" day of March, 1905.

Edw C Griesel
Notary Public.

Applications for Enrollment of Creek Newborn
Act of 1905   Volume VII

BIRTH AFFIDAVIT.

DEPARTMENT OF THE INTERIOR.
COMMISSION TO THE FIVE CIVILIZED TRIBES.

      IN RE APPLICATION FOR ENROLLMENT, as a citizen of the Creek Nation, of   Mary E. Barber, born on the 13 day of February , 1905

Name of Father:	Robert T. Barber	a citizen of the	Creek	Nation.
Name of Mother:	Carrie Barber	a non citizen of the	Creek	Nation.

                     Postoffice   Red Fork, I.T.

AFFIDAVIT OF MOTHER.

UNITED STATES OF AMERICA, Indian Territory,
   Western   DISTRICT.

                                                                 non
     I, Carrie Barber , on oath state that I am 18 years of age and a ^ citizen by *(blank)* , of the *(blank)* Nation; that I am the lawful wife of Robert T. Barber , who is a citizen, by blood of the Creek Nation; that a Female child was born to me on 13th day of February , 1904 , that said child has been named Mary E. Barber , and is now living.

                                         Carrie Barber

Witnesses To Mark:
{

     Subscribed and sworn to before me this 29th day of March , 1905.

                                       Usher Carson
                                              Notary Public.
My Commission Expir Sep 9th 1906.

AFFIDAVIT OF ATTENDING PHYSICIAN OR MID-WIFE.

UNITED STATES OF AMERICA, Indian Territory,
   Western Judicial   DISTRICT.

     I, G.W Jobe , a physician , on oath state that I attended on Mrs. Carrie Barber , wife of Robert T. Barber on the 13" day of Feb. , 1904 ; that there was born to her on said date a Female child; that said child is now living and is said to have been named Mary E. Barber

                                         G.W. Jobe

Witnesses To Mark:
{

Applications for Enrollment of Creek Newborn
Act of 1905   Volume VII

Subscribed and sworn to before me this 16th day of March, 1905.

HR Bonner
Notary Public.

My Com Ex July 1st 1906

NC-520

DEPARTMENT OF THE INTERIOR,
COMMISSIONER TO THE FIVE CIVILIZED TRIBES.

Muskogee, Indian Territory, July 26, 1905

In the matter of the application for the enrollment of Virgie Childers as a citizen by blood of the Creek Nation.

Lydie Childers, being duly sworn, testified as follows:

EXAMINATION BY THE COMMISSIONER:
Q What is your name? A Lydie Childers.
Q How old are you? A I was born in '51.
Q What is your postoffice address? A Broken Arrow.
Q You are citizen of the Creek Nation, are you? A Yes sir.
Q Have you a grand child named Virgie Childers? A Yes sir.
Q Is that child living? A Yes sir.
Q With its mother? A Yes sir.
Q What is the name of its mother? A Daisy Miller now.
Q Did she marry your son? A Yes sir.
Q What is his name? A Pratt.
Q Is he living? A He died.
Q When did he die? A 1902.
Q You said July while ago. A July 19, 1901.
Q How long after he died was this child, Virgie, born? A About--he died July--July, August, September, October and November.
Q The child was born in November of the same year that Pratt died? A Yes sir.
Q Is the child living today? A Yes sir.
Q With its mother or with you? A With its mother.
Q You are sure it was born in 1902, are you? A Yes sir.
Q And you remember that because it was the same year that your son, Pratt, died? A Yes sir.
Q They were married, Pratt and --? A Yes, they was married.
Q Were you present when this child was born? A No, I was not. She was across the river from me when the child was born--with her sister.
Q Who was that? A That, Lula A. Jordan.
Q She acted as midwife? A Yes sir.

Applications for Enrollment of Creek Newborn
Act of 1905 Volume VII

Q How long has she been married to her present husband? You don't know if they were married last Fall? A I could not tell when she was married, because I was--it might have been towards spring.
Q Not much more than a year ago? A No sir.
Q Not a year ago.
Q How many children has she had altogether? A She has two.
Q Just two? A Yes sir.
Q Was you[sic] son, Pratt, the father of both of them? A Yes sir.
Q One of them is enrolled--Richard--and the other is this Virgie? A Yes sir.
Q You are sure that your son, Pratt, was the father of this child? A You mean Virgie? Yes sir.

I, J. Y. Miller, a stenographer to the Commissioner to the Five Civilized Tribes, do hereby certify that the above and foregoing is a true and complete translation of my notes as same appear in my stenographic report of this case.   JY Miller

Sworn to and subscribed before me this the 29th day of July, 1905.

Edw C Griesel   Notary Public.

BIRTH AFFIDAVIT.

DEPARTMENT OF THE INTERIOR.
COMMISSION TO THE FIVE CIVILIZED TRIBES.

IN RE APPLICATION FOR ENROLLMENT, as a citizen of the Creek Nation, of Virgie Childers, born on the 16" day of Nov, 1902

Name of Father: Pratt Childers   a citizen of the Creek   Nation.
Name of Mother: Daisy Childers Miller   a citizen of the   U.S.   Nation.

Postoffice   Broken Arrow, I.T.

AFFIDAVIT OF MOTHER.

UNITED STATES OF AMERICA, Indian Territory, ⎫
     Western   DISTRICT.   ⎭

I, Daisy Childers Miller , on oath state that I am 21 years of age and a citizen ~~by~~ *(blank)* , of the United States ~~Nation~~; that I ~~am~~ was the lawful wife of Pratt Childers , who ~~is~~ was a citizen, by blood of the Creek Nation; that a female child was born to me on 16" day of Nov , 1902 , that said child has been named Virgie Childers , and was living March 4, 1905.

Applications for Enrollment of Creek Newborn
Act of 1905   Volume VII

Daisy Childers Miller

Witnesses To Mark:
{

Subscribed and sworn to before me this 5th day of August, 1905.

N.L. Sanders
Notary Public.

AFFIDAVIT OF ATTENDING PHYSICIAN OR MID-WIFE.

UNITED STATES OF AMERICA, Indian Territory, }
   Western   DISTRICT.

I, Lula A. Jordan, a midwife, on oath state that I attended on Mrs. Daisy Childers Miller, wife of Pratt Childers on the 16" day of Nov., 1902; that there was born to her on said date a female child; that said child was living March 4, 1905, and is said to have been named Virgie Miller

Lula A. Perryman, Jordan

Witnesses To Mark:
{

Subscribed and sworn to before me this 7th day of August, 1905.

My Commission expires July 11, 1906.

H.L. Mars
Notary Public.

Child Present MAR 30 1905 Gr

BIRTH AFFIDAVIT.

DEPARTMENT OF THE INTERIOR.
COMMISSION TO THE FIVE CIVILIZED TRIBES.

IN RE APPLICATION FOR ENROLLMENT, as a citizen of the CREEK Nation, of Virgie Childers, born on the 16 day of Nov., 1902

Name of Father: Pratt Childers (d)   a citizen of the   Creek   Nation.
Name of Mother: Daisy (") (Miller) a citizen of the   U. S.   Nation.

Postoffice   Broken Arrow

Applications for Enrollment of Creek Newborn
Act of 1905   Volume VII

AFFIDAVIT OF MOTHER.

UNITED STATES OF AMERICA, Indian Territory,　}
　　WESTERN　　　　DISTRICT.

     I, Daisy (Childers) Miller , on oath state that I am 21 years of age and a citizen by ----- , of the U. S. Nation; that I am the lawful wife of Pratt Childers (d) , who is a citizen, by blood of the Creek Nation; that a female child was born to me on 16 day of Nov. , 1902 , that said child has been named Virgie (Childers) , and is now living.

Daisy Childers Miller

Witnesses To Mark:
  {

     Subscribed and sworn to before me this 30" day of March , 1905.

Edw C Griesel
Notary Public.

---

grandmother
AFFIDAVIT OF <s>ATTENDING PHYSICIAN OR MID-WIFE</s>.

UNITED STATES OF AMERICA, Indian Territory,　}
　　WESTERN　　　　DISTRICT.

am mother

     I, Lydia Childers , a ----- , on oath state that I <s>attended on Mrs</s>. of Pratt Childers (d) , <s>wife</s> husband of Daisy (Childers) Miller on the 16" day of Nov. , 1902; that there was born to her on said date a female child; that said child is now living and is said to have been named Virgie Childers

Lydia Childers

Witnesses To Mark:
  {

     Subscribed and sworn to before me this 30" day of March , 1905.

Edw C Griesel
Notary Public.

BIRTH AFFIDAVIT.

DEPARTMENT OF THE INTERIOR.
COMMISSION TO THE FIVE CIVILIZED TRIBES.

     IN RE APPLICATION FOR ENROLLMENT, as a citizen of the Creek Nation, of Virgie Childers , born on the 16th day of November, 1903

Applications for Enrollment of Creek Newborn
Act of 1905   Volume VII

Name of Father: Pratt Childers   a citizen of the   Creek   Nation.
Name of Mother: Daisy Childers, Miller   a citizen of the   non-citizen   Nation.

                        Postoffice   Broken Arrow I.T.

AFFIDAVIT OF MOTHER.

UNITED STATES OF AMERICA, Indian Territory, }
    WESTERN   DISTRICT. }

    I, Daisy Childers Miller , on oath state that I am Twenty one years of age and a ~~citizen by~~ non-citizen , of the Creek Nation; that I am the lawful wife of Pratt Childers , who is a citizen, by blood of the Creek Nation; that a Female child was born to me on 16th day of November A.D. , 1903 , that said child has been named Virgie Childers , and is now living.

                                         Daisy Childers Miller

Witnesses To Mark:
{

    Subscribed and sworn to before me this 2 day of May , 1905.

                                         N.L. Gauden
My Com Ex July 25 1906   Notary Public.

AFFIDAVIT OF ATTENDING PHYSICIAN OR MID-WIFE.

UNITED STATES OF AMERICA, Indian Territory, }
    WESTERN   DISTRICT. }

    I, Lula A Perryman Jordan , a midwife , on oath state that I attended on Mrs. Daisy Miller , wife of James Miller on the 16th day of November , 1903; that there was born to her on said date a Female child; that said child is now living and is said to have been named Virgie Childers

                                           Lula A. Jordan

Witnesses To Mark:
{

    Subscribed and sworn to before me this 22nd day of April A.D. , 1905.

My Commission expires July 11, 1906.   H.L. Mars
                                           Notary Public.

Applications for Enrollment of Creek Newborn
Act of 1905   Volume VII

NC520   COPY   HGH

Muskogee, Indian Territory, July 27, 1905.

Daisy Childers Miller,
    Broken Arrow, Indian Territory.

Dear Madam:

    In the matter of the application for the enrollment of your minor child, Virgie Childers, as a citizen by blood of the Creek Nation, you are advised that there [sic] on file in this office affidavits in which the date of her mirth[sic] is given as November 16 1902 and November 16, 1903.

    There is herewith enclosed a form of birth affidavit, and you are requested to have same filled out and properly executed before an officer authorized to administer oaths, and returned to this office in the enclosed envelope.

                      Respectfully,

                      (Signed) Tams Bixby

                                        Commissioner.

JYM-271-

    Sur[sic] there has been a mistake somewhere in this thing so you will have to sine[sic] it over bessure[sic] now it was nove mber[sic] 16-1902 look like some of your folks would come over

                                        (Signed) Daisy

N.C. 521.

DEPARTMENT OF THE INTERIOR,
COMMISSIONER TO THE FIVE CIVILIZED TRIBES.
Near Oktaha, Indian Territory, February 5, 1907.

    In the matter of the application for the enrollment of Ralph Washington, as a citizen by blood of the Creek Nation.

            CILLA HERROD, being duly sworn, by J. McDermott, a notary public, testified as follows:

Applications for Enrollment of Creek Newborn
Act of 1905   Volume VII

BY THE COMMISSIONER:

Q What is your name? A Cilla Herrod.
Q What is your age? A I am about forty.
Q What is your postoffice address? A Oktaha.
Q Have you filed on you land? A Yes sir.
Q Have you your deeds? A Yes sir.

The witness presents deeds issued to Cilla Herrod Creek Indian Roll No. 1411.

Q Do you know Maria Herrod? A Yes sir, she is my daughter[sic].
Q Do you know a child of her's[sic] named Ralph Washington? A Yes sir.
Q When was he born? A 27th of June 1904. He will be three years old next June.
Q What is the name of his father? A Alfred Washington sometimes known as Wallace Washington.
Q Is he a citizen of any of the five nations? A No sir.
Q Were Maria and the father of Ralph lawfully married when he was born, the names of his parents and whether or not he was living on March 4, 1905? A No sir, they never were married.
Q Is Ralph living? A Yes sir, there he is.

The child is present and appears to be about the age as stated above.

Q Where was Ralph born? A Up the river from Fort Gibson on the Grand River.-- on what is known as the "Lemmons Farm".
Q Were you there when he was born, the names of his parents and whether or not he was living on March 4, 1905? A No sir, I was at home.
Q Do you know whether there was anybody present with Maria when Ralph was born? A Mandy Green and Mrs Robbins were there.
Q Where is Maria now? A She is upon Deep Fork visiting Robert Grayson; she will be back here tomorrow. When she comes home I will have her to go over to Fort Gibson and get the affidavit of the midwife.

A blank proof of birth is handed the witness.

I, Jesse McDermott, on oath state that the above and foregoing is a full and true transcript of my notes as taken in said cause on said date.

Jesse McDermott

Subscribed and sworn to before me
this 5th day of Feb., 1907.

Applications for Enrollment of Creek Newborn
Act of 1905   Volume VII

J.D. Springer
Notary Public.

BIRTH AFFIDAVIT.

DEPARTMENT OF THE INTERIOR.
COMMISSION TO THE FIVE CIVILIZED TRIBES.

IN RE APPLICATION FOR ENROLLMENT, as a citizen of the CREEK Nation, of Ralph Washington , born on the 27 day of June , 1904

Name of Father: Alfred Washington	a citizen of the U.S.	Nation.
Name of Mother: Maria Herrod	a citizen of the Creek	Nation.

Postoffice   Oktaha

(Child present)

AFFIDAVIT OF MOTHER.

UNITED STATES OF AMERICA, Indian Territory, ⎱
  WESTERN   DISTRICT. ⎰

I, Maria Herrod , on oath state that I am 19 years of age and a citizen by ~~adoption~~ blood , of the Creek Nation; that I am not the lawful wife of Alfred Washington , who is a citizen, by ----- of the U.S. Nation; that a male child was born to me on 27 day of June , 1904 , that said child has been named Ralph Washington , and is now living.

Maria herd[sic]

Witnesses To Mark:
{

Subscribed and sworn to before me this 1st day of April , 1905.

J McDermott
Notary Public.

(The above Birth Affidavit given again)

NC 521   JLDe
                                                               CM

DEPARTMENT OF THE INTERIOR,
COMMISSIONER TO THE FIVE CIVILIZED TRIBES.

Applications for Enrollment of Creek Newborn
Act of 1905   Volume VII

In the matter of the application for the enrollment of Ralph Washington as a citizen by blood of the Creek Nation.

DECISION.

The record in this case shows that on April 1, 1905, application was made, in affidavit form, supplemented on February 5, 1907 by oral testimony, for the enrollment of Ralph Washington as a citizen by blood of the Creek Nation, under the provisions of the Act of Congress approved March 3, 1905.

It appears from the evidence filed in this cause that said Ralph Washington was born June 27, 1904, was living March 4, 1905, and was the illegitimate child of Alfred Washington, a non-citizen, and Maria Herrod, whose name appears opposite No. 1412 on the approved roll of citizens by blood of the Creek Nation.

It is therefore, ordered and adjudged that said Ralph Washington is entitled to enrollment as a citizen by blood of the Creek Nation in accordance with the provisions of the Act of Congress approved March 3, 1905 (33 Stat. L., 1048), and the application for her enrollment as such is accordingly granted.

Tams Bixby   Commissioner.

Muskogee, Indian Territory.
FEB 23 1907

NC 521 Muskogee I T Aug 8, 1905

Maria Herrod
    Oktaha I T

Dear Madam:

In the matter of the application for the enrollment of your minor son Ralph Washington, born June 27, 1904, as a citizen by blood of the Creek Nation it will be necessary for you to furnish this office with the affidavit of the attending physician or midwife at the birth of said child, relative to his birth. For that purpose there is inclosed herewith a blank for proof of birth.

You are requested to have the same properly executed and return to this office in the inclosed envelope.

In case there was no attending physician or midwife at the birth of said child it will be necessary for you to furnish, in lieu of the affidavit of such attending physician or midwife, the affidavits of two disinterested persons who are acquainted with said child, know when he was born, the names of his parents and whether or not he was living on March 4, 1905.

Resp

Act Comr

Applications for Enrollment of Creek Newborn
Act of 1905   Volume VII

NC-521

Muskogee, Indian Territory, December 13, 1905.

Maria Herrod
        Oktaha I T

Dear Madam:

    In the matter of the application for the enrollment of your minor son Ralph Washington, born June 27, 1904, as a citizen by blood of the Creek Nation, you are advised that it will be necessary for you to furnish this office with the affidavit of the attending physician or midwife at the birth of said child relative to its birth. For this purpose, there is herewith enclosed blank form of birth affidavit. In the event there was no physician or midwife in attendance at the child's birth, this Office requires the affidavit of two disinterested persons relative to its birth, and a blank for that purpose is also enclosed.

    This matter should receive your prompt attention.

                      Respectfully,

1 B A   Commissioner.
Dis

NC 521

Muskogee, Indian Territory, January 11, 1907.

Maria Herrod
    Care of Alfred Washington,
        Oktaha, Indian Territory.

Dear Madam:

    In the matter of the application for the enrollment of your minor son Ralph Washington, as a citizen of the Creek Nation, it will be necessary for you to furnish this office with the affidavit of the attending physician or midwife at the birth of said child and for this purpose there is herewith inclosed blank form of birth affidavit, and in executing same care should be exercised to see that all blanks are properly filled, all names written in full and in the event that either of the persons signing the affidavit is unable to which you are requested to have properly executed and returned to this office within five days from date hereof.

Applications for Enrollment of Creek Newborn
Act of 1905   Volume VII

You are also requested to appear at this office within five days from date hereof in order that you may be examined under oath in this matter.

Respectfully,

Commissioner.

ENC.-JCL.
1-BA.

NC 521.

Muskogee, Indian Territory, March 18, 1907.

Maria Herrod,
    c/o Alfred Washington,
        Oktaha, Indian Territory.

Dear Madam:

You are hereby advised that the Secretary of the Interior under date of March 4, 1907, approved the enrollment of your minor child, Ralph Washington, as a citizen by blood of the Creek Nation, and that the name of said child appears upon the roll of New Born citizens by blood of the Creek Nation, enrolled under the Act of Congress approved March 3, 1905, as number 1285.

This child is now entitled to allotment and application therefor should be made without delay at the Creek Land Office, Muskogee, Indian Territory.

Respectfully,

Commissioner.

DEPARTMENT OF THE INTERIOR,
COMMISSION TO THE FIVE CIVILIZED TRIBES.
Holdenville, I. T., March 27, 1905.

In the matter of the application for the enrollment of Pa-thlum-ka Bighead as a citizen of the Creek Nation.

JENNIE PETER, being duly sworn, testified as follows:

Through Alex Posey Official Interpreter.

Applications for Enrollment of Creek Newborn
Act of 1905   Volume VII

BY COMMISSION:
Q What is your name? A Jennie Peter.
Q How old are you? A About forty.
Q What is your post office address? A Holdenville.
Q Are you a citizen of the Creek Nation? A Yes, sir.
Q To what town do you belong? A Tulsa Little River.
Q Do you make application for the enrollment of your child, Pa-thlum-ka Bighead, as a citizen of the Creek Nation? A Yes, sir.
Q What is the name of his child's father? A George Bighead.
Q Is he living? A He is dead.
Q Was he a citizen of the Creek Nation? A He was a Seminole.
Q Was he your lawfull[sic] husband? A Yes, sir.
Q If it should be found that your child, Pa-thlum-ka Bighead, is entitled to be enrolled in either the Creek or Muskogee Seminole Nations in which nation do you desire to have him enrolled? A In the Creek Nation.

---oooOOOooo---

I, D. C. Skaggs, on oath state that the above and foregoing is a full and true transcript of my stenographic notes as taken in said cause on said date.

DC Skaggs

Subscribed and sworn to before me this 18" day of July, 1905.

Edw C Griesel
Notary Public.

N.C. 522.

DEPARTMENT OF THE INTERIOR,
COMMISSIONER TO THE FIVE CIVILIZED TRIBES.
Bilby, I. T., April 26, 1906.

In the matter of the application for the enrollment of Pathlumka Bighead as a citizen by blood of the Creek Nation.

JENNIE BIGHEAD, being duly sworn, testified as follows

Through Alex Posey official interpreter:

BY THE COMMISSIONER:
Q What is your name? A Jennie Bighead.
Q How old are you? A I am over thirty.
Q What is your post office address? A Bilby.

Applications for Enrollment of Creek Newborn
Act of 1905 Volume VII

Q Have you a child named Pathlumka Bighead? A Yes, sir.
Q What is the name of the child's father? A George Bighead, who is now dead.
Q Was he your lawful husband? A Yes, sir.
Q What was his Creek name? A George Cathlocco.
Q To what town did he belong? A He was a Seminole.
Q Is he enrolled as George Bighead or George Cathlocco? A As George Bighead.
Q Under what name are you enrolled? A As Jennie Peter.
Q To what town do you belong? A Tulsa Little River.
Q When was Pathlumka born? A February 18, 1904.

---oooOOOooo---

I, D. C. Skaggs, on oath state that the above and foregoing is a full and true transcript of my stenographic notes as taken in said cause on said date.

DC Skaggs

Subscribed and sworn to before me this 1st day of May, 1906.

Alex Posey
Notary Public.

N.C. 522   F.HW.

DEPARTMENT OF THE INTERIOR,
COMMISSIONER TO THE FIVE CIVILIZED TRIBES.

In the matter of the application for the enrollment of Pa-thlum-ka Bighead as a citizen by blood of the Creek Nation.

DECISION.

The record in this case shows that on March 27, 1905, Jennie Peter appeared before a Creek enrollment field party, at Holdenville, Indian Territory, and made application for the enrollment of her minor child, Pa-thlum-ka Bighead, as a citizen by blood of the Creek Nation. Further proceedings were had at Bilby, Indian Territory, April 26, 1906. Supplemental affidavits as to the birth of said applicant, executed March 27, 1905, December 16, 1905, and April 26, 1906, are attached to and made part of the record herein.

The evidence shows that the said Pa-thlum-ka Bighead is the child of George Bighead, deceased, a citizen of the Seminole Nation, and of Jennie Bighead, whose name appears as Jennie Peter on a partial schedule of citizens by blood of the Creek Nation, approved by the Secretary of the Interior March 28, 1902, opposite roll No. 7514.

It appears from the evidence that an application was made for the enrollment of the applicant in the Creek Nation. The records of this office show that no application has

Applications for Enrollment of Creek Newborn
Act of 1905   Volume VII

been made for his enrollment in the Seminole Nation, under the Act of Congress approved March 3, 1905.

It further appears that the said Pa-thlum-ka Bighead was born February 18, 1904, and was living on March 4, 1905.

The act of Congress approved March 3, 1905, (33 Stats., 1048), provides in part as follows:

"That the Commission to the Five Civilized Tribes is authorized for sixty days after the date of the approval of this Act to receive and consider applications for enrollments of children born subsequent to May twenty five, nineteen hundred and one, and prior to March fourth, nineteen hundred and five, and living on said latter date, to citizens of the Creek tribe of Indians whose enrollment has been approved by the Secretary of the Interior prior to the approval of this act; and to enroll and make, allotments to such children."

It is therefore, ordered and adjudged that said Pa-thlum-ka Bighead is entitled to be enrolled as a citizen by blood of the Creek Nation, in accordance with the provisions of law above quoted, and the application for her enrollment as such is accordingly granted.

Muskogee, Indian Territory.   Tams Bixby Commissioner.
   JAN 22 1907

AFFIDAVIT OF DISINTERESTED WITNESSES.

United States of America,
          Indian Territory,   ss.
          Western District.

We, the undersigned, on oath state that we are personally acquainted with Jennie Peter (or Bighead) , wife of George Bighead, and that there was born to her on or about the   *(blank)* day of January , 1904, a male child; that said child was living March 4, 1905, and is said to have been named   *(Illegible)* Bighead   .

We further state that we have no interest in this case.

                                                  Burnie McCosar

                                                  Nokos Harjo

(2) Witnesses to mark:

_____

_____

Subscribed and sworn to before me this 16 day of December, 1905.

Applications for Enrollment of Creek Newborn
Act of 1905 Volume VII

          Chas Rider
          Notary Public.
Commission expires July 11th 1905

Indian Territory, I
       I ss
Western District. I

  We, the undersigned, on oath state that we are personally acquainted with Jennie Bighead wife of George Bighead ; that on or about the 18 day of February , 1904, a female[sic] child was born to them and has been named Pathlumka Bighead ; and that said child was living March 4, 1905.

  We further state that we have no interest in this case.

         his
        Party x Beaver
         mark
(2) Witnesses to mark: her
 Alex Posey   Lucy x Beaver
         mark
 DC Skaggs

  Subscribed and sworn to before me this 26 day of April, 1906.

         Alex Posey
         Notary Public.

BIRTH AFFIDAVIT.
      DEPARTMENT OF THE INTERIOR,
COMMISSIONER TO THE FIVE CIVILIZED TRIBES.

   ENROLLMENT OF MINORS. ACT OF CONGRESS, APPROVED APRIL 26, 1906.

  IN RE APPLICATION FOR ENROLLMENT, as a citizen of the Creek Nation, of Pa-thlum-ka Bighead , born on the 8th day of Feby , 1904

Name of Father: George Bighead	a citizen of the Seminole	Nation.
Name of Mother: Jennie Bighead	a citizen of the Creek	Nation.

Tribal enrollment of father Seminole   Tribal enrollment of mother Creek

       Postoffice   Holdenville I.T.

Applications for Enrollment of Creek Newborn
Act of 1905 Volume VII

AFFIDAVIT OF MOTHER.

UNITED STATES OF AMERICA, Indian Territory,
Western District.

I, Jennie Bighead , on oath state that I am about 40 years of age and a citizen by Blood , of the Creek Nation; that I am the lawful wife of George Bighead , who is a citizen, by Blood of the Creek[sic] Nation; that a male child was born to me on 8th day of Feby , 1904 , that said child has been named Pa-thlum-ka , and was living March 4, 1906. and now living her
Jennie x Bighead
mark

WITNESSES TO MARK:
{ John A Jacobs
{ O D Smith

Subscribed and sworn to before me this 19th day of January , 1907.

Com expires July 16th 1910   Chas Rider
                                                Notary Public.

BIRTH AFFIDAVIT.   Supplemental testimony taken.
DEPARTMENT OF THE INTERIOR.
COMMISSION TO THE FIVE CIVILIZED TRIBES.

IN RE APPLICATION FOR ENROLLMENT, as a citizen of the Creek Nation, of Pa-thlum-ka Bighead , born on the 18 day of February , 1904

Name of Father: George Bighead (deceased)   a citizen of the Seminole   Nation.
Name of Mother: Jennie Peter   a citizen of the Creek   Nation.
Tulsa Little River Town
                            Postoffice   Holdenville, Ind. Ter.

AFFIDAVIT OF MOTHER.
                                              Child is present
UNITED STATES OF AMERICA, Indian Territory,
Western   DISTRICT.

I, Jennie Peter , on oath state that I am about 40 years of age and a citizen by blood , of the Creek Nation; that I am the lawful wife of George Bighead, deceased , who is a citizen, by blood of the Seminole Nation; that a male child was born to me on 18 day of February , 1904 , that said child has been named Pa-thlum-ka Bighead ,

Applications for Enrollment of Creek Newborn
Act of 1905   Volume VII

and was living March 4, 1905. That no one attended on me as midwife or physician on the birth of the child.

Witnesses To Mark:
{ Alex Posey
{ DC Skaggs

her
Jennie x Peter
mark

Subscribed and sworn to before me this 27 day of March, 1905.

Drennan C Skaggs
Notary Public.

BIRTH AFFIDAVIT.

DEPARTMENT OF THE INTERIOR.
COMMISSION TO THE FIVE CIVILIZED TRIBES.

IN RE APPLICATION FOR ENROLLMENT, as a citizen of the Creek Nation, of Pathlumka Bighead, born on the 18 day of Feb., 1904

Name of Father: George Bighead	a citizen of the Seminole	Nation.
Name of Mother: Jennie Bighead	a citizen of the Creek	Nation.

Postoffice   Bilby Ind. Ter.

AFFIDAVIT OF MOTHER.

UNITED STATES OF AMERICA, Indian Territory, }
    Western   DISTRICT.

I, Jennie Bighead, on oath state that I am over 30 years of age and a citizen by blood, of the Creek Nation; that I ~~am~~ was the lawful wife of George Bighead, who is a citizen, by blood of the Seminole Nation; that a female child was born to me on 18 day of February, 1904, that said child has been named Pathlumka Bighead, and was living March 4, 1905.

her
Jennie x Bighead
mark

Witnesses To Mark:
{ Alex Posey
{ DC Skaggs

Applications for Enrollment of Creek Newborn
Act of 1905   Volume VII

Subscribed and sworn to before me this 26 day of April, 1906.

Alex Posey
Notary Public.

NC. 522.

Muskogee, Indian Territory, July 14, 1905.

Commissioner to the Five Civilized Tribes,
       Seminole Enrollment Division,
          Muskogee, Indian Territory.

Gentlemen:

    March 29, 1905, application was made to the Commission to the Five Civilized Tribes for the enrollment of Pa-tham-ka[sic] Bighead, born February 18, 1904, as a citizen by blood of the Creek Nation. It is stated in said application that the father of said child was George Bighead, deceased, a citizen of the Seminole Nation, and that the mother is Jennie Peter, a citizen of the Creek Nation.

    You are requested to inform the Creek Enrollment Division as to whether application has been made for the enrollment of said Pa-tham-ka Bighead, as a citizen of the Seminole Nation, and if so, what disposition has been made of the same.

Respectfully,

Commissioner.

DEPARTMENT OF THE INTERIOR.
COMMISSION TO THE FIVE CIVILIZED TRIBES.

Muskogee, Indian Territory, July 19, 1905.

Chief Clerk,
       Creek Enrollment Division.

Dear Sir:

    Receipt is acknowledged of your letter of July 14, 1905 (NC-522) stating that application was made to the Commission to the Five Civilized Tribes for the enrollment of Pa-tham-ka[sic] Bighead, born February 18, 1904, child of George Bighead, deceased, a citizen of the Seminole Nation, and Jennie Peter, a citizen of the Creek Nation, as a

Applications for Enrollment of Creek Newborn
Act of 1905   Volume VII

citizen by blood of the Creek Nation and requesting to be informed as to whether an application was ever made to the Commission to the Five Civilized Tribes for the enrollment of said child as a citizen of the Seminole Nation.

In reply to your letter you are advised that it does not appear from an examination of the records of this office that any application was made to the Commission to the Five Civilized Tribes for the enrollment of said Pa-tham-ka[sic] Bighead as a citizen of the Seminole Nation.

Respectfully,

Tams Bixby   Commissioner.

NC-522.

Muskogee, Indian Territory, August 8, 1905.

Jennie Peter,
    Holdenville, Indian Territory.

Dear Madam:

In the matter of the application for the enrollment of your minor son Pa-thlum-ka Bighead, born February 18, 1904, as a citizen by blood of the Creek Nation it will be necessary for you to furnish this office, relative to the birth of said child, with the affidavits of two disinterested persons; said affidavits to set forth said child's name, the date of his birth, the names of his parents and whether or not he was on living March 4, 1905.

Respectfully,

Acting Commissioner.

HGH

REFER IN REPLY TO THE FOLLOWING:
NC-522

DEPARTMENT OF THE INTERIOR,
COMMISSIONER TO THE FIVE CIVILIZED TRIBES.

Muskogee, Indian Territory, September 11, 1905.

Jennie Peter (or Bighead),
    Holdenville, Indian Territory.

Dear Madam:

In the matter of the application for the enrollment of your minor son, Pa-thlum-ka Bighead, born February 18, 1904, as a citizen by blood of the Creek Nation it will be necessary for you to furnish this office, relative to the birth of said child, with the

Applications for Enrollment of Creek Newborn
Act of 1905 Volume VII

affidavits of two disinterested persons; said affidavits to set forth the name of said child, the date of his birth, the names of his parents and whether or not he was on living March 4, 1905.

Respectfully,

Wm O. Beall
Acting Commissioner.

IC-522

Muskogee, Indian Territory, December 13, 1905.

Jennie Peter (or Bighead),
    Holdenville, Indian Territory.

Dear Madam:

    In the matter of the application for the enrollment of your minor son, Pa-thlum-ka Bighead, born February 18, 1904, as a citizen by blood of the Creek Nation, it will be necessary for you to furnish this Office with the affidavits of two disinterested persons relative to said child's birth. A blank for that purpose is herewith enclosed.

Respectfully,

Commissioner.

REFER IN REPLY TO THE FOLLOWING:
N.C. 522.

**DEPARTMENT OF THE INTERIOR,
COMMISSIONER TO THE FIVE CIVILIZED TRIBES.**

Muskogee, Indian Territory, May 2, 1906.

Commissioner to the Five Civilized Tribes,
    Muskogee, Indian Territory.

Sir:

    There is inclosed herewith testimony and affidavits in the matter of the application for the enrollment of Pathlumka Bighead, as a citizen by blood of the Creek Nation.

Respectfully,
Alex Posey
In Charge of Creek Field Party.

Applications for Enrollment of Creek Newborn
Act of 1905   Volume VII

NC 522.

Muskogee, Indian Territory, August 21, 1906.

Clerk in Charge,
    Seminole Enrollment Division,
        Muskogee, Indian Territory.

Dear Sir:

    Application has been made for the enrollment as a citizen of the Creek Nation of Pa-thlum-ka Bighead, born February 18, 1904, to George Bighead, deceased, a Seminole, and Jennie Peter, a citizen of the Creek Nation.

    You are requested to advise this office if application has been made for the enrollment of said child as a citizen of the Seminole Nation, and if so, please furnish the present status of said application.

                Respectfully,

                            Commissioner.

REFER IN REPLY TO THE FOLLOWING:

DEPARTMENT OF THE INTERIOR,
COMMISSIONER TO THE FIVE CIVILIZED TRIBES.

Muskogee, Indian Territory, August 24, 1906.

Chief Clerk,
    Creek Enrollment Division,
        Muskogee, Indian Territory.

Dear Sir:

    Receipt is hereby acknowledged of your letter of August 21, 1906, asking if application has been made for enrollment as a citizen of the Seminole Nation of Pa-thlum-ka Bighead, child of George Bighead, a citizen of the Seminole Nation, and Jennie Peter, a citizen of the Creek Nation.

    In reply you are advised that it does not appear from the records of this office that application was made on behalf of Pa-thlum-ka Bighead for enrollment as a new born citizen of the Seminole Nation under the Act of Congress approved March 3, 1905.

                Respectfully,

                            Wm O. Beall
                            Acting Commissioner.

Applications for Enrollment of Creek Newborn
Act of 1905   Volume VII

NC 522.

Muskogee, Indian Territory, October 3, 1906.

Jennie Bighead,
    Holdenville, Indian Territory.

Dear Madam:

    In the matter of the application for the enrollment of your child, Pa-thlum-ka Bighead. born February 8, 1904, as a citizen of the Creek Nation, there are on file in this office affidavits in which its sex is given variously as male and female. To correct this discrepancy there is herewith enclosed blank form of birth affidavit which you should have properly executed and returned in the enclosed envelope; it would be well for you to transmit with said corrected affidavit a letter explaining the sex of said child.

                              Respectfully,

1 BA   Commissioner.
Env.

N. C. 522.

Muskogee, Indian Territory, March 7, 1907.

Jennie Bighead (or Jennie Peter),
    Holdenville, Indian Territory.

Dear Madam:

    You are hereby advised that on March 2, 1907, the Secretary of the Interior approved the enrollment of your minor child, Pa-thlum-ka Bighead, as a citizen by blood of the Creek Nation, and that the name of said child appears upon the roll of new born citizens by blood of the Creek Nation, enrolled under the Act of Congress approved March 3, 1905, as number 1230.

    This child is now entitled to allotment and application therefor should be made without delay at the Creek Land Office, Muskogee, Indian Territory.

                              Respectfully,
                                          Commissioner.

Applications for Enrollment of Creek Newborn
Act of 1905 Volume VII

AFFIDAVIT OF DISINTERESTED WITNESS.

United States of America)
Indian Territory) SS.
(blank) District

    I, Malind[sic] Thomas on oath state that I am personally acquainted with Eliza Thomas wife of Sorply[sic] Taylor that there was born to her on or about the 22nd day of Januay[sic] 1904 a male child; that said child was living March 4, 1905 and is said to have been named Ely Taylor
I further state that I have no interest in this case.

                                            her
                                   Malinda x Thomas
Witness to mark.   mark

(Illegible) Gibson

J W Fowler

Subscribed and sworn to before me this 8" day of February 1906.

MY COMMISSION EXPIRES JULY 13th, 1908.   J W Fowler
                                                    Notary Public.

AFFIDAVIT OF DISINTERESTED WITNESS.

United States of America)
Indian Territory) SS.
(blank) District

    I, Katie Thomas on oath state that I am personally acquainted with Eliza Thomas wife of Serpsy[sic] Taylor that there was born to her on or about the 22 day of January 1904 a male child; that said child was living March 4, 1905 and is said to have been named Ely Taylor
I further state that I have no interest in this case.

                                            her
                                   Katie x Thomas
                                       mark

Witness to mark.

Simon Likowski

J W Fowler

Applications for Enrollment of Creek Newborn
Act of 1905   Volume VII

Subscribed and sworn to before me this 8" day of February 1906.

MY COMMISSION EXPIRES JULY 13th, 1908.   J W Fowler
                                          Notary Public.

BIRTH AFFIDAVIT.

DEPARTMENT OF THE INTERIOR.
COMMISSION TO THE FIVE CIVILIZED TRIBES.

IN RE APPLICATION FOR ENROLLMENT, as a citizen of the CREEK Nation, of Eli Taylor, born on the 22 day of Jan. , 1904

Name of Father: Sarpsey Taylor   a citizen of the   Creek   Nation.
Name of Mother: Liza   "   a citizen of the   "   Nation.

                        Postoffice   Henrietta[sic]

(Child present)
                        AFFIDAVIT OF MOTHER.

UNITED STATES OF AMERICA, Indian Territory, ⎱
       WESTERN   DISTRICT.   ⎰

   I, Liza Taylor , on oath state that I am 29 years of age and a citizen by blood , of the Creek Nation; that I am the lawful wife of Sarpsey Taylor , who is a citizen, by blood of the Creek Nation; that a male child was born to me on 22 day of Jan., 1904 , that said child has been named Eli Taylor , and is now living.

                                        Her
                              Liza   x   Taylor
Witnesses To Mark: mark
 ⎰ Jesse McDermott
 ⎱ Edw C Griesel

Subscribed and sworn to before me this 3" day of April , 1905.

                                   Edw C Griesel
                                   Notary Public.

AFFIDAVIT OF ATTENDING PHYSICIAN OR MID-WIFE.

UNITED STATES OF AMERICA, Indian Territory, ⎱
       WESTERN   DISTRICT.   ⎰

Applications for Enrollment of Creek Newborn
Act of 1905 Volume VII

    I, Sarpsey Taylor , a ----- , on oath state that I attended on Mrs. Liza Taylor , wife of myself on the 22" day of Jan. , 1904 ; that there was born to her on said date a male child; that said child is now living and is said to have been named Eli Taylor

his
Sarpsey x Taylor
mark

Witnesses To Mark:
{ Jesse McDermott
{ Edw C Griesel

    Subscribed and sworn to before me this 3" day of April , 1905.

Edw C Griesel
Notary Public.

NC-523

Muskogee, Indian Territory, August 8, 1905.

Sarpsey Taylor,
    Henryetta, Indian Territory.

Dear Sir:

    In the matter of the application for the enrollment of your minor son Eli Taylor, born June[sic] 22, 1904, as a citizen by blood of the Creek Nation, it will be necessary for you to furnish this office, relative to the birth of said child, with the affidavits of two disinterested persons; said affidavits to set forth the name of said child, the names of his parents, the date of his birth and whether or not he was on living March 4, 1905.

Respectfully,

Acting Commissioner.

NC-523

Muskogee, Indian Territory, December 13, 1905.

Sarpecy[sic] Taylor,
    Henryetta, Indian Territory.

Dear Sir:

    In the matter of the application for the enrollment of your minor child Eli Taylor, born June[sic] 22, 1904, as a citizen by blood of the Creek Nation, it will be

Applications for Enrollment of Creek Newborn
Act of 1905   Volume VII

necessary for you to furnish this Office, with the affidavits of two disinterested persons relative to the birth of said child. A blank for that purpose is herewith enclosed.

    This matter should receive your prompt attention.

                Respectfully,

                              Commissioner.

Dis

                              C 524

DEPARTMENT OF THE INTERIOR,
COMMISSION TO THE FIVE CIVILIZED TRIBES.
Holdenville, I. T., I. T.,[sic] March 27, 1905.

    In the matter of the application for the enrollment of Selanie Tiger as a citizen of the Creek Nation.

        CINDA TIGER, being duly sworn, testified as follows:

    Through Alex Posey Official Interpreter:

BY COMMISSION:
Q What is your name? A Cinda Tiger.
Q How old are you? A Thirty.
Q What is your post office address? A Spaulding.
Q To what town do you belong? A Little Rive4[sic] Tulsa.
Q Do you make application for the enrollment of your child Selanie Tiger, as a citizen of the Creek Nation? A Yes, sir.
Q What is the name of the father of this child? A John Tiger.
Q Is he a citizen of the Creek Nation? A He is a citizen of the Seminole Nation.
Q If it should be found that your child, Selanie Tiger, is entitled to enrollment in either the Creek or Seminole Nations, in which nation do you desire to have her enrolled?
A In the Creek Nation.

                ---oooOOOooo---

    I, D. C. Skaggs, on oath state that the above and foregoing is a full and true transcript of my stenographic notes as taken in said cause on said date.

                        DC Skaggs

    Subscribed and sworn to before me this 17" day of July, 1905.

Applications for Enrollment of Creek Newborn
Act of 1905   Volume VII

J McDermott
Notary Public.

AFFIDAVIT OF DISINTERESTED WITNESSES.

United States of America,
   Indian Territory,   ss.
   Western District.

We, the undersigned, on oath state that we are personally acquainted with Cinda Tiger , wife of   John Tiger   ; and that there was born to her on or about the 20th   day of   April   , 1903, a   Female   child; that said child was living March 4, 1905, and is said to have been named   Selanie Tiger   .
We further state that we have no interest in this case.

Watty Hipico

Alfred Frank

(2) Witnesses to mark:

A.F. *(Illegible)*

W.R. Grat

Subscribed and sworn to before me this 13th day of January 1905.

Chas Rider
Notary Public.

My Commission Expires July 11th, 1906.

Post Office address Emahaka Mission I.T.

Supplemental testimony taken.

BIRTH AFFIDAVIT.

DEPARTMENT OF THE INTERIOR.
COMMISSION TO THE FIVE CIVILIZED TRIBES.

IN RE APPLICATION FOR ENROLLMENT, as a citizen of the Creek Nation, of Selanie Tiger, born on the 20 day of April , 1903

Name of Father: John Tiger   a citizen of the Seminole   Nation.
Name of Mother: Cinda Tiger (nee Factor)   a citizen of the   Creek   Nation.
Tulsa Little River Town

Postoffice   Spaulding, Ind. Ter.

Applications for Enrollment of Creek Newborn
Act of 1905 Volume VII

AFFIDAVIT OF MOTHER.

UNITED STATES OF AMERICA, Indian Territory, ⎱
    Western   DISTRICT. ⎰   Child is present

    I, Cinda Tiger , on oath state that I am 20 years of age and a citizen by blood , of the Creek Nation; that I am the lawful wife of John Tiger , who is a citizen, by blood of the Seminole Nation; that a female child was born to me on 20 day of April , 1903 , that said child has been named Selanie Tiger , and was living March 4, 1905. That no one attended on me as midwife or physician at the birth of the child except my husband.

                                              her
                                    Cinda x Tiger
Witnesses To Mark: mark
  ⎰ Alex Posey
  ⎱ DC Skaggs

    Subscribed and sworn to before me this 27 day of March , 1905.

                                      Drennan C Skaggs
                                      Notary Public.

                              Father
AFFIDAVIT OF ~~ATTENDING PHYSICIAN OR MID-WIFE~~.

UNITED STATES OF AMERICA, Indian Territory, ⎱
    Western   DISTRICT. ⎰

                                                             my wife
    I, John Tiger , ~~a~~ (blank) , on oath state that I attended on ^ Mrs. Cinda Tiger , ~~wife of~~ (blank) on the 20 day of April , 1903 ; that there was born to her on said date a (blank) child; that said child was living March 4, 1905, and is said to have been named Selanie Tiger

                                           his
                                     John x Tiger
Witnesses To Mark: mark
  ⎰ Alex Posey
  ⎱ DC Skaggs

    Subscribed and sworn to before me this 27 day of March , 1905.

                                      Drennan C Skaggs
                                      Notary Public.

DEPARTMENT OF THE INTERIOR.
COMMISSION TO THE FIVE CIVILIZED TRIBES.

Applications for Enrollment of Creek Newborn
Act of 1905   Volume VII

Muskogee, Indian Territory, July 19, 1905.

Chief Clerk,
    Creek Enrollment Division.

Dear Sir:

    Receipt is acknowledged of your letter of July 14, 1905 (NC-524) stating that application was made to the Commission to the Five Civilized Tribes for the enrollment of Selanie Tiger, born April 20, 1903, child of John Tiger, a citizen of the Seminole Nation, and Cinda Tiger, a citizen of the Creek Nation, as a citizen by blood of the Creek Nation and requesting to be informed as to whether application was ever made for the enrollment of said child as a citizen of the Seminole Nation.

    In reply to your letter you are advised that it does not appear from an examination of the records of this office that application was made to the Commission to the Five Civilized Tribes for the enrollment of said Selanie Tiger as a citizen of the Seminole Nation.

    Respectfully,

    Tams Bixby   Commissioner.

REFER IN REPLY TO THE FOLLOWING:

NC-524

DEPARTMENT OF THE INTERIOR,
COMMISSIONER TO THE FIVE CIVILIZED TRIBES.

Muskogee, Indian Territory, December 13, 1905.

Cinda Tiger,
    Care of John Tiger,
        Spaulding, Indian Territory.

Dear Madam:
    In the matter of the application for the enrollment of your minor child, Selanie Tiger, born April 20, 1903, as a citizen by blood of the Creek Nation, you are advised that it will be necessary for you to furnish this Office with the affidavits of two disinterested persons relative to the birth of said child. A blank for that purpose is herewith enclosed.

    This matter should receive your prompt attention.

    Respectfully,

    Tams Bixby

    Commissioner.

Dis

Applications for Enrollment of Creek Newborn
Act of 1905 Volume VII

NC. 524.

Muskogee, Indian Territory, July 14, 1905.

Commissioner to the Five Civilized Tribes,
    Seminole Enrollment Division,
        Muskogee, Indian Territory.
Gentlemen:

    March 29, 1905, application was made to the Commission to the Five Civilized Tribes for the enrollment of Selanie Tiger, born April 20, 1903, as a citizen by blood of the Creek Nation. It is stated in said application that the father of said child is John Tiger, a citizen of the Seminole Nation, and that the mother is Cinda Tiger, a citizen of the Creek Nation.

    You are requested to inform the Creek Enrollment Division as to whether application has been made for the enrollment of said Selanie Tiger, as a citizen of the Seminole Nation, and if so, what disposition has been made of the same.

        Respectfully,

                Commissioner.

NC-524.

Muskogee, Indian Territory, August 8, 1905.

John Tiger,
    Spaulding, Indian Territory.

Dear Sir:

    In the matter of the application for the enrollment of your minor daughter Selanie Tiger, born April 20, 1903, as a citizen by blood of the Creek Nation, it will be necessary for you to furnish this office, relative to the birth of said child, with the affidavits of two disinterested persons; said affidavits to set forth the name of the child, the date of her birth, the names of her parents and whether or not he was on living March 4, 1905.

        Respectfully,

                Acting Commissioner.

Applications for Enrollment of Creek Newborn
Act of 1905   Volume VII

NC-524

Muskogee, Indian Territory, December 13, 1905.

Cinda Tiger,
    Care of John Tiger,
        Spaulding, Indian Territory.

Dear Madam:

    In the matter of the application for the enrollment of your minor child, Selanie Tiger, born April 20, 1903, as a citizen by blood of the Creek Nation, You are advised that it will be necessary for you to furnish this office with the affidavits of two disinterested persons relative to the birth of said child. A blank for that purpose is herewith enclosed.

    This matter should receive your prompt attention.

        Respectfully,

                Commissioner.

Dis

NC 524.

Muskogee, Indian Territory, August 21, 1906.

Clerk in Charge,
    Seminole Enrollment Division,
        Muskogee, Indian Territory.

Dear Sir:

    Application has been made for the enrollment as a citizen of the Creek Nation of Selanie Tiger, born April 20, 1903, to John Tiger, a Seminole, and Cindy[sic] Taylor, a citizen of the Creek Nation.

    You are requested to advise this office if application has been made for the enrollment of said child as a citizen of the Seminole Nation, and if so, please furnish the present status of said application.

        Respectfully,

                Commissioner.

Applications for Enrollment of Creek Newborn
Act of 1905 Volume VII

REFER IN REPLY TO THE FOLLOWING:

DEPARTMENT OF THE INTERIOR,
COMMISSIONER TO THE FIVE CIVILIZED TRIBES.

Muskogee, Indian Territory, August 24, 1906.

Chief Clerk,
    Creek Enrollment Division,
        Muskogee, Indian Territory.

Dear Sir:

    Receipt is hereby acknowledged of your letter of August 21, 1906, asking if application has been made for the enrollment of Selanie Tiger, child of John Tiger, a citizen of the Seminole Nation, and Cindy[sic] Tiger, a citizen of the Creek Nation, as a citizen of the Seminole Nation.

    In reply you are advised that it does not appear from the records of this office that any application has been made on behalf of Selanie Tiger for enrollment as a new born citizen of the Seminole Nation under the Act of Congress approved March 3, 1905.

                                    Respectfully,

                                      Wm. O. Beall
                                    Acting Commissioner.

NC-524.

Muskogee, Indian Territory, October 31, 1906.

Chief Clerk,
    Seminole Enrollment Division,
        Muskogee, Indian Territory.
Dear Sir:

    There is on file in the office an application for the enrollment of Selanie Tiger, born April 20, 1903, to John Tiger, a citizen of the Seminole Nation, and Cinda Tiger, who is identified as a citizen of the Creek Nation, opposite Creek Indian Roll No. 7711.

    You are advised that the name of said child is contained in a partial list of new born citizens by blood of the Creek Nation, approved by the Secretary of the Interior October 25, 1906, opposite roll number 1048.

                                    Respectfully,
                                                Commissioner.

Applications for Enrollment of Creek Newborn
Act of 1905   Volume VII

NC-525.

Muskogee, Indian Territory, August 8, 1905.

Buckner McGirt,
    Holdenville, Indian Territory.

Dear Sir:

    In the matter of the application for the enrollment of your minor son John McGirt, born April 6, 2903, as a citizen by blood of the Creek nation, it will be necessary for you to furnish this office, relative to the birth of said child, the affidavits of two disinterested persons; said affidavits to set forth the name of said child, the date of his birth, the names of his parents and whether or not he was on living March 4, 1905.

    This matter should receive your prompt attention.

    Respectfully,

    Acting Commissioner.

Western Dist Ind Ter
    Creek Nation

    Personally appeared before me a Notary Public in and for said Western District Creek Nation Ind Ter. Jim Davis and Henry Long citizens of the Creek (Muskogee) Nation who being duly sworn deposes and say that they were present at the time a male child was born to Buckner and Linda McGirt and that said child was afterward named John McGirt, and that said child John McGirt was alive on March 4th, 1905 and is still living.

                              his
                            Jim x Davis
                              mark

Witness to mark   his
                            Henry x Long
W.R. Clawson   mark
EDC Wisey

Subscribed and sworn to this Aug. 31, 1905.

                            WR Clawson
My Com Ex 6/13 08   Notary Public

BIRTH AFFIDAVIT.

DEPARTMENT OF THE INTERIOR.
COMMISSION TO THE FIVE CIVILIZED TRIBES.

Applications for Enrollment of Creek Newborn
Act of 1905   Volume VII

IN RE APPLICATION FOR ENROLLMENT, as a citizen of the Creek Nation, of John McGirt, born on the 6 day of April, 1902

Name of Father: Buckner McGirt   a citizen of the Creek   Nation.
Tuckabatche Town
Name of Mother: Lindy McGirt (nee Beaver)   a citizen of the Creek   Nation.
Tuckabatche Town
                       Postoffice   Holdenville, Ind. Ter.

AFFIDAVIT OF MOTHER.

UNITED STATES OF AMERICA, Indian Territory,
    Western   **DISTRICT.**   Child is present

I, Lindy McGirt, on oath state that I am about 25 years of age and a citizen by blood, of the Creek Nation; that I am the lawful wife of Buckner McGirt, who is a citizen, by blood of the Creek Nation; that a male child was born to me on 6 day of April, 1902, that said child has been named John McGirt, and was living March 4, 1905.

                                            her
                              Lindy x McGirt
Witnesses To Mark: mark
    { Alex Posey
      DC Skaggs

Subscribed and sworn to before me this 27 day of March, 1905.

                              Drennan C Skaggs
                                   Notary Public.

                          Father
AFFIDAVIT OF ~~ATTENDING PHYSICIAN OR MID-WIFE~~.

UNITED STATES OF AMERICA, Indian Territory,
    Western   **DISTRICT.**

                                                my wife
I, Buckner McGirt, ~~a~~ ------, on oath state that I attended on ^ Mrs. Lindy McGirt, ~~wife of~~ *(blank)* on the 6 day of April, 1902; that there was born to her on said date a *(blank)* child; that said child was living March 4, 1905, and is said to have been named John McGirt   his
                              Buckner x McGirt
Witnesses To Mark: mark
    { Alex Posey
      DC Skaggs

Applications for Enrollment of Creek Newborn
Act of 1905   Volume VII

Subscribed and sworn to before me this 27 day of March, 1905.

                         Drennan C Skaggs
                         Notary Public.

C 526

DEPARTMENT OF THE INTERIOR, COMMISSION TO THE FIVE CIVILIZED TRIBES.
Holdenville, I. T., March 27, 1905.

In the matter of the application for the enrollment of George Factor as a citizen of the Creek Nation.

NANCY FACTOR, being duly sworn, testified as follows:

Through Alex Posey Official Interpreter:

BY COMMISSION:

Q What is your name? A Nancy Factor.
Q How old are you? A I don't know.

Witness appears to be about thirty years old.

Q What is your post office address? A Wewoka.
Q Are you a citizen of the Creek Nation? A Yes, sir.
Q To what town do you belong? A Tuckabatche.
Q Do you know make application for the enrollment of your child, George Factor, as a citizen of the Creek Nation? A Yes, sir.
Q When was George born? A The child was born April 11 and is nearly two years old.
Q In the event that it is found that your child, George, is entitled to be enrolled in either the Creek or Muskogee Seminole nations in which nation do you desire to have him enrolled? A In the Creek Nation.

WILLIAM FACTOR, being duly sworn, testified as follows:

BY COMMISSION:

Q What is your name? A William Factor.
Q How old are you? A Thirty-eight.
Q Are you a citizen of the Seminole Nation? A Yes, sir.

Applications for Enrollment of Creek Newborn
Act of 1905   Volume VII

Q What is your post office address? A Wewoka.
Q Are you the husband of Nancy Factor? A Yes, sir.
Q Have you a child named George Factor? A Yes, sir.
Q Do you know when he was born? A April 11, 1903.
Q Did you make a record of the birth of George? A Yes, sir.
Q Have you that record with you? A No, sir, it is at home.
Q The child is living is it? A Yes, sir.

The child is present and appears to be fully two years old.

Q If it should be found that you[sic] child, George, is entitled to be enrolled in either the Creek or Muskogee Seminole Nations[sic], in which nation do you elect to have him enrolled? A In the Creek Nation.

SUSIE JACKSON, being duly sworn, testified as follows:

BY COMMISSION:
Q What is your name? A Susie Jackson.
Q How old are you? A About forty-three.
Q (Typing with overtyped letters.)
Q What is your post office address? A Wewoka.
Q Are you a citizen of the Creek Nation? A Yes, sir, but I have never been enrolled yet.
Q Do you know Willaim[sic] and Nancy Factor? A Yes, sir.
Q Do you know a child of theirs named George? A Yes, sir.
Q Did you attend on Nancy at the time that child was born? A Yes, sir.
Q Do you know when that was? A It was in April, year before last.
Q The child is living is it? A Yes, sir.
Q Do you know what time in April it was born? A No, sir, I do not know the day of the month. Just know it was in April.

------:O:------

I, D. C. Skaggs, on oath state that the above and foregoing is a full and true transcript of my stenographic notes as taken in said cause on said date.

DC Skaggs

Subscribed and sworn to before me this 17" day of July, 1905.

J McDermott
Notary Public.

NC 526.

DEPARTMENT OF THE INTERIOR,
COMMISSION TO THE FIVE CIVILIZED TRIBES.
Holdenville, I. T., March 27, 1905.

Applications for Enrollment of Creek Newborn
Act of 1905 Volume VII

In the matter of the application for the enrollment of Cogee Factor as a citizen by bloox[sic] of the Creek Nation.

NANCY FACTOR, being duly sworn, testified as follows:

Through Alex Posey Official Interpreter:

BY COMMISSION:
Q What is your name? A Nancy Factor.
Q How old are you? A I do not know.

Witness appears to be about thirty.

Q What is your post office address? A Wewoka.
Q Are you a citizen of the Creek Nation? A Yes, sir.
Q To what town do you belong? A Tuckabatchee.
Q Do you now make application for the enrollment of your child Cogee Factor as a citizen by blood of the Creek Nation? A Yes, sir.
Q Do you know when she was born? A The child will be two months old to-morrow.
Q In what month was she born? A In January.
Q What time in January? A Friday night.
Q Do you know the date? A The last of January 28.
Q Was there a record made of the birth of this child? A Yes, sir.
Q Where is that record? A The record is at home.

The child is present and appears to be as old as claimed.

Q In the event that your child, Cogee, is found to be entitled to enrollment in either the Creek or Seminole Nations, in which nation do you desire that she be enrolled? A In the Creek Nation.

WILLIAM FACTOR, being duly sworn, testified as follows:

BY COMMISSION:
Q What is your name? A William Factor.
Q How old are you? A Thirty-eight.
Q What is your post office address? A Wewoka.
Q Are you a citizen of the Creek Nation? A No, sir, Seminole.
Q Do you make application for the enrollment of your minor child, Cogee Factor, as a citizen by blood of the Creek Nation? A Yes, sir.
Q Do you know when she was born? A Jan 28.
Q What year? A 1905.
Q Was there a record made of the birth of the child? A Yes, sir.
Q Have you that record with you? A No, sir, it is at home.
Q Who made the record? A I did.
Q Have you that record? A No, sir, it is at home.

Applications for Enrollment of Creek Newborn
Act of 1905   Volume VII

Q In the event that it is found that your child is entitled to be enrolled in either the Creek Seminole Nations[sic], in which nation do you desire that she be enrolled? A In the Creek Nation.

COGEE TIGER, being duly sworn, testified as follows:

Through Alex Posey Official Interpreter:

BY COMMISSION:
Q What is your name? A Cogee Tiger.
Q How old are you? A I do not know my age.
   Witness appears to be about fifty years of age.

Q Do you know William and Nancy Factor? A Yes, sir, Nancy is my daughter.
Q Do you know a child of theirs named Cogee? A Yes, sir.
Q Do you know when that child was born? A I only know that the child was born on Friday night.
Q Do you know in what month? A I do not know the month nor the year.
Q Did you attend on Nancy factor as mid-wife at the time the child was born? A Yes, sir.
Q How old is the child? A I do not know.

---oooOOOooo---

I, D. C. Skaggs, on oath state that the above and foregoing is a full and true transcript of my stenographic notes as taken in said cause on said date.

DC Skaggs

Subscribed and sworn to before me this 17th day of July 1905.

Edw C Griesel
Notary Public.

BIRTH AFFIDAVIT.
(clipped off top)
Supplemental ^ taken
DEPARTMENT OF THE INTERIOR.
COMMISSION TO THE FIVE CIVILIZED TRIBES.

IN RE APPLICATION FOR ENROLLMENT, as a citizen of the Creek Nation, of Cogee Factor, born on the 28 day of January , 1905

Name of Father: William Factor   a citizen of the Seminole   Nation.
Name of Mother: Nancy Factor (nee Benton)   a citizen of the   Creek   Nation.
Tuckabatche Town
                    Postoffice   Wewoka, Ind. Ter.

Applications for Enrollment of Creek Newborn
Act of 1905   Volume VII

AFFIDAVIT OF MOTHER.

UNITED STATES OF AMERICA, Indian Territory, }   Child is present
   Western   DISTRICT.

I, Nancy Factor , on oath state that I am about 28 years of age and a citizen by blood , of the Creek Nation; that I am the lawful wife of William Factor , who is a citizen, by blood of the Seminole Nation; that a female child was born to me on 28 day of January , 1905 , that said child has been named Cogee Factor , and is now living.

                                      her
                               Nancy x Factor
                                 mark

Witnesses To Mark:
{ Alex Posey
{ DC Skaggs

Subscribed and sworn to before me this 27 day of March , 1905.

                              Drennan C Skaggs
                              Notary Public.

AFFIDAVIT OF ATTENDING PHYSICIAN OR MID-WIFE.

UNITED STATES OF AMERICA, Indian Territory }
   Western   DISTRICT.

I, Cogee Tiger , a midwife , on oath state that I attended on Mrs. Nancy Factor, wife of William Factor on the (blank) day of (blank) , 1 ; that there was born to her on said date a female child; that said child is now living and is said to have been named Cogee Factor

                                 her
                              Cogee x Tiger
Witnesses To Mark: mark
{ Alex Posey
{ DC Skaggs

Subscribed and sworn to before me this 27 day of March , 1905.

                              Drennan C Skaggs
                              Notary Public.

BIRTH AFFIDAVIT.
                          (clipped off top)
                          Supplemental ^ taken
                      DEPARTMENT OF THE INTERIOR.
          COMMISSION TO THE FIVE CIVILIZED TRIBES.

Applications for Enrollment of Creek Newborn
Act of 1905   Volume VII

IN RE APPLICATION FOR ENROLLMENT, as a citizen of the Creek Nation, of George Factor, born on the 11 day of April, 1903

Name of Father: William Factor a citizen of the Seminole Nation.
Name of Mother: Nancy Factor (nee Benton) a citizen of the Creek Nation.
Tuckabatche Town
                Postoffice   Wewoka, Ind. Ter.

AFFIDAVIT OF MOTHER.

UNITED STATES OF AMERICA, Indian Territory,
    Western   DISTRICT.
                                            Child is present

I, Nancy Factor, on oath state that I am about 28 years of age and a citizen by blood, of the Creek Nation; that I am the lawful wife of William Factor, who is a citizen, by blood of the Seminole Nation; that a male child was born to me on 11 day of April, 1903, that said child has been named George Factor, and is now living.

                                                her
                                            Nancy x Factor
                                              mark

Witnesses To Mark:
  { Alex Posey
    DC Skaggs

Subscribed and sworn to before me this 27 day of March, 1905.

                                          Drennan C Skaggs
                                          Notary Public.

AFFIDAVIT OF ATTENDING PHYSICIAN OR MID-WIFE.

UNITED STATES OF AMERICA, Indian Territory,
    Western   DISTRICT.

I, Susie Jackson, a midwife, on oath state that I attended on Mrs. Nancy Factor, wife of William Factor ~~on the (blank) day of~~ April, 1903; that there was born to her on said date a male child; that said child is now living and is said to have been named George Factor

                                              her
                                          Susie x Jackson
Witnesses To Mark: mark
  { Alex Posey
    DC Skaggs

Applications for Enrollment of Creek Newborn
Act of 1905 Volume VII

Subscribed and sworn to before me this 27 day of March, 1905.

Drennan C Skaggs
Notary Public.

W.F.

DEPARTMENT OF THE INTERIOR.
COMMISSION TO THE FIVE CIVILIZED TRIBES.

Muskogee, Indian Territory, July 19, 1905.

Chief Clerk,
    Creek Enrollment Division.

Dear Sir:

    Receipt is acknowledged of your letter of July 14, 1905 (NC-526) stating that application was made to the Commission to the Five Civilized Tribes for the enrollment of Cogee Factor, born January 28, 1905, and George Factor, born April 11, 1903, children of William Factor, a citizen of the Seminole Nation, and Nancy Factor, a citizen of the Creek Nation, as citizens by blood of the Creek Nation and requesting to be informed as to whether application was made for the enrollment of said children as citizens of the Seminole Nation.

    In reply to your letter you are advised that it does not appear from an examination of the records of this office that any application was made to the Commission to the Five Civilized Tribes for the enrollment of said Cogee Factor and George Factor as citizens of the Seminole Nation.

Respectfully,

Tams Bixby   Commissioner.

NC. 526.

Muskogee, Indian Territory, July 14, 1905.

Commissioner to the Five Civilized Tribes,
    Seminole Enrollment Division,
        Muskogee, Indian Territory.

Gentlemen:

    March 29, 1905, application was made to the Commission to the Five Civilized Tribes for the enrollment of Cogee Factor, born January 28, 1905, and George Factor,

Applications for Enrollment of Creek Newborn
Act of 1905   Volume VII

born April 11, 1903, as citizens by blood of the Creek Nation. It is stated in said application that the father of said children is William Factor, a citizen of the Seminole Nation, and that the mother is Nancy Factor, a citizen of the Creek Nation.

You are requested to inform the Creek Enrollment Division as to whether application has been made for the enrollment of said children as citizens of the Seminole Nation, and if so, what disposition has been made of the same.

Respectfully,

Commissioner.

NC
526

Muskogee, Indian Territory, November 12, 1906.

Chief Clerk,
    Seminole Enrollment Division,
        General Office.

Dear Sir:

You are hereby advised that the names of Cogee and George Factor, children of William Factor, an alleged citizen of the Seminole Nation, and Nancy Factor, a citizen by blood of the Creek Nation, are contained in a schedule of New Born citizens of the Creek Nation, approved by the Secretary of the Interior September 27, 1905, opposite Roll Nos. 516 and 517.

Respectfully,

Commissioner.

NC-527.

Muskogee, Indian Territory, August 8, 1905.

Rhoda Harrison,
    c/o Peter Harrison,
        Holdenville, Indian Territory.

Dear Madam:

In the matter of the application for the enrollment of your minor child, Bettie Harrison, born February 10, 1905, as a citizen by blood of the Creek Nation, it will be necessary for you to furnish this office with the affidavits of two disinterested persons relative to the birth of said child; said affidavits to set forth the name of said child, the

Applications for Enrollment of Creek Newborn
Act of 1905   Volume VII

date of her birth, the names of her parents and whether or not he was on living March 4, 1905.

Respectfully,

Acting Commissioner.

NC-527

Muskogee, Indian Territory, December 13, 1905.

Rhoda Harrison,
    c/o Peter Harrison,
        Holdenville, Indian Territory.
Dear Madam:

    In the matter of the application for the enrollment of your minor child, Bettie Harrison, born February 10, 1905, as a citizen by blood of the Creek Nation, you are advised that this Office requires the affidavit of two disinterested persons relative to the birth of said child. A blank for that purpose is herewith enclosed.

    This matter should receive your prompt attention.

Respectfully,

Commissioner.

Dis

REFER IN REPLY TO THE FOLLOWING:
N.C. 527

DEPARTMENT OF THE INTERIOR,
COMMISSIONER TO THE FIVE CIVILIZED TRIBES.

Muskogee, Indian Territory, April 30, 1905.

Commissioner to the Five Civilized Tribes,
    Muskogee, Indian Territory.

Sir:
    There is inclosed herewith joint affidavit of Ottawa and Mary Cain. in the matter of the application for the enrollment of Bettie Harrison, as a citizen by blood of the Creek Nation.

Respectfully,
Alex Posey
In Charge of Creek Field Party

Applications for Enrollment of Creek Newborn
Act of 1905 Volume VII

Indian Territory, I
               I ss
Western District. I

We, the undersigned, on oath state that we are personally acquainted with Rhoda Harrison wife of Peter Harrison ; that on or about the 10 day of February , 1905, a female child was born to them and has been named Bettie Harrison ; and that said child was living March 4, 1905.

We further state that we have no interest in this case.

                                      his
                                 Ottawa x Cain

Witnesses to mark: mark
  Alex Posey
                                      her
                                 Mary x Cain
  DC Skaggs   mark

Subscribed and sworn to before me this 25 day of April, 1906.

                                        Alex Posey
                                        Notary Public.

AFFIDAVIT OF DISINTERESTED WITNESSES.

United States of America,
   Indian Territory,   ss.
   Western District.

We, the undersigned, on oath state that we are personally acquainted with Rhoda Harrison , wife of Peter Harrison , and that there was born to her on or about the 10th day of February , 1905 , a Female child; that said child was living March 4, 1905, and is said to have been named Bettie Harrison .

We further state that we have no interest in this case.

                                      Alfred Goat

                                      Wardley Goat

(2) Witnesses to mark.

_____

_____

Subscribed and sworn to before me this 29th day of January 1905.

                                   (No name given)
                                        Notary Public.

My Commission Expires July 11th, 1906.

Applications for Enrollment of Creek Newborn
Act of 1905 Volume VII

BIRTH AFFIDAVIT.

DEPARTMENT OF THE INTERIOR.
COMMISSION TO THE FIVE CIVILIZED TRIBES.

IN RE APPLICATION FOR ENROLLMENT, as a citizen of the Creek Nation, of Bettie Harrison, born on the 10 day of February, 1905

Name of Father: Peter Harrison   a citizen of the Creek Nation. Weogufky Town
Name of Mother: Rhoda Harrison (nee Yahola)   a citizen of the Creek Nation. Tuckabatche Town
                      Postoffice   Holdenville, Ind. Ter.

AFFIDAVIT OF MOTHER.

UNITED STATES OF AMERICA, Indian Territory,   Child is present
     Western   DISTRICT.

I, Rhoda Harrison, on oath state that I am 19 years of age and a citizen by blood, of the Creek Nation; that I am the lawful wife of Peter Harrison, who is a citizen, by blood of the Creek Nation; that a female child was born to me on 10 day of February, 1905, that said child has been named Bettie Harrison, and was living March 4, 1905. That no one attended on me as midwife or physician at the birth of the child.
                                       her
                         Rhoda x Harrison
Witnesses To Mark: mark
    { Alex Posey
    { DC Skaggs

Subscribed and sworn to before me this 27 day of March, 1905.

                         Drennan C Skaggs
                             Notary Public.

N.C. 528.

DEPARTMENT OF THE INTERIOR,
COMMISSIONER TO THE FIVE CIVILIZED TRIBES.
Bernard, I. T., April 22, 1906.

In the matter of the application for the enrollment of Jennie Lowe as a citizen by blood of the Creek Nation.

Applications for Enrollment of Creek Newborn
Act of 1905   Volume VII

NANCY LEADER, being duly sworn, testified as follows:

Through Alex Posey official interpreter:

BY THE COMMISSIONER:
Q What is your name? A Nancy Leader.
Q How old are you? A About twenty-six.
Q What is your post office address? A Bernard.
Q Do you know Tobler and Sallie Lowe? A Yes, sir, Sallie was my sister.
Q Do you know a child of theirs named Jennie Lowe: A Yes, sir.
Q Did you attend on Sallie at the birth of the child? A Yes, sir.
Q When was the child born? A The child was born September 22, but I do not know in what year.
Q According to affidavits executed by you and the child's mother the child was born September 22, 1901. Is that correct? A The month and the day is correct but the year is wrong. The child was born in 1902.
Q Is the child living? A Yes sir.
Q Did Sallie Lowe have any other children? A Yes, sir, she had a child that died last year unnamed. It was about three months old. She has two other children who are dead, both boys.
Q What were their names? A One was named Millie and the other named Joe. Millie was named and enrolled before it was born. It happened to be a boy instead of a girl.
Q Do you know when Millie and Joe were born and died? A I do not know. I was not present at the birth or death of either. I think Millie was born in October. I do not know in what year and am not positive as to the month.
Q How old was Millie at the time he died? A About six months old, I think.
Q How old was Joe at the time of his death? A Joe died three days after he was born.
Q Why did you make an affidavit stating that Jennie was born September 22, 1901, when in fact she was born September 22, 1902? A I stated at the time the affidavit was made that the child was born September 22, 1902, but Daniel McGert, who assisted the mother in making out the affidavits insisted thath[sic] the child was born September 22, 1901, and the notary public must have put down the date given by him, which is incorrect.
    There is on file in the office of the Commissioner an affidavit executed by Sallie Lowe, September 6, 1901, stating that Jennie Lowe was born September 31, 1900, and died the same day. Does that refer to the Jennie who is living or to another child named Jennie who is dead? A That affidavit no doubt refers to Millie Lowe, the child she named and enrolled before it was born. After the birth of the child she named it Jennie. I think she made that affidavit when the Commission was at Wetumka.

    I, D. C. Skaggs, on oath state that the above and foregoing is a full and true transcript of my stenographic notes as taken in said cause on said date.
                                                                DC Skaggs

Subscribed and sworn to before me this 18 day of April, 1906.

                                                                Alex Posey
                                                                Notary Public.

Applications for Enrollment of Creek Newborn
Act of 1905 Volume VII

N.C. 528.

DEPARTMENT OF THE INTERIOR,
COMMISSIONER TO THE FIVE CIVILIZED TRIBES.
Bernard, I.T., April 11, 1906.

In the matter of the application for the enrollment of Jennie Lowe as a citizen by blood of the Creek Nation.

COLUMBUS LOWE, being duly sworn, testified as follows:

Through Alex Posey official interpreter.

BY THE COMMISSIONER:
Q What is your name? A Columbus Lowe.
Q How old are you? A About twenty-three.
Q What is your post office address? A Wetumka.
Q Are you a citizen of the Creek Nation? A Yes, sir.
Q Do you know Tobler Lowe and Sallie Lowe? A Yes, sir.
Q What relation are they to you? A Tobler is my brother.
Q Are they both dead? A Sallie is dead.
Q Do you know a child of theirs named Jennie Lowe? A Yes, sir.
Q Is that child living? A Yes, sir.
Q Do you know when the child was born? A I do not remember when the child was born. It is four years old or over.

The child is present and appears to be about four years of age.

Q There is on file in the office of the Commissioner an affidavit executed by the mother, September 6, 1901, stating that the child was born December 31, 1900, and died the same day. Another affidavit executed by the mother is on file giving the same date of birth and erasing the words "and now living." April 1, 1905, the mother and Nancy Leader executed affidavits stating that the child was born September 22, 1901, and was living March 4, 1905 March 4, 1905. Do these affidavits refer to different children? A She never had any other child named Jennie. She lost a child about ten years ago but that child was a boy.
Q Do you know what that child's name was? A No, sir.
Q Do you know whether or not Sallie Lowe had a child which was born and died the same day? A No, sir. Sallie never had but three children. Her last child died when it was about a month old and it was born since Jennie was born. It was a boy.
Q When was it born? A In August, 1905. And it died about the middle of October, 1905.
Q Where does Tobler Lowe live? A Near Bernard but he is now in Muskogee.

Applications for Enrollment of Creek Newborn
Act of 1905   Volume VII

---oooOOOooo---

I, D. C. Skaggs, on oath state that the above and foregoing is a full and true transcript of my stenographic notes as taken in said cause on said date.

DC Skaggs

Subscribed and sworn to before me this 17th day of April, 1906.

Alex Posey
Notary Public.

N.C. 528

DEPARTMENT OF THE INTERIOR,
COMMISSIONER TO THE FIVE CIVILIZED TRIBES.
Muskogee, Indian Territory, April 11, 1906.

In the matter of the application for the enrollment of Jennie Lowe as a citizen by blood of the Creek Nation.

TOBLER LOWE, being duly sworn, testified as follows through Jesse McDermott official interpreter.

Q What is your name? A Tobler Lowe.
Q What is your age? A I am over fifty years old.
Q What is your post office address? A Barnard.
Q What is the name of your wife? A Sallie Lowe. Sallie is now dead. Died last summer.
Q Did she have two children, your t-step children, named McGirt? A Yes, Mongie and John.

Tobler and Sallie Lowe are identified on Creek Indian care #1726 opposite roll Nos. 5545 and 5546, respectively.

Q Did you ever have any children by Sallie? A Yes
Q How many children by her? A There were four children born to us but three are dead.
Q What was the names of those dead children beginning with the oldest? A Andy, Joseph and Mille.
Q That's all you had by her that are dead? A Yes, sir.
Q Were any of them ever called anything else? A No.
Q How many children have you by her living? A One.
Q You are sure you have only one child by her living? A Yes
Q What is its name? A Jennie.
Q Is that the only child you have had by her whose name is Jennie? A Yes, sir
Q Didn't have another child by her named Jennie that is dead? A No.
Q You are sure that Jennie is living? A She was in Wetumka yesterday.

Applications for Enrollment of Creek Newborn
Act of 1905   Volume VII

Q Explain this, in 1901 September 6 you yourself and Sallie Lowe executed an affidavit before William T. Martin in which you stated that a child was born to you December 31, 1900 named Jennie Jennie[sic] Lowe and the words "is now living" were scratched out in the affidavit. On September 6, 1901, Sallie Lowe executed another affidavit in which she said that Jennie Lowe was born to her December 31, 1900 and that the child died on the same 31 day of December 1900. March 27, 1905, Sallie Lowe and a midwife executed an affidavit stating that a child was born to said Sallie Named Jennie Lowe, on September 22, 1901 and was living March 4, 1905 March 4, 1905 which of those is true? A I am sure the midwife and mother were mistaken in the dates because the child was born five days before the last of September 1901 and the child will be five years old this coming September.

The witness presents a letter written to him by this office telling him of this discrepancy in the affidavits on file and advising him that we will be allowed a certain time to appear at this office with the midwife in attendance at the birth of said child and at least one other witness.
Q Who was the midwife when Jennie Lowe was born? A Nannie Leader.
Q Is she living? A Yes, sir.
Q Why didn't you bring her in today as the letter told you? A I asked her to come but she refused.
Q Is this Jennie whom you now state is living and will be five years old next September according to the last affidavit made by Sallie is this one the same for whom you made an affidavit some time ago and said it was born at a different time from this and signed an affidavit which had scratched out the words now living? A Yes
Q The same child is referred to in these different affidavits is it? A Yes
Q You never had but one child named Jennie? A No, sir.
Q Look here, it wasn't the midwife and the mother alone who made that mistake before, you signed an affidavit yourself which gave the date of its birth as December 31, 1900 and had scratched out the words "is now living". You signed that yourself as well as the mother Sallie Lowe? A I recollect signing some affidavits at Barnard some time ago but those affidavits were not explained to me fully so I could understand them.
Q In addition to those affidavits on the same day Sallie Lowe executed an affidavit stating that the child was born December 31, 1900 and died on the same 31 December 1900 how do you account for that? A I am unable to explain the differences in the dates. I will read the affidavits to you so you will understand them:

SARTY COWEE, being duly sworn, testified as follows: through Jesse McDermott official interpreter.

Q What is your name? A Sarty Cowee.
Q What is your age? A I am over fifty.
Q What is your post office address? A Wetumka.
Q Do you know Tobler Lowe here? A Yes, sir.
Q How long have you known him? A We were raised up together.
Q Do you know a child he has now by Sallie Lowe? A The only thing that I know is that they have had this child with them all the time.

Applications for Enrollment of Creek Newborn
Act of 1905 Volume VII

Q They have a child living now? A Yes, sir
Q Do you know the name of that child? A No, sir I don't
Q Do you know how old it is? A From the size I should judge that she is past three; according to the Indian custom they judge ages by the summers.
Q Is that the only child he has living that you know of? A Yes
Q Is the mother of that child living? A No
Q How long has she been dead? A I am not sure of that. I never heard of her death until some time after she died.
Q Did she have this child with her the last time you saw her? A Yes
Q And did you see her and the child as recently as a year ago? A Yes
Q That child you say then was living March 4, 1905 was it? A Yes, sir
Q Do you know it to be the child of Tobler and Sallie Lowe? A Yes
Q Do you know anything about these affidavits executed by Tobler and Sallie Lowe which indicate that that same child died about the time of its birth? A No, sir I don't know anything about the affidavits

TOBLER LOWE RECALLED:

Q Where is that child living now? A She is in the custody of my brother & wife, Mary Lowe, who lives at Wetumka. We had a child born a short time after Christmas that died the same day it was born.
Q Was that child name? A No but in making out the affidavit they might have called it Jennie.
Q How long before the affidavits were made out by that field party at Wetumka was it that this child -this dead child, was born and died? A The child had been dead a good while before the Commission was out at Wetumka, we never had thought anything about it but they got to asking us about our children and it may be the mother gave the child's name a Jennie in making out these affidavits.
Q I asked you several times to tell how many children you had and you mentioned only four, and this one you say lived only a day why didn't you mention it then? A The reason I didn't say anything about this child was it was so small when it died. I also have another one that died last summer unnamed of which I didn't say anything about.
Q How long after the birth of that unnamed child which died the same day was it before this child that is now living was born? A It was nearly a year after this unnamed child died that the one that is living now was born.
Q At the time this field party came there and you and Sallie made out an affidavit about that one that died so young was your living child born then? A No
Q How long after the field party had been at Wetumka was it before this living child was born? A I am unable to state just how long it was but it wasn't very long afterwards.
Q The affidavit says the living child was born September 22, and that field party was there the 6th of September of the same year, it that about right? A Yes

I, Anna Garrigues, on oath state that the above and foregoing is a true and correct copy of my stenographic notes taken in said case on said date.

Anna Garrigues

Applications for Enrollment of Creek Newborn
Act of 1905   Volume VII

Subscribed and sworn to before me this
11 day of April 1906.

          J McDermott
            Notary Public.

N.C. 528   F.H.W.

DEPARTMENT OF THE INTERIOR,
COMMISSIONER TO THE FIVE CIVILIZED TRIBES.

In the matter of the application for the enrollment of Jennie Lowe as a citizen by blood of the Creek Nation.

DECISION.

The record in this case shows that on September 6, 1901, application was filed, in affidavit form, for the enrollment of Jennie Lowe as a citizen by blood of the Creek Nation. Supplementary affidavits filed September 6, 1901, and April 1, 1905, are attached to and made part of the record herein. Further proceedings were had April 11, 1905, before the Commission to the Five Civilized Tribes, at Muskogee, Indian Territory and on the same date before a Creek enrollment field party, at Barnard, Indian Territory.

The evidence shows that said Jennie Lowe is the child of Tobler Lowe and Sallie Lowe, who are identified on the approved roll of citizens by blood of the Creek Nation, opposite roll Nos. 5545 and 5546 respectively, approved by the Secretary of the Interior March 28, 1902.

The evidence is conflicting as to the date of birth of said applicant, but by a preponderance of testimony it is clearly established that the said Jennie Lowe was born either September 22, 1901 or September 1902, and was living March 4, 1905 April 11, 1906.

The Act of Congress approved March 3, 1905 (33 Stat. L., 1048), provides in part as follows:

> "That the Commission to the Five Civilized Tribes is authorized for sixty days after the date of the approval of this act to receive and consider applications for enrollment, of children, born subsequent to May twenty-fifth, nineteen hundred and one, and prior to March fourth, nineteen hundred and five, and living on said latter date, to citizens of the Creek tribe of Indians whose enrollment has been approved by the Secretary of the Interior prior to the approval of this act; and to enroll and make allotments to such children."

It is therefore, ordered and adjudged that the said Jennie Lowe is entitled to be enrolled as a citizen by blood of the Creek Nation, in accordance with the provisions of law above quoted, and the application for her enrollment as such is accordingly granted.

Applications for Enrollment of Creek Newborn
Act of 1905   Volume VII

Tams Bixby Commissioner.

Muskogee, Indian Territory.
January 14-1907

BIRTH AFFIDAVIT.

Department of the Interior,
COMMISSION TO THE FIVE CIVILIZED TRIBES.

IN RE Application for Enrollment, as a citizen of the Creek Nation, of Jennie Lowe , born on the 31 day of December , 1900

Name of Father: Tobler Lowe   a citizen of the Creek   Nation.
Name of Father: Sallie Lowe   a citizen of the Creek   Nation.

Post-office   Wetumka I.T.

AFFIDAVIT OF MOTHER.

UNITED STATES OF AMERICA,
    INDIAN TERRITORY,
    Northern   District.

I, Sallie Lowe , on oath state that I am 35 years of age and a citizen by blood , of the Creek Nation; that I am the lawful wife of Tobler Lowe , who is a citizen, by blood of the Creek Nation; that a female child was born to me on 31 day of December , 1900 , that said child has been named Jennie Lowe , ~~and is now living.~~

                                     her
                                Sallie x Lowe
WITNESSES TO MARK: mark
    { Charles Coachman
    { Walter Gray

Subscribed and sworn to before me this 6 day of September , 1901.

                             William T Martin
                                   NOTARY PUBLIC.

AFFIDAVIT OF ATTENDING PHYSICIAN OR MID-WIFE.

UNITED STATES OF AMERICA,
    INDIAN TERRITORY,
    Northern   District.

Applications for Enrollment of Creek Newborn
Act of 1905   Volume VII

I, Tobler Lowe , a Creek Citizen by blood 50 years of age , on oath state that was present when my wife Sallie Lowe was confined I attended on Mrs.   , wife of   on the 31 day of December , 1900 ; that there was born to her on said date a female child; ~~that said child is now living and is said to have been named~~ Jennie Lowe   that said child was named his
Tobler x Lowe
mark

WITNESSES TO MARK:
{ Charles Coachman
{ Walter Gray

Subscribed and sworn to before me this 6 day of September , 1901.

William T Martin
NOTARY PUBLIC.

BIRTH AFFIDAVIT.

DEPARTMENT OF THE INTERIOR.
COMMISSION TO THE FIVE CIVILIZED TRIBES.

IN RE APPLICATION FOR ENROLLMENT, as a citizen of the Creek Nation, of Jennie Lowe, born on the 22 day of Sept , 1901

Name of Father: Tobeler[sic] Lowe   a citizen of the Creek   Nation.
Name of Mother: Sallie Lowe   a citizen of the   Creek   Nation.

Postoffice   Barnard I.T.

AFFIDAVIT OF MOTHER.

UNITED STATES OF AMERICA, Indian Territory,
(blank)   **DISTRICT.**

I, Sallie Lowe , on oath state that I am 45 years of age and a citizen by blood , of the Creek   Nation; that I am the lawful wife of Tobeler Lowe , who is a citizen, by blood of the Creek   Nation; that a female   child was born to me on 22^d day of Sept , 1901 , that said child has been named Jennie Lowe , and was living March 4, 1905.

her
Sallie x lowe[sic]
mark

Witnesses To Mark:
{ Goliah Jones
{ Timmie Stidham

Applications for Enrollment of Creek Newborn
Act of 1905 Volume VII

Subscribed and sworn to before me this 27" day of March, 1905.

J.R. Dunzy
Notary Public.

AFFIDAVIT OF ATTENDING PHYSICIAN OR MID-WIFE.

UNITED STATES OF AMERICA, Indian Territory,
Western DISTRICT.

I, Nancy Leader, a mid-wife, on oath state that I attended on Mrs. Sallie Lowe, wife of Tobeler Lowe on the 22^d day of Sept, 1901 ; that there was born to her on said date a female child; that said child was living March 4, 1905, and is said to have been named Jennie Lowe

his
Nancy x Leader
mark

Witnesses To Mark:
  Goliah Jones
  Timmie Stidham

Subscribed and sworn to before me this 27 day of March, 1905.

J.R. Dunzy

Notary Public.

SUPPLEMENTAL PROOF.

DEPARTMENT OF THE INTERIOR,
COMMISSION TO THE FIVE CIVILIZED TRIBES.

IN RE Application for Enrollment, as a citizen of the Creek (or Muskogee) Nation, of Jennie Lowe, born on the 31 day of December, 1900

Name of Father: Tobler Lowe   a citizen of the   Creek   Nation.
Name of Mother: Sallie Lowe   a citizen of the   Creek   Nation.

Postoffice   Wetumka I.T.

Applications for Enrollment of Creek Newborn
Act of 1905 Volume VII

AFFIDAVIT OF PARENT.
(To be made if child is now living)

UNITED STATES OF AMERICA,
Indian Territory,
Northern DISTRICT.

    I, Sallie Lowe, on oath state that I am 35 years of age and a citizen by blood , of the Creek (or Muskogee) Nation; that I am the Mother of Jennie Lowe a female child who was born on the 31 day of December , 1900, that said child died on the same 31st day of December , 1900

                                        her
                                Sallie x Lowe

Witnesses To Mark: mark
    Charles Coachman
    Walter Gray
    Subscribed and sworn to before me this 6 *day of* September, *19*01.

                                        William T Martin
                                        Notary Public.

NC 528.

                              Muskogee, Indian Territory, July 20, 1905.

Salle Lowe,
    Barnard, Indian Territory.

Dear Madam:

    In the matter of the application for the enrollment of your minor child, Jennie Lowe, as a citizen of the Creek Nation, you are advised that you will be allowed fifteen days from date hereof which to appear at the office of the Commission to the Five Civilized Tribes, in Muskogee, Indian Territory, for the purpose of testifying under oath.

                                      Respectfully,

                                                Commissioner.

REFER IN REPLY TO THE FOLLOWING:
N.C.528

DEPARTMENT OF THE INTERIOR,
COMMISSIONER TO THE FIVE CIVILIZED TRIBES.

                            Muskogee, Indian Territory, September 11, 1905.

Tobler Lowe,
    Barnard, Indian Territory.

Applications for Enrollment of Creek Newborn
Act of 1905   Volume VII

Dear Sir:

Receipt is acknowledged of your letter of September 7, 1905, in which you state that your wife, Sallie Lowe, is dead.

There is on file at this office an application for the enrollment of your minor child, Jennie Lowe, deceased.

It is stated that Sallie Lowe, deceased, was the mother of said child.

In order to determine whether said Jennie Lowe is entitled to be enrolled as a citizen by blood of the Creek Nation, it will be necessary for you to furnish this office with the names of the parents of yourself and wife, the Creek Indian town to which each of you belongs, the maiden name of said Sallie Lowe, deceased and any other information that will help to identify either of you as citizens of the Creek Nation.

When this information has been furnished the matter of the enrollment of said Jennie Lowe, deceased, will be further investigated.

Respectfully,

Wm. O. Beall
Acting Commissioner.

ATKINS & HICKS,
  Law & Insurance,
    Wetumka, I.T.

COPY

October 28th, 1905.

Hon. William O. Beall, Acting Commissioner,
   Muskogee, I.T.

Dear Sir:

I herewith enclose information concerning citizenship of myself and wife. The names of the parents of myself, Tobler Lowe, are Ahalokoce and Soke. The parents of my wife are Cendey Lone and Loseluse. I, Tobler Lowe, belong to the Town of Tokpvce and my wife Sallie Lowe, belonged to the Reuale.

Mose Respectfully,

(Signed) TOBLER LOWE,

By B.N. Hicks.

Applications for Enrollment of Creek Newborn
Act of 1905 Volume VII

FOOT NOTE. The words "Tokpvce" and Rueale"[sic] are interpreted by Jesse McDermott, official interpreter, as Tuckabatche and Thlewarthle, respectively.

NC 528.　　　　　　　　　　　　Muskogee, Indian Territory, December 13, 1905.

Tobler Lowe,
　　Barnard, Indian Territory.

Dear Sir:

　　There are on file in this office affidavits executed by you and by your deceased wife, Sallie Lowe, relative to the birth of your minor child, Jennie Lowe, in which you state that said child was born December 31, 1900, and that she died the same day. There are also on file affidavits executed by you and by said Sallie Lowe relative to the birth of said Jennie Lowe, in which it is stated that said Jennie Lowe was born September 22, 1901, and that she was living March 4, 1905.

　　In order that you may explain what appears to be discrepancies in said affidavits, you will be allowed twenty days from date within which to appear at the office of the Commissioner to the Five Civilized Tribes, in Muskogee, Indian Territory, with the midwife who attended at the birth of said Jennie Lowe, and at least one other witness who knows the exact date of her birth, for the purpose of being examined under oath.

　　　　　　　　　　　　　　　　Respectfully,

　　　　　　　　　　　　　　　　　　　　　　　　Commissioner.
Register.

NC 528.

　　　　　　　　　　　　　　　　Wetumka, Indian Territory, April 19, 1905.

Commissioner to the Five Civilized Tribes,
　　Muskogee, Indian Territory.

Sir:

　　There is enclosed herewith the testimony of Columbus Lowe and Nancy Leader, taken April 11, 1906, in the matter of the application for the enrollment of Jennie Lowe, as a citizen by blood of the Creek Nation.

　　The testimony of Tobler Lowe which is desired in this case will follow as soon as same can be secured.

　　　　　　　　　　　　　　　　Respectfully,

Applications for Enrollment of Creek Newborn
Act of 1905   Volume VII

Signed   Alex Posey,
In Charge Creek Field Party.

N C 528

JWH

Muskogee, Indian Territory, March 1, 1907.

Tobeler[sic] Lowe,
   Barnard, Indian Territory.

Dear Sir:

You are hereby advised that on February 15, 1907, the Secretary of the Interior approved the enrollment of your minor child, Jennie Lowe, as a citizen by blood of the Creek Nation, and that the name of said child appears upon the roll of New Born citizens by blood of the Creek Nation, enrolled under the Act of Congress approved March 3, 1905, as number 1155.

This child is now entitled to allotment and application therefor should be made without delay at the Creek Land Office, Muskogee, Indian Territory.

Respectfully,

Commissioner.

BIRTH AFFIDAVIT.

DEPARTMENT OF THE INTERIOR.
COMMISSION TO THE FIVE CIVILIZED TRIBES.

IN RE APPLICATION FOR ENROLLMENT, as a citizen of the Creek Nation, of Diamond Jackson , born on the 18 day of January , 1903

Name of Father: Anton Jackson   a citizen of the United States Nation.
Name of Mother: Sally Jackson (nee Beaver)   a citizen of the   Creek   Nation.
Tulsa Canadian Town
                     Postoffice   Holdenville, Ind. Ter.

AFFIDAVIT OF MOTHER.

UNITED STATES OF AMERICA, Indian Territory,
   Western   DISTRICT.

Child is present

Applications for Enrollment of Creek Newborn
Act of 1905 Volume VII

I, Sally Jackson , on oath state that I am 30 years of age and a citizen by blood, of the Creek Nation; that I am the lawful wife of Anton Jackson , who is a citizen, by *(blank)* of the United States Nation; that a male child was born to me on 18 day of January, 1903 , that said child has been named Diamond Jackson , and was living March 4, 1905.

Sallie Jackson

Witnesses To Mark:

{

Subscribed and sworn to before me this 27 day of March , 1905.

Drennan C Skaggs
Notary Public.

AFFIDAVIT OF ATTENDING PHYSICIAN OR MID-WIFE.

UNITED STATES OF AMERICA, Indian Territory, }
Western   DISTRICT.

I, H.A. Howell , a physician , on oath state that I attended on Mrs. Sally Jackson , wife of Anton Jackson on the 18 day of January , 1903 ; that there was born to her on said date a male child; that said child was living March 4, 1905, and is said to have been named Diamond Jackson

H.A. Howell, M.D.

Witnesses To Mark:

{

Subscribed and sworn to before me this 27 day of March , 1905.

Drennan C Skaggs
Notary Public.

DEPARTMENT OF THE INTERIOR.
COMMISSION TO THE FIVE CIVILIZED TRIBES.

In the matter of the death of Sosee Leader a citizen of the Creek Nation, who formerly resided at or near Barnard , Ind. Ter., and died on the 17th day of May , 1904

AFFIDAVIT OF RELATIVE.

UNITED STATES OF AMERICA, Indian Territory, }
Western   DISTRICT.

Applications for Enrollment of Creek Newborn
Act of 1905   Volume VII

I, Nancy Leader, on oath state that I am 27 years of age and a citizen by blood, of the Creek Nation; that my postoffice address is Barnard, Ind. Ter.; that I am the mother of Sosee Leader who was a citizen, by blood, of the Creek Nation and that said Sosee Leader died on the 17th day of May, 1904.

her
Nancy x Leader
mark

Witnesses To Mark:
{ Goliah Jones
{ Timmie Stidham

Subscribed and sworn to before me this 27th day of March, 1905.

J.R. Dunzy
Notary Public.

AFFIDAVIT OF ACQUAINTANCE.

UNITED STATES OF AMERICA, Indian Territory, }
    Western   DISTRICT.

I, Sallie Lowe, on oath state that I am 45 years of age, and a citizen by blood of the Creek Nation; that my postoffice address is Barnard, Ind. Ter.; that I was personally acquainted with Sosee Leader who was a citizen, by blood, of the Creek Nation; and that said Sosee Leader died on the 17th day of May, 1904.

her
Sallie x Lowe
mark

Witnesses To Mark:
{ Goliah Jones
{ Timmie Stidham

Subscribed and sworn to before me this 27th day of March, 1905.

J.R. Dunzy
Notary Public.

NC 530   JLD
DEPARTMENT OF THE INTERIOR,
COMMISSIONER TO THE FIVE CIVILIZED TRIBES.

In the matter of the application for the enrollment of Sosee Leader, deceased, as a citizen by blood of the Creek Nation.

. . . .

Applications for Enrollment of Creek Newborn
Act of 1905   Volume VII

STATEMENT AND ORDER.

The record in this case shows that on April 1, 1905, application was made, in affidavit form, for the enrollment of Sosee Leader, deceased, as a citizen by blood of the Creek Nation, under the provisions of the act of Congress approved March 3, 1905.

It appears from the affidavit filed in this matter that said Sosee Leader, deceased, was born May 7, 1904, and died May 17, 1904.

The act of Congress approved March 3, 1905, (33 Stats., 1048), provides:

"That the Commission to the Five Civilized Tribes is authorized for sixty days after the date of the approval of this act to receive and consider applications for enrollment, of children, born subsequent to May twenty-fifth, nineteen hundred and one, and prior to March fourth, nineteen hundred and five, and living on said latter date, to citizens of the Creek tribe of Indians whose enrollment has been approved by the Secretary of the Interior prior to the approval of this act; and to enroll and make allotments to such children."

It is, therefore, ordered that the application for the enrollment of Sosee Leader, deceased, as a citizen by blood of the Creek Nation be, and the same is, hereby dismissed.

Tams Bixby Commissioner.

Muskogee, Indian Territory.
JAN 4 – 1907

BIRTH AFFIDAVIT.

DEPARTMENT OF THE INTERIOR.
COMMISSION TO THE FIVE CIVILIZED TRIBES.

IN RE APPLICATION FOR ENROLLMENT, as a citizen of the Creek Nation, of   Allice Leader, born on the 3^d day of Oct , 1901

Name of Father: Dave Leader	a citizen of the	Creek	Nation.
Name of Mother: Nancy Leader	a citizen of the	Creek	Nation.

Postoffice   Barnard, I.T.

AFFIDAVIT OF MOTHER.

UNITED STATES OF AMERICA, Indian Territory, ⎫
   (blank)   DISTRICT.   ⎬

Applications for Enrollment of Creek Newborn
Act of 1905   Volume VII

I, Nancy Leader , on oath state that I am 27 years of age and a citizen by blood, of the Creek Nation; that I am the lawful wife of Dave Leader , who is a citizen, by blood of the Creek Nation; that a female child was born to me on 3^d day of Oct , 1901 , that said child has been named Allice Leader , and was living March 4, 1905.

                                                                   her
                                           Nancy x Leader

Witnesses To Mark: mark
  { Goliah Jones
    Timmie Stidham

Subscribed and sworn to before me this 27th day of March , 1905.

                                              J.R. Dunzy
                                                  Notary Public.

AFFIDAVIT OF ATTENDING PHYSICIAN OR MID-WIFE.

UNITED STATES OF AMERICA, Indian Territory, }
    (blank)   DISTRICT.

I, Mary Lowe , a mid-wife , on oath state that I attended on Mrs. Nancy Leader, wife of Dave Leader on the 3^d day of Oct , 1901 ; that there was born to her on said date a female child; that said child was living March 4, 1905, and is said to have been named Allice Leader

                                              her
                                         Mary x Lowe

Witnesses To Mark: mark
  { Goliah Jones
    Timmie Stidham

Subscribed and sworn to before me this 27th day of March , 1905.

                                              J.R. Dunzy
                                                Notary Public.

BIRTH AFFIDAVIT.
DEPARTMENT OF THE INTERIOR.
COMMISSION TO THE FIVE CIVILIZED TRIBES.

IN RE APPLICATION FOR ENROLLMENT, as a citizen of the Creek Nation, of Lizzie Leader, born on the 17th day of May , 1903

Name of Father:	Dave Leader	a citizen of the	Creek	Nation.
Name of Mother:	Nancy Leader	a citizen of the	Creek	Nation.

                                  Postoffice   Barnard, I.T.

Applications for Enrollment of Creek Newborn
Act of 1905 Volume VII

AFFIDAVIT OF MOTHER.

UNITED STATES OF AMERICA, Indian Territory, }
    Western   DISTRICT.

I, Nancy Leader, on oath state that I am 27 years of age and a citizen by blood, of the Creek Nation; that I am the lawful wife of Dave Leader, who is a citizen, by blood of the Creek Nation; that a female child was born to me on 17th day of May, 1903, that said child has been named Lizzie Leader, and was living March 4, 1905.

                                        her
                                 Nancy x Leader
Witnesses To Mark: mark
 { Goliah Jones
   Timmie Stidham

Subscribed and sworn to before me this 27th day of March, 1905.

                                        J.R. Dunzy
                                              Notary Public.

AFFIDAVIT OF ATTENDING PHYSICIAN OR MID-WIFE.

UNITED STATES OF AMERICA, Indian Territory, }
    (blank)   DISTRICT.

I, Sallie Lowe, a mid-wife, on oath state that I attended on Mrs. Nancy Leader, wife of Dave Leader on the 17th day of May, 1903; that there was born to her on said date a female child; that said child was living March 4, 1905, and is said to have been named Lizzie Leader

                                        her
                                Sallie x Lowe
Witnesses To Mark: mark
 { Goliah Jones
   Timmie Stidham

Subscribed and sworn to before me this 27th day of March, 1905.

                                      J.R. Dunzy
                                         Notary Public.

Applications for Enrollment of Creek Newborn
Act of 1905   Volume VII

NC-531.

Muskogee, Indian Territory, August 8, 1905.

Kizzie Bear,
    c/o Polar Bear,
        Barnard, Indian Territory.

Dear Madam:

    In the matter of the application for the enrollment of your minor daughter Lillie Barnard[sic] as a citizen by blood of the Creek Nation this office is unable to identify you upon the final roll of citizens by blood of the Creek Nation. It is necessary that you be identified before the rights of said child can be finally determined.

    You are, therefore, requested to state the name under which you were finally enrolled, the names of your parents and other members of your family, the Creek Indian town to which you belong and your roll number as the same appears upon your allotment certificate and deeds.

                Respectfully,

                Acting Commissioner.

#3-C 1021

(Copy)   Cr 2449-B

DEPARTMENT OF THE INTERIOR,
COMMISSION TO THE FIVE CIVILIZED TRIBES.
Near Weleetka, I. T. April 25, 1905.

    In the matter of the application for new born children concerning whose enrollment no affidavits could be obtained in time.

    James Spaniard, being duly sworn, testified as follows through Alex Posey, Official Interpreter:

Examination by the Commission:

Q What is your name? A James Spaniard.
Q How old are you? A About 42.
Q What is your postoffice address? A Carson.

    Statement: Tommie Lott of Cheyarhar Town and Tena Lott of Tulmochuss Town, have two children both girls, the oldest Lucy, and the other Jennie. They are both living. I don't know their ages exactly, but they are new borns. Their post office is Carson.

Applications for Enrollment of Creek Newborn
Act of 1905   Volume VII

Ceasar Johnson, of Tookpufka and Eliza John, probably of Eufaula Canadian, have two children. I don't know their names or ages, but they are new borns. Both are living and boys. Their post office is Carson, Indian Territory. and I think the oldest is named Wesley and the youngest Hotulke.

Boley and Kizzie----of Thlewarthle and Tulmochuss respectively--I just know they have a child, whose name or sex I am unfamiliar with. Don't know its age. It's a young child something over a year old I think.

(Note beside entry: See NC 531)

Dave Hullie of Tookpufka and Eliza Hullie, deceased, of Kialigee, have a boy about three or under and living, named Tarpie. Their post office is Carson.

Thomas Wilson of Hickory Ground and Bettie Wilson of Tulmochuss have two children both girls. The oldest is named Wisey and the youngest Minnie. Wisey is three or nearly so and Minnie is about two years old. Both living. Post Office, Carson.

Timmie Stidham of Cheyahar and Liza Stidham of Weogufky have two children. The oldest a girl named Mattie, and the youngest a boy, don't know the name. Both living, the youngest about a year old and the other over two years old. Post Office, Carson.

Henry G. Hains, being duly sworn, on his oath, states that the above and foregoing is a true and correct transcript of his stenographic notes as taken in said cause on said date.

      (signed)   HENRY G. HAINS.

Subscribed and sworn to before me this 10th day of May, 1905.

      (signed)   DRENNAN C SKAGGS,
              Notary Public.

(SEAL)

INDIAN TERRITORY, Western District.

I, J. Y. Miller, a stenographer to the Commissioner to the Five Civilized Tribes, do hereby certify that the above and foregoing is a true and correct copy of its original to be found in the records of the aforesaid office.

          JY Miller

Sworn to and subscribed before
me this the 18th day of
July, 1905.   Edw C Griesel
            Notary Public.

N.C. 1021.

DEPARTMENT OF THE INTERIOR,
COMMISSIONER TO THE FIVE CIVILIZED TRIBES.
Bernard, I.T., April 11, 1906.

In the matter of the application for the enrollment of an unnamed minor child of Boley and Kizzie as a citizen by blood of the Creek Nation.

Applications for Enrollment of Creek Newborn
Act of 1905   Volume VII

POLAR BEAR, being duly sworn, testified as follows:

Through Alex Posey official interpreter:

BY THE COMMISSIONER:
Q What is your name? A Polar Bear.
Q Are you sometimes know simply as Boley? A Yes, sir.
Q How old are you? A About forty-two.
Q What is your post office address? A Wetumka.
Q Are you a citizen of the Creek Nation? A Yes, sir.
Q To what town do you belong? A Thlewathlee[sic].
Q What is the name of your wife? A Kizzie.
Q Application has been made for an unnamed minor child of yours. Have you such child? A I had the child. It died January, this year.
Q What was the name of that child? A Lillie Bear.
Q Had you made application for the enrollment of this child at the time it died? A Yes, sir, I had made application and filed for the child.
Q When was Lillie born? A The child was born in August.
Q What year? A 1904. I had another child named Wisey who was born May 7, 1903, and died July 10, 1903.

---oooOOOooo---

I, D. C. Skaggs, on oath state that the above and foregoing is a full and true transcript of my stenographic notes as taken in said cause on said date.

D.C. Skaggs

Subscribed and sworn to before meu[sic] this 17th day of April, 1906.

Alex Posey
Notary Public.

BIRTH AFFIDAVIT.

DEPARTMENT OF THE INTERIOR.
COMMISSION TO THE FIVE CIVILIZED TRIBES.

IN RE APPLICATION FOR ENROLLMENT, as a citizen of the Creek Nation, of Lillie Bear, born on the 24th day of August, 1904

Name of Father: Poley Bear   a citizen of the   Creek   Nation.
Name of Mother: Kizzie Bear   a citizen of the   Creek   Nation.

Postoffice   Barnard, I.T.

Applications for Enrollment of Creek Newborn
Act of 1905   Volume VII

AFFIDAVIT OF MOTHER.

UNITED STATES OF AMERICA, Indian Territory, ⎫
    Western   DISTRICT. ⎭

    I, Kizzie Bear, on oath state that I am 23 years of age and a citizen by blood, of the Creek Nation; that I am the lawful wife of Poley Bear, who is a citizen, by blood of the Creek Nation; that a female child was born to me on 24th day of August, 1904, that said child has been named lillie[sic] Bear, and was living March 4, 1905.

                                           her
                                 Kizzie x Bear
                                       mark

Witnesses To Mark:
   { Goliah Jones
     Timmie Stidham

Subscribed and sworn to before me this 27th day of March, 1905.

                                   J.R. Dunzy
                                       Notary Public.

AFFIDAVIT OF ATTENDING PHYSICIAN OR MID-WIFE.

UNITED STATES OF AMERICA, Indian Territory, ⎫
    Western   DISTRICT. ⎭

    I, Mary Lowe, a mid-wife, on oath state that I attended on Mrs. Kizzie Bear, wife of Poley Bear on the 24th day of August, 1904; that there was born to her on said date a female child; that said child was living March 4, 1905, and is said to have been named Lillie Bear

                                       her
                                 Mary x Lowe

Witnesses To Mark: mark
   { Goliah Jones
     Timmie Stidham

Subscribed and sworn to before me this 27th day of March, 1905.

                                   J.R. Dunzy
                                     Notary Public.

DEPARTMENT OF THE INTERIOR.
COMMISSION TO THE FIVE CIVILIZED TRIBES.

Applications for Enrollment of Creek Newborn
Act of 1905   Volume VII

IN RE APPLICATION FOR ENROLLMENT, as a citizen of the Creek Nation, of Hazel Irene Wills, born on the 31st day of August, 1901

Name of Father: Henry F. Wills   a citizen of the   Creek   Nation.
Name of Mother: Mary A. Wills, a non-citizen ~~a citizen~~ of the   Creek   Nation.

Postoffice   Mounds, Indian Territory

AFFIDAVIT OF MOTHER.

UNITED STATES OF AMERICA, Indian Territory, ⎫
    Western   DISTRICT. ⎬
                                 ⎭

non-
I, Mary A. Wills, on oath state that I am 25 years of age and a citizen by blood, of the Creek Nation; that I am the lawful wife of Henry F. Wills, who is a citizen, by blood of the Creek Nation; that a female child was born to me on 31st day of August, 1901, that said child has been named Hazel Irene Wills, and was living March 4, 1905.

                              Mary A Wills

Witnesses To Mark:
{

Subscribed and sworn to before me this 27 day of March, 1905.

                              DJ Red
                              Notary Public.

AFFIDAVIT OF ATTENDING PHYSICIAN OR MID-WIFE.

UNITED STATES OF AMERICA, Indian Territory, ⎫
    Western   DISTRICT. ⎬

I, D. D. Ellis, a physician, on oath state that I attended on Mrs. Mary A. Wills, wife of Henry F. Wills on the 31st day of August, 1901; that there was born to her on said date a female child; that said child was living March 4, 1905, and is said to have been named Hazel Irene Wills

                        ⟨sign here⟩ D^{avid} D. Ellis M.D.

Witnesses To Mark:
{ J^{ason} Best Bixby I.T

Subscribed and sworn to before me this 29th day of March, 1905.

                            Francis R. Brennan
                            Notary Public.

Applications for Enrollment of Creek Newborn
Act of 1905   Volume VII

Department of the Interior,
COMMISSION TO THE FIVE CIVILIZED TRIBES.

IN RE Application for Enrollment, as a citizen of the Creek Nation, of Hazel I. Wills, born on the 31" day of August, 1901

Name of Father: Henry F. Wills   a citizen of the   Creek   Nation.
Name of Father: Mary A. Wills   a citizen of the   U.S.   Nation.

Post-office   Mounds, Ind. Ter.

AFFIDAVIT OF MOTHER.

UNITED STATES OF AMERICA, }
    INDIAN TERRITORY, }
Northern District[sic] District. }

I, Mary A Wills, on oath state that I am 22 years of age and a citizen by Blood, of the U.S. Nation; that I am the lawful wife of Henry F. Wills, who is a citizen, by Blood of the Creek Nation; that a Female child was born to me on 31" day of August, 1901, that said child has been named Hazel I. Wills, and is now living.

                      Mary A Wills

WITNESSES TO MARK:
{

Subscribed and sworn to before me this 28" day of September, 1901.

                      Will S. Hines
                           NOTARY PUBLIC.

AFFIDAVIT OF ATTENDING PHYSICIAN OR MID-WIFE.

UNITED STATES OF AMERICA, }
    INDIAN TERRITORY, }
Northern District[sic] District. }

I, D.D. Ellis, a M D, on oath state that I attended on Mrs. Mary A Wills, wife of Henry Wills on the 31" day of August, 1901; that there was born to her on said date a female child; that said child is now living and is said to have been named Hazel I. Wills

                      D.D. Ellis M.D.

Applications for Enrollment of Creek Newborn
Act of 1905 Volume VII

WITNESSES TO MARK:
{

Subscribed and sworn to before me this 28" *day of* September , *1901*.

Will S. Hines
NOTARY PUBLIC.

NC. 533.

Muskogee, Indian Territory, July 14, 1905.

Commissioner to the Five Civilized Tribes,
    Seminole Enrollment Division,
        Muskogee, Indian Territory.
Gentlemen:

    March 28, 1905, application was made to the Commission to the Five Civilized Tribes for the enrollment of Cheparney Barnett, born March 10, 1903, as a citizen by blood of the Creek Nation. It is stated in said application that the father of said child is Jimmie Barnett, a citizen of the Seminole Nation, and that the mother is Mahaly Barnett, a citizen of the Creek Nation.

    You are requested to inform the Creek Enrollment Division as to whether application has been made for the enrollment of said Cheparney Barnett as a citizen of the Seminole Nation, and if so, what disposition has been made of the same.

Respectfully,

Commissioner.

NC 533.

Muskogee, Indian Territory, July 18, 1905.

Mahaly Barnett,
    Sasakwa, Indian Territory.

Dear Madam:

    In the matter of the application for the enrollment of your minor child, Cheparney Barnett, as a citizen of the Creek Nation, you are advised that this office requires further information in order to identify you as a citizen of said Nation.

Applications for Enrollment of Creek Newborn
Act of 1905 Volume VII

You are requested to furnish this office with your maiden name, the names of your parents, the Creek Indian Town to which you belong, and, if possible, the numbers which appear on your deeds to land in the Creek Nation, and any other information that will help to identify you as a citizen of the Creek Nation.

Respectfully,

Commissioner.

W.F.

DEPARTMENT OF THE INTERIOR.
COMMISSION TO THE FIVE CIVILIZED TRIBES.

Muskogee, Indian Territory, July 19, 1905.

Chief Clerk,
    Creek Enrollment Division.
Dear Sir:

    Receipt is acknowledged of your letter of July 14, 1905 (NC-5336) stating that application was made to the Commission to the Five Civilized Tribes for the enrollment of Cheparney Barnett, born March 10, 1903, child of Jimmie Barnett, a citizen of the Seminole Nation, and Mahaly Barnett, a citizen of the Creek Nation, as a citizen by blood of the Creek Nation and requesting to be informed as to whether application was ever made for the enrollment of said child as a citizen of the Seminole Nation.

    In reply to your letter your[sic] are advised that it does not appear from an examination of the records of this office that any application was made for the enrollment of the said Cheparney Barnett as a citizen of the Seminole Nation.

Respectfully,

Tams Bixby   Commissioner.

NC 533.

Muskogee, Indian Territory, November 12, 1906.

Chief Clerk,
    Seminole Enrollment Division,
        General Office.

Dear Sir:

Applications for Enrollment of Creek Newborn
Act of 1905 Volume VII

You are hereby advised that the name of Cheparney Barnett born March 10, 1903, to Jimmie Barnett, an alleged citizen of the Seminole Nation, and Mahaly Barnett, a citizen by blood of the Creek Nation, is contained in a schedule of New Born citizens of the Creek Nation, approved by the Secretary of the Interior September 27, 1905, opposite Roll No. 523.

Respectfully,

Commissioner.

C 533.

DEPARTMENT OF THE INTERIOR,
COMMISSION TO THE FIVE CIVILIZED TRIBES.
Holdenville, I. T., March 27, 1905.

In the matter of the application for the enrollment of Cheparne[sic] Barnett as a citizen of the Creek Nation.

Mahaly Barnett, being first duly sworn, testified as follows:

Through Alex Posey Official Interpreter.

BY COMMISSION:
Q What is your name? A Mahaly Barnett.
Q How old are you? A About thirty.
Q What is your post office address? A Sasakawa[sic].
Q Are you a citizen of the Creek Nation? A Yes, sir.
Q To what town to you belong? A Hillabee.
Q Do you make application for the enrollment of your child, Cheparne[sic] Barnett as a citizen of the Creek Nation? A Yes, sir.
Q What is the name of the father of this child? A Jimmie Barnett.
Q Is he a citizen of the Creek Nation? A He is a Seminole.
Q Is he your lawful husband? A Yes, sir.
Q If it should be found that your child, Cheparne[sic], is entitled to be enrolled in either the Creek or Muskogee Seminole Nations in which nation do you desire to have him enrolled? A In the Creek Nation.

---oooOOOooo---

I, D. C. Skaggs, on oath state that the above and foregoing is a full and true transcript of my stenographic notes as taken in said cause on said date.

DC Skaggs

Applications for Enrollment of Creek Newborn
Act of 1905 Volume VII

Subscribed and sworn to before me this 18" day of July, 1905.

                         Edw C Griesel
                                   Notary Public.

BIRTH AFFIDAVIT.   Supplemental testimony taken
DEPARTMENT OF THE INTERIOR.
COMMISSION TO THE FIVE CIVILIZED TRIBES.

IN RE APPLICATION FOR ENROLLMENT, as a citizen of the Creek Nation, of Cheparney Barnett , born on the 10 day of March , 1903

Name of Father: Jimmie Barnett   a citizen of the Seminole Nation.
Name of Mother: Mahaly Barnett   a citizen of the Creek Nation.
Hillabee Town
                    Postoffice   Sasakwa, Ind. Ter.

AFFIDAVIT OF MOTHER.

UNITED STATES OF AMERICA, Indian Territory,   Child is present
    Western   **DISTRICT.**

     I, Mahaly Barnett , on oath state that I am about 30 years of age and a citizen by blood , of the Creek Nation; that I am the lawful wife of Jimmie Barnett , who is a citizen, by blood of the Seminole Nation; that a male child was born to me on 10 day of March , 1903 , that said child has been named Cheparney Barnett , and was living March 4, 1905.

                              her
                        Mahaly x Barnett
Witnesses To Mark: mark
   { Alex Posey
   { DC Skaggs

     Subscribed and sworn to before me this 27 day of March , 1905.

                             Drennan C Skaggs
                                 Notary Public.

Applications for Enrollment of Creek Newborn
Act of 1905   Volume VII

AFFIDAVIT OF ATTENDING PHYSICIAN OR MID-WIFE.

UNITED STATES OF AMERICA, Indian Territory,　⎫
　　Western　　　　DISTRICT.　　　　　　⎭

I, Millie Barnett , a midwife , on oath state that I attended on Mrs. Mahaly Barnett , wife of Jimmie Barnett on the 10 day of March , 1903 ; that there was born to her on said date a male child; that said child was living March 4, 1905, and is said to have been named Cheparney Barnett

　　　　　　　　　　　　　　　　　her
　　　　　　　　　　　　　　Millie x Barnett
　　　　　　　　　　　　　　　　mark

Witnesses To Mark:
　⎧ Alex Posey
　⎩ DC Skaggs

Subscribed and sworn to before me this 27 day of March , 1905.

　　　　　　　　　　　　　Drennan C Skaggs
　　　　　　　　　　　　　　Notary Public.

NC-534.

　　　　　　　　　　　Muskogee, Indian Territory, August 8, 1905.

Katie Downing,
　　　Burney, Indian Territory.

Dear Madam:

In the matter of the application for the enrollment of your minor son Jesse Downing, born February 21, 1904, as a citizen by blood of the Creek Nation, it will be necessary for you to file with this office, relative to the birth of you said child, the affidavits of two disinterested persons; said affidavits to set forth the name of said child, the date of his birth, the names of his parents and whether or not he was on living March 4, 1905.

　　　Please give this matter your prompt attention.

　　　　　　　　　　　　　Respectfully,

　　　　　　　　　　　　　Acting Commissioner.

Applications for Enrollment of Creek Newborn
Act of 1905 Volume VII

NC-534

Muskogee, Indian Territory, December 14, 1905.

Katy Downing,
    Care of Ambrose Downing,
        Burney, Indian Territory.

Dear Madam:

    In the matter of the application for the enrollment of your minor child, Jesse Downing, born February 21, 1904, as a citizen by blood of the Creek Nation, you are advised that this Office requires the affidavits of two disinterested persons relative to the birth of said child. A blank for that purpose is herewith enclosed.

    This matter should receive your prompt attention.

        Respectfully,

                Commissioner.

Dis

UNITED STATES OF AMERICA,
    WESTERN DISTRICT,
    INDIAN TERRITORY.

    We, the undersigned, on oath state that we are personally acquainted with Katie Downing wife of Ambros Downing and that on or about the 21 day of February, 1904, a male child was born to her and has been named Jessie Downing; and that said child was living March 4, 1905.

    We further state that we have no interest in this case.

                F E Lamb

Witness to mark.

                S. F. Jones

N. P. Lamb

My Commission Expires July 20, 1907.

Subscribed and sworn to before me this 3rd day of January 1906.

                Henry A McDaniel
                    Notary Public.

Applications for Enrollment of Creek Newborn
Act of 1905 Volume VII

BIRTH AFFIDAVIT.

DEPARTMENT OF THE INTERIOR.
COMMISSION TO THE FIVE CIVILIZED TRIBES.

IN RE APPLICATION FOR ENROLLMENT, as a citizen of the CREEK Nation, of Jesse Downing, born on the 21" day of Feb., 1904

                                                                                                       (Creek?)

Name of Father: Ambrose Downing   a citizen of the   U.S.   Nation.
Name of Mother: Katy Downing   a citizen of the   Creek   Nation.

                             Postoffice   ~~Coweta~~   Burney

(Child present)

AFFIDAVIT OF MOTHER.

UNITED STATES OF AMERICA, Indian Territory, ⎫
    WESTERN   DISTRICT. ⎭

    I, Katy Downing , on oath state that I am *(blank)* years of age and a citizen by blood , of the Creek Nation; that I am the lawful wife of Ambrose Downing , who is a citizen, by blood of the Creek Nation; that a male child was born to me on 21" day of Feby , 1904 , that said child has been named Jesse Downing , and is now living.

                                              Her
                                      Katy x Downing
Witnesses To Mark: mark
 ⎰ Jesse McDermott
 ⎱ EC Griesel

    Subscribed and sworn to before me this 3" day of April , 1905.

                                         Edw C Griesel
                                                  Notary Public.

AFFIDAVIT OF ATTENDING PHYSICIAN OR MID-WIFE.

UNITED STATES OF AMERICA, Indian Territory, ⎫
    WESTERN   DISTRICT. ⎭   No one else present ---

    I, , a , on oath state that I attended on Mrs. , wife of on the day of , 190 ; that there was born to her on said date a male child; that said child is now living and is said to have been named

Witnesses To Mark:
 ⎰
 ⎱

    Subscribed and sworn to before me this day of, 190_ .

Applications for Enrollment of Creek Newborn
Act of 1905   Volume VII

BIRTH AFFIDAVIT.

DEPARTMENT OF THE INTERIOR.
COMMISSION TO THE FIVE CIVILIZED TRIBES.

IN RE APPLICATION FOR ENROLLMENT, as a citizen of the Creek Nation, of John J. Fleet, born on the 29th day of June, 1904

Name of Father: James H. Fleet   a citizen of the U.S.   Nation.
Name of Mother: Alice J. Fleet   a citizen of the Creek Nation.

Postoffice   Sasakwa I.T.

AFFIDAVIT OF MOTHER.

UNITED STATES OF AMERICA, Indian Territory,
   Western   DISTRICT.

I, Alice J. Fleet, on oath state that I am 21 years of age and a citizen by Blood, of the Creek Nation; that I am the lawful wife of James H. Fleet, who is a citizen, by of[sic] of the U.S. ~~Nation~~; that a male child was born to me on 29th day of June, 1904, that said child has been named John J. Fleet, and was living March 4, 1905.

Alice J. Fleet

Witnesses To Mark:

Subscribed and sworn to before me this 21st day of March, 1905.

My Com Expires 7/24/1906   Savil H. Miller
                                Notary Public.

AFFIDAVIT OF ATTENDING PHYSICIAN OR MID-WIFE.

UNITED STATES OF AMERICA, Indian Territory,
   Western   DISTRICT.

I, Dr. J. M. McPherson, a Doctor, on oath state that I attended on Mrs. Alice J. Fleet, wife of James H. Fleet on the 29th day of June, 1904; that there was born to her on said date a male child; that said child was living March 4, 1905, and is said to have been named John J. Fleet

Dr. J. M. McPherson

Applications for Enrollment of Creek Newborn
Act of 1905   Volume VII

Witnesses To Mark:
{

Subscribed and sworn to before me this 21st day of March, 1905.

My Com Expires 7/24/1906   Savil H. Miller
                                  Notary Public.

BIRTH AFFIDAVIT.

DEPARTMENT OF THE INTERIOR.
COMMISSION TO THE FIVE CIVILIZED TRIBES.

IN RE APPLICATION FOR ENROLLMENT, as a citizen of the Creek Nation, of Jesey Fife, born on the 10th day of February, 1903

Name of Father: James Fife   a citizen of the   Creek   Nation.
Name of Mother: Lucy Fife   a citizen of the   Creek   Nation.

Postoffice   Sonora, I.T.

AFFIDAVIT OF MOTHER.

UNITED STATES OF AMERICA, Indian Territory, }
    Western   DISTRICT.

    I, Lucy Fife, on oath state that I am Twenty Four years of age and a citizen by Blood, of the Creek Nation; that I am the lawful wife of James Fife, who is a citizen, by Blood of the Creek Nation; that a Male child was born to me on 10th day of February, 1903, that said child has been named Jesey Fife, and was living March 4, 1905.

                                           Her
Witnesses To Mark: Lucy x Fife
  { C.M. Osborn   mark
    J.N. Willhite

Subscribed and sworn to before me this 29th day of March, 1905.

                                      J. W. Fowler
MY COMMISSION EXPIRES JULY 13th 1908.   Notary Public.

Applications for Enrollment of Creek Newborn
Act of 1905   Volume VII

AFFIDAVIT OF ATTENDING PHYSICIAN OR MID-WIFE.

UNITED STATES OF AMERICA, Indian Territory,
    Western   DISTRICT

    I, Maula Yarhola, a Midwife, on oath state that I attended on Mrs. Lucy Fife, wife of James Fife on the 10th day of February, 1903 ; that there was born to her on said date a male child; that said child was living March 4, 1905, and is said to have been named Jesey Fife

                                                       her
                                      Maula x Yarhola
Witnesses To Mark: mark
    C.M. Osborn
    J.N. Willhite

    Subscribed and sworn to before me this 29th day of March, 1905.

                                           J. W. Fowler
MY COMMISSION EXPIRES JULY 13th 1908.   Notary Public.

BIRTH AFFIDAVIT.

DEPARTMENT OF THE INTERIOR.
COMMISSION TO THE FIVE CIVILIZED TRIBES.

    IN RE APPLICATION FOR ENROLLMENT, as a citizen of the Creek Nation, of John Randolph Williams, born on the 8 day of December, 1903

Name of Father: Charley Williams   a citizen of the   Creek   Nation.
Coweta Town
Name of Mother: Emma Williams   a citizen of the   Creek   Nation.
Cheyaha Town
                                Postoffice   Calvin, Ind. Ter.

AFFIDAVIT OF MOTHER.

UNITED STATES OF AMERICA, Indian Territory
    Western   DISTRICT.   <u>Child</u> is present

    I, Emma Williams, on oath state that I am 37 years of age and a citizen by blood, of the Creek Nation; that I am the lawful wife of Charley Williams, who is a citizen, by blood of the Creek Nation; that a male child was born to me on 8 day of December, 1903, that said child has been named John Randolph Williams, and was living March 4, 1905. That no one attended on me as midwife or physician at the birth of the child.

Applications for Enrollment of Creek Newborn
Act of 1905 Volume VII

Emma Williams

Witnesses To Mark:
{

Subscribed and sworn to before me this 27 day of March, 1905.

Drennan C Skaggs
Notary Public.

(The above Birth Affidavit given again.)

DEPARTMENT OF THE INTERIOR.
COMMISSION TO THE FIVE CIVILIZED TRIBES.

In the matter of the death of   Benjamin Franklin Williams   a citizen of the Creek Nation, who formerly resided at or near   Calvin   , Ind. Ter., and died on the 18 day of April , 1904

AFFIDAVIT OF RELATIVE.

UNITED STATES OF AMERICA, Indian Territory, }
    Western   DISTRICT.

I, Emma Williams , on oath state that I am 37 years of age and a citizen by blood , of the Creek Nation; that my postoffice address is Calvin , Ind. Ter.; that I am the mother   of Benjamin Franklin Williams   who was a citizen, by blood , of the Creek   Nation and that said Benjamin Franklin Williams   died on the 18   day of   April   , 1904

Emma Williams

Witnesses To Mark:
{

Subscribed and sworn to before me this 30 day of March, 1905.

Drennan C Skaggs
Notary Public.

Applications for Enrollment of Creek Newborn
Act of 1905   Volume VII

AFFIDAVIT OF ACQUAINTANCE.

UNITED STATES OF AMERICA, Indian Territory, ⎫
    Western   DISTRICT. ⎬

I, Jane Frank , on oath state that I am 62 years of age, and a citizen by blood of the Creek   Nation; that my postoffice address is   Sasakwa   , Ind. Ter.; that I was personally acquainted with   Benjamin Franklin Williams   who was a citizen, by blood , of the Creek   Nation; and that said   Benjamin Franklin Williams   died on the   18   day of   April   , 1904

                                    Jane Frank

Witnesses To Mark:
⎰ Alex Posey
⎱

Subscribed and sworn to before me this 30 day of March, 1905.

                                      Drennan C Skaggs
                                      Notary Public.

NC 537   JLD

DEPARTMENT OF THE INTERIOR,
COMMISSIONER TO THE FIVE CIVILIZED TRIBES.

In the matter of the application for the enrollment of Benjamin Franklin Williams, deceased, as a citizen by blood of the Creek Nation.

STATEMENT AND ORDER.

The record in this case shows that on April 1, 1905, application was made, in affidavit form, for the enrollment of Benjamin Franklin Williams, deceased, as a citizen by blood of the Creek Nation, under the provisions of the act of Congress approved March 3, 1905.

It appears from the affidavit filed in this matter that said Benjamin Franklin Williams, deceased, was born December 8, 1903 and died April 18, 1904.

The Act of Congress approved March 3, 1905, (33 Stats., 1048), provides:

"That the Commission to the Five Civilized Tribes is authorized for sixty days after the date of the approval of this act to receive and consider applications for enrollment, of children, born subsequent to May twenty-fifth, nineteen hundred and one, and prior to March fourth, nineteen hundred and five, and living on said latter date, to citizens of the Creek tribe of Indians whose enrollment has been approved by the Secretary of the Interior prior to the approval of this act; and to enroll and make allotments to such children."

It is, therefore, ordered that the application for the enrollment of Benjamin Franklin Williams, deceased, as a citizen by blood of the Creek Nation be, and the same is, hereby dismissed.

Applications for Enrollment of Creek Newborn
Act of 1905 Volume VII

Muskogee, Indian Territory.
JAN 4 – 1907

Tams Bixby Commissioner.

United States of America)
Western District)
(
Indian Territory)

Personally appeared before me John R. Goat a creek[sic] citizen by birth, and ___ years of age, and upon their oath state that thy[sic] are well acquainted with Emma Williams, a citizen of the creek[sic] Nation I.T. And know that a male child was born to her on the 8th day of December 1903 that said child was named John Randolph Williams. The father of said child was Charley Williams, and his mother is named Emma Williams, and said child is now liveing[sic]. I have no interst[sic] in this case whatever, and make this statement as a disinterested person.

John R. Goat

Subscribed and Sworn to before me this the 17th day of August, 1905

Chas Rider
Notary Public.

My Commission Expires July 11th, 1906.

United States of America)
Western District)
(
Indian Territory)

Personally appeared before me Burnie McCosar a creek[sic] citizen by birth, and 42 years of age, and upon their oath state that thy[sic] are well acquainted with Emma Williams, a citizen of the creek[sic] Nation I.T. And know that a male child was born to her on the 8th day of December 1903 that said child was named John Randolph Williams. The father of said child was Charley Williams, and his mother is named Emma Williams, and said child is now liveing[sic]. I have no interst[sic] in this case whatever, and make this statement as a disinterested person.

Burnie McCosar

Subscribed and Sworn to before me this the 17th day of August, 1905

Chas Rider
Notary Public.

My Commission Expires July 11th, 1906.

Applications for Enrollment of Creek Newborn
Act of 1905   Volume VII

United States of America
Western District   )
Indian Territory   )

Personally appeared before me a Notary Public in and for the western District, Jane Frank and states upon oath that she is the mother of Emma Williams, and a citizen of the Creek Nation I.T. and that on the 8th day of December 1903 their[sic] was born to Emma Williams a male child who has been named John Randolph Williams, and that the child is now liveing[sic], the father of the above said child was Charley Williams, deceased.

Jane Frank

Sworn and subscribed to before me this 14th day of August 1905

Chas Rider
Notary Public.

My Commission Expires July 11th, 1906

NC-537.

Muskogee, Indian Territory, August 8, 1905.

Emma Williams,
    c/o Charley Williams,
        Calvin, Indian Territory.

Dear Madam:

In the matter of the application for the enrollment of your minor son John Randolph Williams, born December 8, 1903, as a citizen by blood of the Creek Nation, it will be necessary for you to furnish this office with the affidavits of two disinterested persons; said affidavits to set forth the name of said child, the date of his birth, the names of his parents and whether or not he was on living March 4, 1905.

Please give this matter your prompt attention.

Respectfully,

Acting Commissioner.

Applications for Enrollment of Creek Newborn
Act of 1905   Volume VII

C 538

DEPARTMENT OF THE INTERIOR,
COMMISSIONER TO THE FIVE CIVILIZED TRIBES.
Holdenville, I. T., March 27, 1905.

In the matter of the application for the enrollment of Johnson Frank as a citizen by blood of the Creek Nation.

SISSIE FRANK, being duly sworn, testified as follows:

Through Alex Posey, Official Interpreter:

BY COMMISSION:
Q What is your name? A Sissie Frank.
Q How old are you? A About twenty.
Q What is your post office address? A Emahaka.
Q Are you a citizen of the Creek Nation? A Yes, sir.
Q To what town to you belong? A Little River Tulsa.
Q Do you make application for the enrollment of your child, Johnson Frank, as a citizen of the Creek Nation? A Yes, sir.
Q What is the name of the father of Johnson? A Albert Frank.
Q Is he a citizen of the Creek Nation? A He is a seminole[sic].
Q Is he your lawful husband? A Yes, sir.
Q If it should be found that Johnson Frank is entitled to enrollment in either the Creek or Seminole Nations in which nation do you desire to have him enrolled? A In the Creek Nation.

---oooOOOooo---

I, D. C. Skaggs, on oath state that the above and foregoing is a full and true transcript of my stenographic notes as taken in said cause on said date.

DC Skaggs

Subscribed and sworn to before me this 18" day of July, 1905.

Edw C Griesel
Notary Public.

Supplemental testimony taken.
DEPARTMENT OF THE INTERIOR.
COMMISSION TO THE FIVE CIVILIZED TRIBES.

IN RE APPLICATION FOR ENROLLMENT, as a citizen of the Creek Nation, of Johnson Frank, born on the 11 day of February , 1904

Applications for Enrollment of Creek Newborn
Act of 1905   Volume VII

Name of Father: Albert Frank   a citizen of the Seminole   Nation.
Name of Mother: Sissy Frank (nee Factor)   a citizen of the   Creek   Nation.
Tulsa Little River Town
                 Postoffice   Emahaka, Indian Territory

AFFIDAVIT OF MOTHER.

UNITED STATES OF AMERICA, Indian Territory, }
     Western   DISTRICT. }

     I, Sissy Frank , on oath state that I am 20 years of age and a citizen by blood , of the Creek Nation; that I am the lawful wife of Albert Frank , who is a citizen, by blood of the Seminole Nation; that a male child was born to me on 11 day of February , 1904 , that said child has been named Johnson Frank , and was living March 4, 1905.

                           her
                       Sissy x Frank
Witnesses To Mark: mark
   { Alex Posey
   { DC Skaggs

     Subscribed and sworn to before me this 27 day of March , 1905.

                     Drennan C Skaggs
                        Notary Public.

                    Father
AFFIDAVIT OF ~~ATTENDING PHYSICIAN OR MID-WIFE~~.

UNITED STATES OF AMERICA, Indian Territory, }
     Western   DISTRICT. }

                                         my wife
     I, Albert[sic] Frank , a *(blank)* , on oath state that I attended on ^ Mrs. Sissy Frank , ~~wife of~~ *(blank)* on the 11 day of February , 1904 ; that there was born to her on said date a male child; that said child was living March 4, 1905, and is said to have been named Johnson Frank

                     Alfred Frank
Witnesses To Mark:
   {

     Subscribed and sworn to before me this 27 day of March, 1905.

                     Drennan C Skaggs
                        Notary Public.

Applications for Enrollment of Creek Newborn
Act of 1905   Volume VII

DEPARTMENT OF THE INTERIOR.
COMMISSION TO THE FIVE CIVILIZED TRIBES.

Muskogee, Indian Territory, July 18, 1905.

Chief Clerk,
  Creek Enrollment Division.

Dear Sir:

  Receipt is hereby acknowledged of your letter of July 14, 1905 (NC-538) stating that an application was made to the Commission to the Five Civilized Tribes for the enrollment of Johnson Frank, born February 11, 1904, child of Albert Frank, a citizen of the Seminole Nation, and Sissie Frank, a citizen of the Creek Nation, as a citizen by blood of the Creek Nation and requesting to be informed as to whether application has been made for the enrollment of said Johnson Frank as a citizen of the Seminole Nation.

  In reply to your letter you are advised that it does not appear from an examination of the records of this office that any application was made to the Commission to the Five Civilized Tribes for the enrollment of said Johnson Frank as a citizen of the Seminole Nation.

        Respectfully,

          Tams Bixby Commissioner.

NC. 538.

Muskogee, Indian Territory, July 14, 1905.

Commissioner to the Five Civilized Tribes,
  Seminole Enrollment Division,
    Muskogee, Indian Territory.

Gentlemen:

  March 28, 1905, application was made to the Commission to the Five Civilized Tribes for the enrollment of Johnson Frank, born February 11, 1904, as a citizen by blood of the Creek Nation. It is stated in said application that the father of said child is Albert Frank, a citizen of the Seminole Nation, and that the mother is Sissie Frank, a citizen of the Creek Nation.
  You are requested to inform the Creek Enrollment Division as to whether application has been made for the enrollment of Johnson Frank, as a citizen of the Seminole Nation, and if so, what disposition has been made of the same.

Applications for Enrollment of Creek Newborn
Act of 1905   Volume VII

Respectfully,

Commissioner.

UNITED STATES OF AMERICA,
WESTERN DISTRICT,
INDIAN TERRITORY.

--ooOoo--

We, the undersigned, on oath state that we are personally acquainted with Sissie Frank   wife of   Alfred Frank   and that on or about the   11th day of February , 1904   , a   male   child was born to her and has been named   Johnson Frank ; and that said child was living March 4, 1905.

We further state that we have no interest in this case.

John Tiger

Witnesses to mark.
  A.F. Goat

Watty Fixico

W.A. Goat

Subscribed and sworn to before me this 13th day of January 1906

Chas Rider
Notary Public.

My Commission Expires July 11th. 1906

NC-558.

Muskogee, Indian Territory, August 8, 1905.

Alfred Frank
  Emahaka, Indian Territory.

Dear Sir:

In the matter of the application for the enrollment of your minor son Johnson Frank, born February 11, 1904, as a citizen by blood of the Creek Nation, it will be necessary for you to furnish this office with the affidavits of two disinterested persons, relative to the birth of said child; said affidavits to set forth the name of said child, the date of his birth, the names of his parents and whether or not he was on living March 4, 1905.

Applications for Enrollment of Creek Newborn
Act of 1905   Volume VII

Respectfully,

Acting Commissioner.

HGH

REFER IN REPLY TO THE FOLLOWING:
NC-538

DEPARTMENT OF THE INTERIOR,
COMMISSIONER TO THE FIVE CIVILIZED TRIBES.

Muskogee, Indian Territory, December 14, 1905.

Alfred Frank,
    Emahaka, Indian Territory.

Dear Sir:

In the matter of the application for the enrollment of your minor child, Johnson Frank, born February 11, 1904, as a citizen by blood of the Creek Nation, You are advised that it will be necessary for you to furnish this Office with the affidavits of two disinterested persons relative to the birth of said child. A blank for that purpose is herewith enclosed.

This matter should receive your prompt attention.

Respectfully,

Tams Bixby   Commissioner.

Dis

HGH

REFER IN REPLY TO THE FOLLOWING:

DEPARTMENT OF THE INTERIOR,
COMMISSIONER TO THE FIVE CIVILIZED TRIBES.

Muskogee, Indian Territory, October 23, 1906.

Sissy Frank,
    Emahaka, Indian Territory.

Dar Madam:

You are hereby advised that the name of your minor child, Johnson Frank, is contained in the partial list of citizens by blood of the Creek Nation, approved by the Secretary of the Interior October 15, 1906, and that a selection of land may now be made in the Creek Nation for said child at the Creek Land Office in Muskogee, Indian Territory.

Applications for Enrollment of Creek Newborn
Act of 1905 Volume VII

This matter should receive your prompt attention.

Respectfully,

Tams Bixby   Commissioner.

NC 538.

Muskogee, Indian Territory, October 31, 1906.

Chief Clerk,
    Seminole Enrollment Division,
        Muskogee, Indian Territory.

Dear Sir:

There is on file in this office an application for the enrollment of Johnson Frank, born February 11, 1904, to Alfred Frank, a citizen of the Seminole Nation, and Sissy Frank, who is identified as Sissie Factor, a citizen of the Creek Nation, opposite Creek Indian roll number 7708.

You are advised that the name of said child is contained in a partial list of new born citizens by blood of the Creek Nation, approved by the Secretary of the Interior October 15, 1906, opposite roll number 10510.

Respectfully,

Commissioner.

NC-539.

Muskogee, Indian Territory, August 8, 1905.

Mattie Riley,
    Yeager, Indian Territory.

Dear Madam:

In the matter of the application for the enrollment of your minor children Claud Riley, born June 28, 1902, and Henry E. Riley, born June 15, 1904, as citizens by blood of the Creek Nation, it will be necessary for you to file with this office either the original or a certified copy of the marriage license and certificate showing the marriage between you and Horace Riley, the father of said children.

Applications for Enrollment of Creek Newborn
Act of 1905   Volume VII

It will also be necessary for you to file, in the matter of the enrollment of said children, the affidavits of two disinterested persons as to their birth; said affidavits to set forth the names of the children, the date of their birth, the names of their parents and whether or not they were living on March 4, 1905.

Respectfully,

Acting Commissioner.

NC-539.

Muskogee, Indian Territory, August 19, 1905.

Mattie Riley,
    Care of Horace Riley,
        Yeager, Indian Territory.

Dear Madam:

Your letter of August 14, 1905, asking for a duplicate of your marriage certificate, which was burned, has been referred by the United States Indian Agent to this Office for appropriate reply.

You are advised that a certified copy of your marriage license and certificate should be procured from the Clerk of the United States Court who issued same.

You are again advised that it will be necessary for you to file, in the matter of the enrollment of your minor children, Claud A. and Henry E. Riley, as citizens of the Creek nation, the affidavits of two disinterested persons as to their births; said affidavits to set forth the names of the children, the dates of their birth, the names of their parents, and whether or not they were living on March 4, 1905.

Respectfully,

Acting Commissioner.

❋   **MARRIAGE LICENSE**   ❋

UNITED STATES OF AMERICA ⎫
    Indian Territory   ⎬ ss.   No. 1651
Northern ~~Western~~ District ⎭

To Any Person Authorized by Law to Solemnize Marriage---Greeting:

Applications for Enrollment of Creek Newborn
Act of 1905 Volume VII

You are Hereby Commanded to Solemnize the Rite and Publish the Banns of Matrimony between Mr. Horace Riley *of* Holdenville *in the Indian Territory, aged* 16 *years and Miss* Mattie Cock *of* Holdenville *in the Indian Territory aged* 17 *years according to law, and do you officially sign and return this license to the parties therein named.*

WITNESS my hand and official seal ~~at Muskogee Indian Territory~~ *this* 24 *day of* June *A.D. 190*1

(Seal)

Chas. A. Davidson
Clerk of the U S Court.

By M.T. Manville Deputy.

| 🙠 🙠 | CERTIFICATE OF MARRIAGE | 🙢 🙢 |

UNITED STATES OF AMERICA
Indian Territory } ss.
Northern ~~Western~~ District

I, Rev. T.B. Clark *, a Minister of the Gospel, DO HEREBY CERTIFY that on the* 30 *day of* June *A. D. 19*01 *did duly and according to law as commanded in the foregoing License, solemnize the Rite and Publish the Banns of Matrimony between the parties therein named.*

WITNESS my hand this 1 *day of* July *A. D. 19*01

My credentials are recorded in the office of the Clerk of the United States Court, Indian Territory ~~Western~~ Northern District Book A Page 344

Rev. T.B. Clark
A Minister of the Gospel

Note This license and certificate of marriage must be returned to the office of the Clerk of the United States court in the Western District Indian Territory from whence it was issued within sixty days from the date thereof of the party to whom the license was issued will be liable in the amount of the one hundred dollars ($100.00).

Filed and duly recorded this 3 day of October, 1901
Book L page 233   Chas. A. Davidson Clrk of the United
States Court.

CERTIFICATE OF TRUE COPY.

United States of America,
Indian Territory, } ss.
Western District.

I, R. P. HARRISON, *Clerk of the United States Court in the Western District, Indian Territory, do hereby certify that the instrument*

Applications for Enrollment of Creek Newborn
Act of 1905   Volume VII

hereto attached is a full, true and correct copy of a Marriage License *as the same appears from the records of my office.*

WITNESS my hand and seal of said Court at Muskogee *in said Territory, this* 24" *day of* August   *A. D. 1905*

By   John Harlan   R. P. Harrison
         Deputy Clerk   *Clerk and Ex-Officio Recorder.*

Book L   page 233

B. H. MILLS   NAT WILLIAMS

Real Estate Agents
and
Notary Public

Wetumka, Ind. Ter.,   *190*

UNITED STATES OF AMERICA,

    INDIAN TERRITORY,   s s:

WESTERN JUDICIAL DISTRICT,

I, Mrs M E Kendrick do solumly[sic] swear that I am acquainted with Horace Riley and Mattie Riley, and know them to be Man and wife, and know that there was a child born to them on the 28th day of June 1902, and that the said child was named Claud Riley, and that there was a child born to the said above named couple on the 15th June 1904, and that the said child was named Henry Earl Riley, and that both of the above named children were liveing[sic] on the 4th day of March, 1905.

                                      Mrs. M. E. Kendrick

Subscribed and sworn to before me this 19th day of Aug 1905.

                                      B.H. Mills
My commission Expires Aug 15th 1906.   Notary Public.

Applications for Enrollment of Creek Newborn
Act of 1905 Volume VII

B. H. MILLS   NAT WILLIAMS

Real Estate Agents
and
Notary Public

Wetumka, Ind. Ter.,   190

UNITED STATES OF AMERICA,

    INDIAN TERRITORY,   s s:

WESTERN JUDICIAL DISTRICT,

I, Mary Emiline Simson, do solumly[sic] swear that I am acquainted with Horace Riley and Mattie Riley, and know them to be man and wife, and know that there was a child born to them on the 28th day of June 1902, and that the said child was named Claud Riley, and that there was a child born to the said above named couple on the 15th June 1904, and the said child was named Henry Earl Riley, and that both of the above named children were liveing[sic] on the 4th day of March, 1905.

                                                        her
                                    Mary Emeline-Simson x
                                                       mark

Subscribed and sworn to before me this 19th day of Aug 1905.
        Witness to mark
            Nat Williams   B.H. Mills
            Louis Curtain   Notary Public.
My commission Expires Aug 15th 1906.

BIRTH AFFIDAVIT.

DEPARTMENT OF THE INTERIOR.
COMMISSION TO THE FIVE CIVILIZED TRIBES.

    IN RE APPLICATION FOR ENROLLMENT, as a citizen of the Creek Nation, of Henry Earl Riley, born on the 15 day of June , 1904

Name of Father: Horace R Riley   a citizen of the   Creek   Nation.
Name of Mother: Mattie Riley   a citizen of the   Creek   Nation.

                              Postoffice   Wetumka I.T.

Applications for Enrollment of Creek Newborn
Act of 1905   Volume VII

AFFIDAVIT OF MOTHER.

UNITED STATES OF AMERICA, Indian Territory,
Western Judicial   DISTRICT.

                                                    non

I, Mattie Riley, on oath state that I am 20 years of age and a ^ citizen by Birth, of the Creek Nation; that I am the lawful wife of Horace R. Riley, who is a citizen, by Birth of the Creek Nation; that a male child was born to me on 15 day of June, 1904, that said child has been named Henry Earl Riley, and was living March 4, 1905.

                                      Mattie Riley

Witnesses To Mark:
- W.A. McCoy
- B.H. Mills

Subscribed and sworn to before me this 19 day of Aug, 1905.

My Com Exp. July 1-1906   Nat Williams
                                           Notary Public.

AFFIDAVIT OF ATTENDING PHYSICIAN OR MID-WIFE.

UNITED STATES OF AMERICA, Indian Territory,
Western Judicial   DISTRICT.

I, M. E. Stewart, a mid wife, on oath state that I attended on Mrs. Mattie Riley, wife of Horace R. Riley on the 15 day of June, 1904; that there was born to her on said date a male child; that said child was living March 4, 1905, and is said to have been named Henry Earl Riley

                                      M. E. Stewart

Witnesses To Mark:
- B.H. Mills
- R. Phelps

Subscribed and sworn to before me this 19 day of Aug, 1905.

My Com Exp. July 1-1906   Nat Williams
                                           Notary Public.

BIRTH AFFIDAVIT.

DEPARTMENT OF THE INTERIOR.
COMMISSION TO THE FIVE CIVILIZED TRIBES.

IN RE APPLICATION FOR ENROLLMENT, as a citizen of the Creek Nation, of Henry E. Riley, born on the 15 day of June, 1904

Applications for Enrollment of Creek Newborn
Act of 1905   Volume VII

Name of Father: Horace R Riley   a citizen of the   Creek   Nation.
Eufaula Canadian Town
Name of Mother: Mattie Riley   a citizen of the United States Nation.

Postoffice   Yeager, Ind. Terr.

AFFIDAVIT OF MOTHER.

UNITED STATES OF AMERICA, Indian Territory, ⎱
    Western   DISTRICT. ⎰

    I, Mattie Riley , on oath state that I am 20 years of age and a citizen ~~by~~ *(blank)*, of the United States Nation; that I am the lawful wife of Horace Riley , who is a citizen, by blood of the Creek Nation; that a male child was born to me on 15 day of June , 1904 , that said child has been named Henry E. Riley , and was living March 4, 1905.

                                   Mrs. Mattie Riley

Witnesses To Mark:
⎰
⎱ Subscribed and sworn to before me this 30 day of March , 1905.

                                   Drennan C Skaggs
                                   Notary Public.

AFFIDAVIT OF ATTENDING PHYSICIAN OR MID-WIFE.

UNITED STATES OF AMERICA, Indian Territory, ⎱
    Western   DISTRICT. ⎰

    I, Mrs. H.E. Cook , a mid-wife , on oath state that I attended on Mrs. Mattie Riley , wife of Horace Riley on the 15 day of June , 1904 ; that there was born to her on said date a male child; that said child was living March 4, 1905, and is said to have been named Henry E. Riley

                                   her
                           Mrs. H. E. x Cook
Witnesses To Mark: mark
⎰ DC Skaggs
⎱ Alex Posey
Subscribed and sworn to before me this 30 day of March , 1905.

                                   Drennan C Skaggs
                                   Notary Public.

Applications for Enrollment of Creek Newborn
Act of 1905   Volume VII

BIRTH AFFIDAVIT.

DEPARTMENT OF THE INTERIOR.
COMMISSION TO THE FIVE CIVILIZED TRIBES.

IN RE APPLICATION FOR ENROLLMENT, as a citizen of the Creek Nation, of Claud Riley, born on the 28 day of June, 1902

Name of Father: Horace R Riley   a citizen of the   Creek   Nation.
Name of Mother: Mattie Riley   a citizen of the   Creek   Nation.

Postoffice   Wetumka I.T.

AFFIDAVIT OF MOTHER.

UNITED STATES OF AMERICA, Indian Territory,
Western Judicial   DISTRICT.

                                                                                                        non

I, Mattie Riley, on oath state that I am 20 years of age and a ^ citizen by Birth, of the Creek Nation; that I am the lawful wife of Horace R. Riley, who is a citizen, by Birth of the Creek Nation; that a male child was born to me on 28 day of June, 1902, that said child has been named Claud Riley, and was living March 4, 1905.

                                                                                  Mattie Riley

Witnesses To Mark:
{ W.A. McCoy
  Louis Curtain

Subscribed and sworn to before me this 19 day of Aug, 1905.

My Com Exp. July 1-1906   Nat Williams
                                                                            Notary Public.

AFFIDAVIT OF ATTENDING PHYSICIAN OR MID-WIFE.

UNITED STATES OF AMERICA, Indian Territory,
Western Judicial   DISTRICT.

I, Mary Emiline Simpson, a midwife, on oath state that I attended on Mrs. Mattie Riley, wife of Horace R. Riley on the 28 day of June, 1902; that there was born to her on said date a male child; that said child was living March 4, 1905, and is said to have been named Claud Riley   her
                                                      Mary Emiline Simpson x
Witnesses To Mark: mark
{ W.A. McCoy
  Louis Curtain

Applications for Enrollment of Creek Newborn
Act of 1905 Volume VII

Subscribed and sworn to before me this 19 day of Aug , 1905.

My Com Exp. July 1-1906

Nat Williams
Notary Public.

BIRTH AFFIDAVIT.

DEPARTMENT OF THE INTERIOR.
COMMISSION TO THE FIVE CIVILIZED TRIBES.

IN RE APPLICATION FOR ENROLLMENT, as a citizen of the Creek Nation, of Claud Riley, born on the 28 day of June , 1902

Name of Father: Horace Riley   a citizen of the   Creek   Nation.
Eufaula Canadian Town
Name of Mother: Mattie Riley   a citizen of the United States Nation.

Postoffice   Yeager, Ind. Terr.

AFFIDAVIT OF MOTHER.

Child present

UNITED STATES OF AMERICA, Indian Territory,
Western   DISTRICT.

I, Mattie Riley , on oath state that I am 20 years of age and a citizen ~~by~~ *(blank)*, of the United States   Nation; that I am the lawful wife of Horace Riley   , who is a citizen, by blood of the Creek Nation; that a male child was born to me on 28 day of June , 1902 , that said child has been named Claud Riley , and was living March 4, 1905. That the mid-wife who attended on me at the birth of the child is dead.

Mrs. Mattie Riley

Witnesses To Mark:

Subscribed and sworn to before me this 30 day of March , 1905.

Drennan C Skaggs
Notary Public.

Applications for Enrollment of Creek Newborn
Act of 1905   Volume VII

AFFIDAVIT OF ATTENDING PHYSICIAN OR MID-WIFE.

UNITED STATES OF AMERICA, Indian Territory,
Western   DISTRICT.

am the mother of
I, Mrs. H.E. Cook , a *(blank)* , on oath state that I ~~attended on~~ Mrs. Mattie Riley , wife of Horace Riley; that on the 28 day of June , 1902 ; that there was born to her on said date a male child; that said child was living March 4, 1905, and is said to have been named Claud Riley

her
Mrs. H. E. x Cook
mark

Witnesses To Mark:
  { DC Skaggs
    Alex Posey

Subscribed and sworn to before me this 30 day of March , 1905.

Drennan C Skaggs
Notary Public.

NC 540.

Muskogee, Indian Territory, May 31, 1906.

Lena Harrison,
    Holdenville, Indian Territory.

Dear Madam:

In the matter of the application for the enrollment of your minor child, Louisa Sewell, as a citizen by blood of the Creek Nation, you are advised that it is required the your furnish this office with the affidavits of yourself, and the midwife in attendance at the birth of said child, said affidavits showing the name of the child, the names of its parents, the date of the birth, and whether said child was living March 4, 1905. For this purpose there is herewith enclosed blank form of birth affidavit.

This matter should receive your prompt attention.

Respectfully,

1 BA   Commissioner.

Applications for Enrollment of Creek Newborn
Act of 1905   Volume VII

BIRTH AFFIDAVIT.

DEPARTMENT OF THE INTERIOR.
COMMISSION TO THE FIVE CIVILIZED TRIBES.

IN RE APPLICATION FOR ENROLLMENT, as a citizen of the Creek Nation, of George Hill, born on the 9 day of August, 1904

Name of Father: Mitchell Hill   a citizen of the   Creek   Nation.
Hitchita Town
Name of Mother: Hilly Hill (nee Robison)   a citizen of the   Creek   Nation.
Tuckabatche Town
                              Postoffice   Yeager, Ind. Ter.

AFFIDAVIT OF MOTHER.

UNITED STATES OF AMERICA, Indian Territory,
    Western   DISTRICT.   Child is present

I, Hilly Hill, on oath state that I am about 20 years of age and a citizen by blood, of the Creek Nation; that I am the lawful wife of Mitchell Hill, who is a citizen, by blood of the Creek Nation; that a male child was born to me on 9 day of August, 1904, that said child has been named George Hill, and was living March 4, 1905.
                                                    her
                                        Hilly x Hill
Witnesses To Mark: mark
{ Alex Posey
{ DC Skaggs

Subscribed and sworn to before me this 30 day of March, 1905.

                              Drennan C Skaggs
                                Notary Public.

AFFIDAVIT OF ATTENDING PHYSICIAN OR MID-WIFE.

UNITED STATES OF AMERICA, Indian Territory,
    Western   DISTRICT.

I, Liza Bruner, a -----, on oath state that I attended on Mrs. Hilly Hill, wife of Mitchell Hill on the 9 day of August, 1904; that there was born to her on said date a male child; that said child was living March 4, 1905, and is said to have been named George Hill
                              Liza Bruner
Witnesses To Mark:
{
{

Applications for Enrollment of Creek Newborn
Act of 1905   Volume VII

Subscribed and sworn to before me this 30 day of March, 1905.

Drennan C Skaggs
Notary Public.

C 542

DEPARTMENT OF THE INTERIOR,
COMMISSION TO THE FIVE CIVILIZED TRIBES.
Holdenville, I. T., March 27, 1905.

In the matter of the application for the enrollment of Roman Tiger as a citizen of the Creek Nation.

MINNIE TIGER, being duly sworn, testified as follows:

Through Alex Posey Official Interpreter:

BY COMMISSION:
Q What is your name? A Minnie Tiger.
Q How old are you? A Twenty.
Q What is your post office address? A Emahaka.
Q Are you a citizen of the Creek Nation? A Yes, sir.
Q To what town do you belong? A Little River Tulsa.
Q Do you make application for the enrollment of your child, Roman Tiger, as a citizen of the Creek Nation? A Yes, sir.
Q Who is the father of Toman[sic]? A Cheparne Simon.
Q Is he a citizen of the Creek Nation? A Seminole.
Q Is he your lawful husband? A No, sir.
Q Are you married to him according to Indian custom? A No, sir.
Q Do you live together as man and wife? A No, sir.
Q If it should be found that your child, Roman Tiger, is entitled to enrollment in either the Creek or Muskogee Seminole Nations in which nation do you desire to have him enrolled? A In the Creek Nation.

---oooOOOooo---

I, D. C. Skaggs, on oath state that the above and foregoing is a full and true transcript of my stenographic notes as taken in said cause on said date.

DC Skaggs

Subscribed and sworn to before me this 18" day of July, 1905.

Applications for Enrollment of Creek Newborn
Act of 1905 Volume VII

Edw C Griesel
Notary Public.

BIRTH AFFIDAVIT.

DEPARTMENT OF THE INTERIOR.
COMMISSION TO THE FIVE CIVILIZED TRIBES.

IN RE APPLICATION FOR ENROLLMENT, as a citizen of the Creek Nation, of Roman Tiger, born on the 19 day of May, 1903

Name of Father: Cheparney Simon   a citizen of the Seminole Nation.
Name of Mother: Minnie Tiger   a citizen of the Creek Nation.
Tulsa L.R. Town
            Postoffice   Emahaka, I.T.

AFFIDAVIT OF MOTHER.

Child is present

UNITED STATES OF AMERICA, Indian Territory, }
     Western   DISTRICT.

I, Minnie Tiger, on oath state that I am 20 years of age and a citizen by blood, of the Creek Nation; that I am not the lawful wife of Cheparney Simon, who is a citizen, by blood of the Seminole Nation; that a male child was born to me on 19" day of May, 1903, that said child has been named Roman Tiger, and was living March 4, 1905.

                   her
           Minnie x Tiger
Witnesses To Mark: mark
   { Alex Posey
   { DC Skaggs

Subscribed and sworn to before me this 27" day of March, 1905.

                 Drennan C Skaggs
                      Notary Public.

AFFIDAVIT OF ATTENDING PHYSICIAN OR MID-WIFE.

UNITED STATES OF AMERICA, Indian Territory, }
     Western   DISTRICT.

I, Lizzie Harjo, a midwife, on oath state that I attended on Mrs. Minnie Tiger, ~~wife of~~ *(blank)* on the 19" day of May, 1903; that there was born to her on said date a male child; that said child was living March 4, 1905, and is said to have been named Roman Tiger

Applications for Enrollment of Creek Newborn
Act of 1905   Volume VII

Witnesses To Mark:

                            her
                           Lizzie x Harjo
                           mark

{ Subscribed and sworn to before me this 28 day of March, 1905.

                                      Notary Public.

(The above Birth Affidavit given again)

Indian Territory, I
               I ss:
Western District. I
    I   my
    ~~We~~, the undersigned, do hereby elect to have ~~our~~ child, Roman Tiger , born on the 19 day of May , 1903 , enrolled as a citizen of the Creek Nation, and to have said child receive his allotment of land and distribution of moneys in said nation.

                                 her

Witnesses to mark: Manie x Cumseh[sic]
                               mark
J McDermott

W R Jackson

Subscribed and sworn to before me this 1 day of Nov 1906.

                                    J McDermott
                                    Notary Public.

                                      NC 542.

            Muskogee, Indian Territory, July 14, 1905.

Commissioner to the Five Civilized Tribes,
        Seminole Enrollment Division,
            Muskogee, Indian Territory.

Gentlemen:
    March 28, 1905, application was made to the Commission to the Five Civilized Tribes for the enrollment of Roman Tiger, born May 19, 1903, as a citizen by blood of the Creek Nation. It is stated in said application that the father of said child is Cheparney

Applications for Enrollment of Creek Newborn
Act of 1905   Volume VII

Simon, a citizen of the Seminole Nation, and that the mother is Minnie Tiger, a citizen of the Creek Nation.

You are requested to inform the Creek Enrollment Division as to whether application has been made for the enrollment of said Roman Tiger as a citizen of the Seminole Nation, and if so, what disposition has been made of the same.

Respectfully,

Commissioner.

N.C. 542

Muskogee, I T July 17, 1905

Minnie Tiger
    Emahaka I T

Dear Madam:

In the matter of the application for the enrollment of your minor child, Roman Tiger, as a citizen of the Creek Nation you are advised that without further information it is impossible for this office to identify you on its rolls of citizens of said nation.

You are requested to furnish this office with your maiden name, the names of your parents, the Creek Indian Town to which you belong, and, if possible, the numbers which appear on your deeds to land in the Creek Nation, and any other information that will help to identify you as a citizen of the Creek Nation.

Respectfully,

Commissioner.

DEPARTMENT OF THE INTERIOR.
COMMISSION TO THE FIVE CIVILIZED TRIBES.

Muskogee, Indian Territory, July 19, 1905.

Chief Clerk,
    Creek Enrollment Division.

Dear Sir:
Receipt is acknowledged of your letter of July 14, 1905 (NC-542) stating that application was made to the Commission to the Five Civilized Tribes for the enrollment

Applications for Enrollment of Creek Newborn
Act of 1905   Volume VII

of Roman Tiger, born May 19, 1903, child of Cheparney Simon, a citizen of the Seminole Nation, and Minnie Tiger, a citizen of the Creek Nation, and requesting to be informed as to whether application was made for the enrollment of said child as a citizen of the Seminole Nation.

In reply to your letter you are advised that it does not appear from an examination of the records of this office that any application was made to the Commission to the Five Civilized Tribes for the enrollment of said as a citizen of the Seminole Nation.

Respectfully,

Tams Bixby   Commissioner.

N C 542

Muskogee, Indian Territory, March 1, 1907.

Manie Cumseh
% Cheparney Simon,
Emahaka, Indian Territory.

Dear Madam :--

You are hereby advised that on February 15, 1907, the Secretary of the Interior approved the enrollment of your minor child, Roman Tiger, as a citizen by blood of the Creek Nation, and that the name of said child appears upon the roll of New Born citizens by blood of the Creek Nation, enrolled under the Act of Congress approved March 3, 1905, as number 1156.

This child is now entitled to allotment and application therefor should be made without delay at the Creek Land Office, Muskogee, Indian Territory.

Respectfully,

Commissioner.

Applications for Enrollment of Creek Newborn
Act of 1905   Volume VII

BIRTH AFFIDAVIT.

DEPARTMENT OF THE INTERIOR.
COMMISSION TO THE FIVE CIVILIZED TRIBES.

    IN RE APPLICATION FOR ENROLLMENT, as a citizen of the Creek Nation, of Nettie McCoy, born on the 27 day of April, 1902

Name of Father: William A. McCoy   a citizen of the United States Nation.
Name of Mother: Ida McCoy (nee Carr)   a citizen of the Creek Nation.
Euche[sic] Town
                Postoffice   Wetumka, Ind. Ter.

AFFIDAVIT OF MOTHER.

UNITED STATES OF AMERICA, Indian Territory,   <u>Child</u> is <u>present</u>
     Western   **DISTRICT.**

    I, Ida McCoy, on oath state that I am 23 years of age and a citizen by blood, of the Creek Nation; that I am the lawful wife of William A. McCoy, who is a citizen, by *(blank)* of the United States Nation; that a female child was born to me on 27 day of April, 1902, that said child has been named Nettie McCoy, and was living March 4, 1905.

                                     Ida McCoy
Witnesses To Mark:
   {

    Subscribed and sworn to before me this 30 day of March, 1905.

                               Drennan C Skaggs
                                   Notary Public.

AFFIDAVIT OF ATTENDING PHYSICIAN OR MID-WIFE.

UNITED STATES OF AMERICA, Indian Territory,
     Western   **DISTRICT.**

    I, Bettie Carr, a midwife, on oath state that I attended on Mrs. Ida McCoy, wife of William A. McCoy on the 27 day of April, 1902; that there was born to her on said date a female child; that said child was living March 4, 1905, and is said to have been named Nettie McCoy
                                  her
                             Bettie x Carr
Witnesses To Mark: mark
   { Alex Posey
     DC Skaggs

Applications for Enrollment of Creek Newborn
Act of 1905   Volume VII

Subscribed and sworn to before me this 30 day of March, 1905.

                        Drennan C Skaggs
                        Notary Public.

BIRTH AFFIDAVIT.

DEPARTMENT OF THE INTERIOR.
COMMISSION TO THE FIVE CIVILIZED TRIBES.

IN RE APPLICATION FOR ENROLLMENT, as a citizen of the Creek Nation, of Robert Elihu McCoy, born on the 3 day of January , 1905

Name of Father: William A. McCoy   a citizen of the United States Nation.
Name of Mother: Ida McCoy (nee Carr)   a citizen of the Creek Nation.
Euche[sic] Town

                Postoffice   Wetumka, Ind. Ter.

AFFIDAVIT OF MOTHER.

UNITED STATES OF AMERICA, Indian Territory,   Child is present
    Western   **DISTRICT.**

    I, Ida McCoy , on oath state that I am 23 years of age and a citizen by blood , of the Creek Nation; that I am the lawful wife of William A. McCoy , who is a citizen, ~~by~~ *(blank)* of the United States Nation; that a male child was born to me on 3 day of January , 1905 , that said child has been named Robert Elihu McCoy , and was living March 4, 1905.

                        Ida McCoy

Witnesses To Mark:

    Subscribed and sworn to before me this 30 day of March , 1905.

                        Drennan C Skaggs
                        Notary Public.

AFFIDAVIT OF ATTENDING PHYSICIAN OR MID-WIFE.

UNITED STATES OF AMERICA, Indian Territory,
    Western   **DISTRICT.**

    I, Bettie Carr , a midwife , on oath state that I attended on Mrs. Ida McCoy , wife of William A. McCoy on the 3 day of January , 1905 ; that there was born to her

Applications for Enrollment of Creek Newborn
Act of 1905   Volume VII

on said date a male child; that said child was living March 4, 1905, and is said to have been named Robert Elihu McCoy

Witnesses To Mark:
{ Alex Posey
DC Skaggs

Bettie x Carr
her   mark

Subscribed and sworn to before me this 30 day of March, 1905.

Drennan C Skaggs
Notary Public.

DEPARTMENT OF THE INTERIOR,
COMMISSION TO THE FIVE CIVILIZED TRIBES.
Holdenville, I. T., March 30, 1905.

In the matter of the application for the enrollment of Leah Bruner as a citizen by blood of the Creek Nation.

LITTLE CHARLIE, being duly sworn, testified as follows:

Through Alex Posey Official Interpreter:

BY COMMISSION:
Q What is your name? A Little Charlie.
Q How old are you? A About fifty.
Q What is your post office address? A Holdenville.
Q Are you a citizen of the Creek Nation? A Yes, sir.
Q to what town do you belong? A Little River Tulsa.
Q Do you make application for the enrollment of Leah Bruner as a citizen by blood of the Creek Nation? A Yes, sir.
Q What relation is the child to you? A My grandchild.
Q What are the names of the parents? A Addie and William Bruner.
Q Is Addie Bruner your daughter? A Yes, sir.
Q Is she a citizen of the Creek Nation? A Yes, sir.
Q To what town does she belong? A Little River Tulsa.
Q Why does not the mother herself make application for the enrollment of Leah? A Her husband has forbidden her. He is a member of the Snake Faction and has always refused to make application for the enrollment of any of his children.
Q When was Leah born? A The child was born in July, 1903, I do not know what day.

---oooOOOooo---

Applications for Enrollment of Creek Newborn
Act of 1905   Volume VII

I, D. C. Skaggs, on oath state that the above and foregoing is a full and true transcript of my stenographic notes as taken in said cause on said date.

DC Skaggs

Subscribed and sworn to before me this 20" day of July, 1905.

Edw C Griesel
Notary Public.

2450-B.
N.C. 484.

DEPARTMENT OF THE INTERIOR,
COMMISSIONER TO THE FIVE CIVILIZED TRIBES.
CALVIN, I. T., September 4, 1906.

In the matter of the application for the enrollment of two unnamed minor children of Willie and Addie Bruner, as citizens by blood of the Creek Nation.

ADDIE BRUNER being duly sworn, testified as follows:
Through Alex Posey, Official Interpreter.

BY THE COMMISSIONER:

Q What is your name? A Addie Bruner.
Q How old are you? A About 25.
Q What is your postoffice address? A Calvin.
Q Are you a citizen of the Creek Nation? A Yes sir.
Q To what Creek town do you belong? A Little River Tulsa.
Q Have you any minor children for whom you have not made application? A Yes sir, I have two.
Q What are their names? A The oldest child is variously named Sadie, Susie, Katie and Mary, we have never decided upon a name for her but you may put her down as Susie.
Q When was Susie born? A On or about July 3, 1902.
Q Susie is living, is she? A Yes, sir, this is the child present.
Q Who is the father of the child? A Willie Bruner.
Q Is he a citizen of the Creek Nation? A Yes sir.
Q To what Creek town does he belong? A Weagufky[sic].
Q Is Willie Bruner your lawful husband? A We are living together as husband and wife according to Indian custom.
Q What is the name of your other child? A Losanna Bruner.
Q When was she born? A Sometime in April of this year.
Q 1906? A Yes sir.
Q Can you not state exactly what time in April? A No sir.
Q You are positive it was in April, are you? A Yes sir.

Applications for Enrollment of Creek Newborn
Act of 1905   Volume VII

Q Is Willie Bruner also the father of this child? A Yes sir.
Q Who attended on you as mid-wife at the birth of Susie and Losanna? A There was no mid-wife present at the birth of either.
Q Why have you not looked after the rights of these children before now? A Because the father is opposed to having them enrolled, and I am running the risk of incurring his displeasure by giving information about them today.
Q Where is the father today? A He has gone to attend a meeting of the Snakes down at Weagufky[sic].

James B. Myers, being first duly sworn, states, that as stenographer to the Commissioner to the Five Civilized Tribes, he recorded the testimony in the foregoing proceedings, and that the above is a true, and correct transcript of his stenographic notes thereof.

                              James B Myers

Subscribed and sworn to before me, this
the *(illegible)* day of October, 1906.
                              Alex Posey
JBM   Notary Public.

Supplemental testimony taken

BIRTH AFFIDAVIT.

DEPARTMENT OF THE INTERIOR.
COMMISSION TO THE FIVE CIVILIZED TRIBES.

IN RE APPLICATION FOR ENROLLMENT, as a citizen of the Creek Nation, of Leah Bruner, born on the *(blank)* day of July, 1903

Name of Father: William Bruner   a citizen of the Creek Nation.
Tokpafka[sic] Town
Name of Mother: Addie Bruner (nee Charlie) a citizen of the Creek Nation.
Tulsa Little River Town
                          Postoffice   Calvin, Ind. Ter.

AFFIDAVIT OF MOTHER.

UNITED STATES OF AMERICA, Indian Territory, ⎫
    Western   DISTRICT. ⎭   Child is present.

    I, Little Charlie, on oath state that I am about 50 years of age and a citizen by blood, of the Creek Nation; that I am the ~~lawful wife~~ father of Addie Bruner, who is a citizen, by blood of the Creek Nation; that a female child was born to ~~me on~~ her *(blank)* ~~day of~~ July, 1903, that said child has been named Leah Bruner, and was living March 4, 1905. That the mother refused to make application for the enrollment of the child.

Applications for Enrollment of Creek Newborn
Act of 1905   Volume VII

<table>
<tr><td>Witnesses To Mark:
  { Alex Posey
    DC Skaggs</td><td>his
Little x Charlie
mark</td></tr>
</table>

Subscribed and sworn to before me this 30 day of March , 1905.

                                  Drennan C Skaggs
                                  Notary Public.

NC 544.

                         Muskogee, Indian Territory, January 13, 1907.

Addie Bruner (or Ida Bruner,)
    c/o William Bruner,
        Calvin, Indian Territory.

Dear Madam:

    In the matter of the application for the enrollment of your minor child, Lean Bruner, as a citizen by blood of the Creek Nation, you are advised that this office requires your affidavit and the affidavit of the midwife or physician in attendance at its, and a blank form for that purpose is herewith enclosed, which you are requested to have properly executed and returned to this office within ten days.

    You are requested to write this office giving the names of all your children and the dates of their birth.

                         Respectfully,

                                    Commissioner.

1 BA

NC 544.

                         Muskogee, Indian Territory, January 16, 1907.

Little Charlie,
    Calvin, Indian Territory.

Dear Sir:

    In the matter of the application for the enrollment of Leah Bruner, minor child of your daughter, Addie Bruner or Ida Bruner, as a citizen of the Creek Nation, you are advised that this office requires her affidavit and the affidavit of the midwife or physician

Applications for Enrollment of Creek Newborn
Act of 1905   Volume VII

in attendance at the birth of said child and ten days[sic] time has been granted to furnish same.

You are requested to write this office at once stating the names of the children of your said daughter and the dates of their birth.

Respectfully,

1 BA

Commissioner.

N.C. 545

DEPARTMENT OF THE INTERIOR,
COMMISSION TO THE FIVE CIVILIZED TRIBES.
Muskogee, Indian Territory, June 16, 1905.

In the matter of the application for the enrollment of Lillie Wills as a citizen of the Creek Nation.

Joseph Wills, being duly sworn, testified as follows:

By Commission.

Q What is your name? A Joseph Wills.
Q How old are you? A About twentyfive.
Q What is your post office address? A Burney.
Q You are a citizen of the Creek Nation, are you? A Yes, sir.
Q Well when was your child Lilly ----Witness---I spell that Lillie--Q Well when was that child born? A Born February 27, 1904 I maybe said 1905 when I made that affidavit, because every time I write I think of this year 1905. I made a mistake in that affidavit because it was born in 1904. This last February it was a year old.
Q You are sure that this child Lillie is a little over a year old? A Yes, sir.
Q And is living? A Yes, sir.
Q The other child died a long time ago? A Yes, sir, in 1902.
Q You are a full blood Indian are you, Creek? A Yes, sir.

I, Henry G. Hains, on oath state that the above and foregoing is a full and true transcript of my stenographic notes as taken in said cause on said date.

Henry G. Hains

Subscribed and sworn to before me this 29 day of June, 1905.

J McDermott
Notary Public.

Applications for Enrollment of Creek Newborn
Act of 1905 Volume VII

BIRTH AFFIDAVIT.

DEPARTMENT OF THE INTERIOR.
COMMISSION TO THE FIVE CIVILIZED TRIBES.

IN RE APPLICATION FOR ENROLLMENT, as a citizen of the CREEK Nation, of Lillie Wills, born on the 27 day of Feb , 1905

Name of Father: Joseph Wills   a citizen of the   Creek   Nation.
Name of Mother: Nancy   "   a citizen of the   Creek   Nation.
                       Postoffice   Burney, I.T.

                       Father
AFFIDAVIT OF MOTHER.

UNITED STATES OF AMERICA, Indian Territory, }
       WESTERN   DISTRICT.

     I, Joseph Wills , on oath state that I am 25" years of age and a citizen by blood, of the Creek Nation; that I am the lawful ~~wife~~ husband of Nancy Wills , who is not a citizen, by *(blank)* of the Creek Nation; that a female child was born to me on 27" day of Feb , 1905 , that said child has been named Lillie Wills , and is now living.

                       Joseph Wills
Witnesses To Mark:
   {

     Subscribed and sworn to before me this 30 day of March , 1905.

                       J McDermott
                       Notary Public.

BIRTH AFFIDAVIT.

DEPARTMENT OF THE INTERIOR.
COMMISSION TO THE FIVE CIVILIZED TRIBES.

IN RE APPLICATION FOR ENROLLMENT, as a citizen of the Creek Nation, of Lilly Wills, born on the 27th day of February , 1904

Name of Father: Joseph Wills   a citizen of the   Creek   Nation.
Name of Mother: Nancy Wills   a citizen of the   Creek   Nation.

                       Postoffice   Burney Ind. Ter

Applications for Enrollment of Creek Newborn
Act of 1905 Volume VII

AFFIDAVIT OF MOTHER.

UNITED STATES OF AMERICA, Indian Territory, ⎱
    Western   DISTRICT.   ⎰

    I, Nancy Wills, on oath state that I am Ninteen[sic] years of age and a citizen by Blood, of the Creek Nation; that I am the lawful wife of Joseph Wills, who is a citizen, by Blood of the Creek Nation; that a Female child was born to me on 27th day of February, 1904, that said child has been named Lilly Wills, and is now living.

                                            Nancy Wills

Witnesses To Mark:
  { J.N. Willhite
    Senora E. Likowski

    Subscribed and sworn to before me this 10th day of April, 1905.

        MY COMMISSION EXPIRES JULY 13th 1908.   J W Fowler
                                                       Notary Public.

AFFIDAVIT OF ATTENDING PHYSICIAN OR MID-WIFE.

UNITED STATES OF AMERICA, Indian Territory, ⎱
    Western   DISTRICT.   ⎰

    I, Clara Cole, a Midwife, on oath state that I attended on Mrs. Nancy Wills, wife of Joseph Wills on the 27th day of February, 1904; that there was born to her on said date a female child; that said child is now living and is said to have been named Lilly Wills
                                            her
                                        Clara x Cole
Witnesses To Mark: mark
  { J.N. Willhite
    Senora E. Likowski

    Subscribed and sworn to before me this 10th day of April, 1905.

        MY COMMISSION EXPIRES JULY 13th 1908   J W Fowler
                                                         Notary Public.

Applications for Enrollment of Creek Newborn
Act of 1905   Volume VII

BIRTH AFFIDAVIT.

DEPARTMENT OF THE INTERIOR.
COMMISSION TO THE FIVE CIVILIZED TRIBES.

IN RE APPLICATION FOR ENROLLMENT, as a citizen of the CREEK Nation, of Sandy Wills, born on the 7 day of Apr , 1902

Name of Father: Joseph Wills	a citizen of the	Creek	Nation.
Name of Mother: Nancy "	not a citizen of the	Creek	Nation.

Postoffice   Burney, I.T.

Father

AFFIDAVIT OF ~~MOTHER~~.

UNITED STATES OF AMERICA, Indian Territory, }
   WESTERN   DISTRICT.

I, Joseph Wills , on oath state that I am 25 years of age and a citizen by blood , of the Creek Nation; that I am the lawful ~~wife~~ husband of Nancy Wills, who is not a citizen, by *(blank)* of the Creek Nation; that a male child was born to ~~me~~ her on 7" day of Apr   , 1902 , that said child has been named Sandy Wills , and is now ~~living~~ dead. having died Aug. 21st 1902

Joseph Wills

Witnesses To Mark:
{

Subscribed and sworn to before me this 30" day of March, 1905.

J McDermott
Notary Public.

NC 545.   JLD.

DEPARTMENT OF THE INTERIOR,
COMMISSIONER TO THE FIVE CIVILIZED TRIBES.
....

In the matter of the application for the enrollment of Sandy Wills, deceased, as a citizen by blood of the Creek Nation.
....

STATEMENT AND ORDER.

The record in this case shows that on March 30, 1905, application was made, in

Applications for Enrollment of Creek Newborn
Act of 1905   Volume VII

affidavit form, for the enrollment of Sandy Wills, deceased, as a citizen by blood of the Creek Nation, under the provisions of the act of Congress approved March 3, 1905.

It appears from the afficavit filed in this matter that said Sandy Wills, deceased, was born April 7, 1902, and died August 31, 1902.

The Act of Congress approved March 3, 1905, (33 Stats., 1048), provides:

"That the Commission to the Five Civilized Tribes is authorized for sixty days after the date of the approval of this act to receive and consider applications for enrollment, of children, born subsequent to May twenty-fifth, nineteen hundred and one, and prior to March fourth, nineteen hundred and five, and living on said latter date, to citizens of the Creek tribe of Indians whose enrollment has been approved by the Secretary of the Interior prior to the approval of this act; and to enroll and make allotments to such children."

It is, therefore, ordered that the application for the enrollment of Sandy Wills, deceased, as a citizen by blood of the Creek Nation be, and the same is, hereby dismissed.

Tams Bixby   Commissioner.

Muskogee, Indian Territory.
JAN 4 – 1907

DEPARTMENT OF THE INTERIOR,
COMMISSION TO THE FIVE CIVILIZED TRIBES.
Holdenville, I.T., March 30, 1905.

In the matter of the application for the enrollment of Freeman and Harry Kernells as citizens by blood of the Creek Nation.

ARRETTA KERNELLS, being duly sworn, testified as follows:

Through Alex Posey Official Interpreter:

BY COMMISSION:
Q What is your name? A Arretta Kernells.
Q How old are you? A Twenty.
Q What is your post office address? A Earlsboro, O. T.
Q Are you a citizen of the Creek Nation? A Seminole.
Q Do you make application for the enrollment of your minor children, Freeman and Harry Kernells, as citizens by blood of the Creek Nation? A Yes, sir.
Q What is the name of their father? A George Kernells.
Q Is he a citizen of the Creek Nation? A Yes, sir.
Q To what town does he belong? A Eufaula Canadian.
Q Is he your lawfull[sic] husband? A Yes, sir.
Q If it should be found that your children, Freeman and Harry Kernells, are entitled to be enrolled in either the Creek or Seminole Nations in which nation do you desire to have them enrolled? A In the Creek Nation.

Applications for Enrollment of Creek Newborn
Act of 1905   Volume VII

---oooOOOooo---

I, D. C. Skaggs, on oath state that the above and foregoing is a full and true transcript of my stenographic notes as taken in said cause on said date.

DC Skaggs

Subscribed and sworn to before me this 20 day of July, 1905.

Edw C Griesel
Notary Public.

BIRTH AFFIDAVIT.

DEPARTMENT OF THE INTERIOR.
COMMISSION TO THE FIVE CIVILIZED TRIBES.

IN RE APPLICATION FOR ENROLLMENT, as a citizen of the Creek Nation, of Freeman Kernel, born on the 28th day of February, 1905

Name of Father: George Kernel   a citizen of the   Creek   Nation.
Name of Mother: Arretta Kernel   a citizen of the   Seminole   Nation.

Postoffice   Earlsboro, Oklahoma Ter

AFFIDAVIT OF ~~MOTHER~~. Father

UNITED STATES OF AMERICA, Indian Territory, }
      (blank)   DISTRICT.   }

I, George Kernel, on oath state that I am about 23 years of age and a citizen by blood, of the Creek Nation; that I am the lawful ~~wife of~~ husband of Arretta Kernel, who is a citizen, by blood of the Seminole Nation; that a male child was born to ~~me~~ her on 28th day of February, 1905, that said child has been named Freeman Kernel, and was living March 4, 1905. and I elect for said child to be enrolled as a citizen of the Creek Nation

George Kernel
Witnesses To Mark:
{

Subscribed and sworn to before me this 29 day of August, 1905.

My com exp's Oct 5, 1906   John W. Willmott
                                   Notary Public.

Applications for Enrollment of Creek Newborn
Act of 1905 Volume VII

BIRTH AFFIDAVIT.

Supplemental testimony taken

DEPARTMENT OF THE INTERIOR.
COMMISSION TO THE FIVE CIVILIZED TRIBES.

IN RE APPLICATION FOR ENROLLMENT, as a citizen of the Creek Nation, of Freeman Kernells, born on the 28 day of February, 1905

Name of Father: George Kernells   a citizen of the   Creek   Nation.
Eufaula Canadian
Name of Mother: Arretta Kernells   a citizen of the   Seminole   Nation.
         Postoffice   Earlsboro, Okla.

AFFIDAVIT OF MOTHER.

UNITED STATES OF AMERICA, Indian Territory, }
     Western   DISTRICT.

Child is present

I, Arretta Kernells, on oath state that I am 20 years of age and a citizen by blood, of the Seminole Nation; that I am the lawful wife of George Kernells, who is a citizen, by blood of the Creek Nation; that a male child was born to me on 28 day of February, 1905, that said child has been named Freeman Kernells, and was living March 4, 1905.

                       Arretta Kernells

Witnesses To Mark:
{

Subscribed and sworn to before me this 30 day of March, 1905.

                       Drennan C Skaggs
                       Notary Public.

AFFIDAVIT OF ATTENDING PHYSICIAN OR MID-WIFE.

UNITED STATES OF AMERICA, Indian Territory, }
     Western   DISTRICT.

I, Lou Smith, a midwife, on oath state that I attended on Mrs. Arretta Kernells, wife of George Kernells on the 28 day of February, 1905 ; that there was born to her on said date a male child; that said child was living March 4, 1905, and is said to have been named Freeman Kernells

                       her
                       Lou x Smith
                       mark

Applications for Enrollment of Creek Newborn
Act of 1905   Volume VII

Witnesses To Mark:
{ Alex Posey
{ DC Skaggs

Subscribed and sworn to before me this 30 day of March, 1905.

Drennan C Skaggs
Notary Public.

BIRTH AFFIDAVIT.

Supplemental testimony taken

DEPARTMENT OF THE INTERIOR.
COMMISSION TO THE FIVE CIVILIZED TRIBES.

IN RE APPLICATION FOR ENROLLMENT, as a citizen of the Creek Nation, of Harry Kernells, born on the 27 day of October, 1902

Name of Father: George Kernells   a citizen of the   Creek   Nation.
Eufaula Canadian
Name of Mother: Arretta Kernells   a citizen of the   Seminole   Nation.

Postoffice   Earlsboro, Okla.

AFFIDAVIT OF MOTHER.

UNITED STATES OF AMERICA, Indian Territory, }
    Western   DISTRICT.   }   Child is present

I, Arretta Kernells, on oath state that I am 20 years of age and a citizen by blood, of the Seminole Nation; that I am the lawful wife of George Kernells, who is a citizen, by blood of the Creek Nation; that a male child was born to me on 27 day of October, 1902, that said child has been named Harry Kernells, and was living March 4, 1905.

Arretta Kernells

Witnesses To Mark:
{
{

Subscribed and sworn to before me this 30 day of March, 1905.

Drennan C Skaggs
Notary Public.

171

Applications for Enrollment of Creek Newborn
Act of 1905 Volume VII

AFFIDAVIT OF ATTENDING PHYSICIAN OR MID-WIFE.

UNITED STATES OF AMERICA, Indian Territory,
Western DISTRICT.

I, Lou Smith , a midwife , on oath state that I attended on Mrs. Arretta Kernells, wife of George Kernells on the 27 day of October , 1902 ; that there was born to her on said date a male child; that said child was living March 4, 1905, and is said to have been named Harry Kernells

                                        her
                                  Lou x Smith
                                    mark

Witnesses To Mark:
{ Alex Posey
{ DC Skaggs

Subscribed and sworn to before me this 30 day of March, 1905.

                                  Drennan C Skaggs
                                  Notary Public.

DEPARTMENT OF THE INTERIOR
COMMISSIONER TO THE FIVE CIVILIZED TRIBES.

In the matter of the application for the enrollment of ARRA[sic] KERNEL, born on the 27th day of October, 1902 and FREEMAN KERNEL, born on the 28th day of February, 1905, as citizens of the Creek Nation.

Name of Father, George Kernel, a citizen of the Creek Nation.
Name of Mother, Arretta Kernel, [sic] citizen of the Seminole Nation.

                              Post Office, Earlboro[sic]. O.T.

United States of America, Indian Territory,
        Western Judicial District.

Affiant, Hettie Coker, being of lawful age, and first duly sworn, on her oath states, that she is a citizen of the Seminole Nation, Indian Territory; that she is said has been for many years well acquainted with George Kernel, a citizen of the Creek Nation, and Arretta Kernel, his wife, a citizen of the Seminole Nation; that said George Kernel and Arretta Kernel were married about eight years ago, according to the Indian laws and customs of the country, and have since that time been living as husband and wife, together.   her
                                  Hettie Coker x
                                      mark

Applications for Enrollment of Creek Newborn
Act of 1905 Volume VII

Attest:
E M Thorn
Jno W Willmott

Subscribed and sworn to before me this the 29th day of August, A.D., 1905.

John W Willmott

United States of America, Indian Territory,
Western Judicial District.

Affiant, Wysenda Harjo, being of lawful age and first duly sworn, on his oath states, that he is a Seminole Indian by blood, of the age of over fifty years, that he has long known George Kernel, a citizen of the Creek Nation, Indian Territory, and his wife, Arretta Kernel, who is a citizen of the Seminole Nation; that said George Kernel and Arretta Kernel were married about eight or nine years ago, according to the laws and customs prevailing among the Indians, and have been living in the Seminole Nation, near Mekusukey as husband and wife ever since the time of their marriage; that they now are, and for years have held themselves out as husband and wife, have borne children as such, and are so regarded by all the people.

his
Wysenda Harjo x
mark

Attest:
E M Thorn
Jno W Willmott

Subscribed and sworn to before me this the 29th day of August, A.D., 1905.

John W Willmott

My com. expires *(nothing else given)*

DEPARTMENT OF THE INTERIOR.
COMMISSION TO THE FIVE CIVILIZED TRIBES.

In the matter of the death of George Kernel a citizen of the Creek Nation, who formerly resided at or near Tidmore , Ind. Ter., and died on the 12" day of March , 1906

Applications for Enrollment of Creek Newborn
Act of 1905   Volume VII

AFFIDAVIT OF RELATIVE.

UNITED STATES OF AMERICA, Indian Territory, }
   Western   DISTRICT.

      I, Arreta[sic] Kernel , on oath state that I am 21 years of age and a citizen by blood , of the Seminole Nation; that my postoffice address is Tidmore , Ind. Ter.; that I ~~am~~ was the wife of George Kernel who was a citizen, by blood , of the Creek Nation and that said George Kernel died on the 12" day of March , 1906

                                       Arreta Kernel

Witnesses To Mark:
{

      Subscribed and sworn to before me this 9" day of November, 1906.

      My Commission   J McDermott

      Expires July 25" 1907   Notary Public.

Indian Territory, I
            I SS:
Western District. I
     I   my
      ~~We~~, the undersigned, do hereby elect to have ~~our~~ child, Harry Kernel , born on the 27 day of October , 1902 , enrolled as a citizen of the Creek Nation, and to have said child receive his allotment of land and distribution of moneys in said nation.

Witnesses to mark: Arreta Kernel

_____
_____   _____
_____

      Subscribed and sworn to before me this 9 day of Nov, 1906.
My Commission
Expires July 25", 1907.   J McDermott
                                      Notary Public.

BIRTH AFFIDAVIT.
DEPARTMENT OF THE INTERIOR.
COMMISSION TO THE FIVE CIVILIZED TRIBES.

      IN RE APPLICATION FOR ENROLLMENT, as a citizen of the Creek Nation, of Harry Kernel, born on the 27" day of Oct, 1902

Applications for Enrollment of Creek Newborn
Act of 1905   Volume VII

Name of Father: George Kernel   a citizen of the   Creek   Nation.
Name of Mother: Arretta Kernel   a citizen of the   Seminole   Nation.

                 Postoffice   Tidmore, IT

AFFIDAVIT OF MOTHER.

UNITED STATES OF AMERICA, Indian Territory,
     Western   DISTRICT.

     I, Arreta Kernel , on oath state that I am 20 years of age and a citizen by blood , of the Seminole Nation; that I am the lawful wife of George Kernell , who is a citizen, by blood of the Creek Nation; that a male child was born to me on 27" day of October , 1902 , that said child has been named Harry Kernel , and was living March 4, 1905. and is now living

                 Arreta Kernel

Witnesses To Mark:

     Subscribed and sworn to before me this 9 day of November , 1906.

My Commission   J McDermott
Expires July 25" 1907   Notary Public.

(Testimony of ARRETTA KERNELLS, March 30, 1905, given again)

BIRTH AFFIDAVIT.

DEPARTMENT OF THE INTERIOR.
COMMISSION TO THE FIVE CIVILIZED TRIBES.

     IN RE APPLICATION FOR ENROLLMENT, as a citizen of the Creek Nation, of Harry Kernel, born on the 27th day of October , 1902

Name of Father: George Kernel   a citizen of the   Creek   Nation.
Name of Mother: Arretta Kernel   a citizen of the   Seminole   Nation.

                 Postoffice   Earlsboro, Oklahoma Ter

Applications for Enrollment of Creek Newborn
Act of 1905 Volume VII

AFFIDAVIT OF ~~MOTHER~~. Father

UNITED STATES OF AMERICA, Indian Territory, }
    (blank)   DISTRICT.

I, George Kernel , on oath state that I am about 23 years of age and a citizen by blood , of the Creek Nation; that I am the lawful ~~wife of~~ husband of Arretta Kernel , who is a citizen, by blood of the Seminole Nation; that a male child was born to ~~me~~ her on 27th day of October , 1902 , that said child has been named ~~Harry~~ Arra Kernel , and was living March 4, 1905. and I elect for said child to be enrolled as a citizen of the Creek Nation

                                  George Kernel

Witnesses To Mark:
{

Subscribed and sworn to before me this 29 day of August, 1905.

My com exp's Oct 5, 1906   John W. Willmott
                                  Notary Public.

BIRTH AFFIDAVIT.

Supplemental testimony taken
DEPARTMENT OF THE INTERIOR.
COMMISSION TO THE FIVE CIVILIZED TRIBES.

IN RE APPLICATION FOR ENROLLMENT, as a citizen of the Creek Nation, of Harry Kernells , born on the 27" day of October, 1902

Name of Father: George Kernells   a citizen of the   Creek   Nation.
Eufaula Canadian
Name of Mother: Arretta Kernells   a citizen of the   Seminole   Nation.

                     Postoffice   Earlsboro, Okla.

AFFIDAVIT OF MOTHER.

UNITED STATES OF AMERICA, Indian Territory, }   Child present
     Western   DISTRICT.

I, Arretta Kernells , on oath state that I am 20 years of age and a citizen by blood , of the Seminole Nation; that I am the lawful wife of George Kernells , who is a citizen, by blood of the Creek Nation; that a male child was born to me on 27"

Applications for Enrollment of Creek Newborn
Act of 1905   Volume VII

day of October , 1902 , that said child has been named Harry Kernells , and was living March 4, 1905.

Arretta Kernells

Witnesses To Mark:
{

Subscribed and sworn to before me this 30 day of March , 1905.

Drennan C Skaggs
Notary Public.

AFFIDAVIT OF ATTENDING PHYSICIAN OR MID-WIFE.

UNITED STATES OF AMERICA, Indian Territory, }
   Western   DISTRICT.

I, Lou Smith , a midwife , on oath state that I attended on Mrs. Arretta Kernells, wife of George Kernells on the 27" day of October , 1902 ; that there was born to her on said date a *(blank)* child; that said child was living March 4, 1905, and is said to have been named Harry Kernells

her
Lou x Smith
mark

Witnesses To Mark:
{ Alex Posey
  DC Skaggs

Subscribed and sworn to before me this 30 day of March, 1905.

Drennan C Skaggs
Notary Public.

(Testimony of ARRETTA KERNELLS, March 30, 1905, given again)

(Birth Affidavit of ~~Harry~~ Arra Kernel given again)

NC 546.

Muskogee, Indian Territory, July 14, 1905.

Commissioner to the Five Civilized Tribes,
   Seminole Enrollment Division,
      Muskogee, Indian Territory.

Applications for Enrollment of Creek Newborn
Act of 1905   Volume VII

Gentlemen:

April 1, 1905, application was made to the Commission to the Five Civilized Tribes for the enrollment of Harry Kernells, born October 27, 1902, and Freeman Kernells, born February 28, 1905, as citizens by blood of the Creek Nation. It is stated in said application that the father of said children is George Kernells, a citizen of the Creek Nation, and that the mother is Erretta[sic] Kernells, a citizen of the Seminole Nation.

You are requested to inform the Creek Enrollment Division as to whether application has been made for the enrollment of , as a citizen of the Seminole Nation, and if so, what disposition has been made of the same.

Respectfully,

Commissioner.

DEPARTMENT OF THE INTERIOR.
COMMISSION TO THE FIVE CIVILIZED TRIBES.

Muskogee, Indian Territory, July 19, 1905.

Chief Clerk,
    Creek Enrollment Division.
Dear Sir:

Receipt is acknowledged of your letter of July 14, 1905 (NC-546) stating that application was made to the Commission to the Five Civilized Tribes for the enrollment of Harry Kernells, born October 27, 1902, and Freeman Kernells, born February 28, 1905, children of George Kernells, a citizen of the Creek Nation, and Erretta[sic] Kernells, a citizen of the Seminole Nation, as citizens by blood of the Creek Nation, and requesting to be informed as to whether application was made for the enrollment of said child as a citizen of the Seminole Nation.

In reply to your letter you are informed that it does not appear from an examination of the records of this office that application was made for the enrollment of said Harry Kernells and Freeman Kernells as citizens of the Seminole Nation.

Respectfully,

Tams Bixby   Commissioner.

Applications for Enrollment of Creek Newborn
Act of 1905   Volume VII

NC 546.

Muskogee, Indian Territory, August 8, 1905.

Arretta Kernel,
    Earlsboro, Oklahoma Territory.

Dear Madam:

    In the matter of the application for the enrollment of your minor children Harry Kernel and Freeman Kernel, as citizens by blood of the Creek Nation You are advised that it will be necessary for you to furnish this office with evidence of your marriage to George Kernel, the father of said children.

    It will also be necessary for you to furnish this office with the affidavits of said George Kenerl[sic] as to the birth of said children and two blanks for that purpose which have been filled out are inclosed herewith. You are requested to have the said George Kernel appear before a notary public and swear to said affidavits and return the same to this office in the inclosed envelope together with the evidence of marriage above referred to.

                    Respectfully,

                      Acting Commissioner.

END.35.

NC 546.

Muskogee, Indian Territory, August 21, 1906.

Chief Clerk,
    Seminole Enrollment Division,
        Muskogee, Indian Territory.

Dear Sir:

    Application has been made for the enrollment as a citizen of the Creek Nation of Freeman Kernells, born February 28, 1905, to George Kernells, a citizen of the Creek Nation, and Arretta Kernells, a citizen of the Seminole Nation.

    You are requested to advise this office if application has been made for the enrollment of said child as a citizen of the Seminole Nation, and if so, please furnish the present status of said application.

                    Respectfully,

                      Commissioner.

Applications for Enrollment of Creek Newborn
Act of 1905 Volume VII

Wewoka, I.T. December 5th, 1905.

Hon. Tams Bixby,
    Muskogee, I.T.

Dear Sir:

    George Colonel, of Earlboro[sic], O.T., desires to know if any further evidence is needed in the matter of the enrollment of his children, Arra Colonel & Freeman Colonel, as citizens of the Seminole Nation, or Creek Nation, he doesn't know which. He is a Creek and his wife, Retta Colonel, is a Seminole. He claims to have made an application first to have the children enrolled as Creeks; then as Seminoles; We shall thank you for some information upon the subject as to the status of the application.

                Respectfully,

                Signed McKennon & Willmott,
                Attorneys for the Seminoles.

                Muskogee, Indian Territory, December 8, 1905.

McKennon & Willmott,
    Wewoka, Indian Territory.

Gentlemen:

    Receipt is acknowledged of your letter of December 5, 1905, in which you state that George Colonel of Earlsboro, Oklahoma. Oklahoma, desires to know if any further evidence is needed in the matter of the enrollment of Arra and Freeman Colonel, as citizens of the Seminole or Creek Nation.

    In reply you are advised that the name of said child is given variously as Arra and Harry and the surname of said children is given in affidavits in this case as Kernel and Kernells; and that the father of said children is enrolled as a citizen of the Creek Nation under the name of George Kernel.

    It is required that the affidavit of the parents be furnished this office, giving the correct names of said children.

                Respectfully,

                Acting Commissioner.

Applications for Enrollment of Creek Newborn
Act of 1905   Volume VII

REFER IN REPLY TO THE FOLLOWING:
_____

DEPARTMENT OF THE INTERIOR,
COMMISSIONER TO THE FIVE CIVILIZED TRIBES.

Muskogee, Indian Territory, August 24, 1906.

Chief Clerk,
    Creek Enrollment Division,
        Muskogee, Indian Territory.

Dear Sir:

    Receipt is hereby acknowledged of your letter of August 21, 1906, asking if application has been made for enrollment as a citizen of the Seminole Nation of Freeman Kernells, child of George Kernells, a citizen of the Creek Nation, and Arretta Kernells, a citizen of the Seminole Nation.

    In reply you are advised that it does not appear from the records of this office that any application has been made on behalf of Freeman Kernells, for enrollment as a new born citizen of the Seminole Nation under the Act of Congress approved March 3, 1905.

                Respectfully,

                          Wm. O. Beall
                          Acting Commissioner.

HGH

REFER IN REPLY TO THE FOLLOWING:
_____

DEPARTMENT OF THE INTERIOR,
COMMISSIONER TO THE FIVE CIVILIZED TRIBES.

Muskogee, Indian Territory, October 23, 1906.

George Kernal[sic],
    Earlsboro, Oklahoma Territory.

Dear Sir:

    You are hereby advised that the name of your minor child, Freeman Kernal, is contained in the partial list of citizens by blood of the Creek Nation, approved by the Secretary of the Interior October 15, 1906, and that a selection of land in the Creek Nation may now be made for said child at the Creek Land Office in Muskogee.

    This matter should receive your prompt attention.

Applications for Enrollment of Creek Newborn
Act of 1905   Volume VII

Respectfully,

Tams Bixby   Commissioner.

NC 546.

Muskogee, Indian Territory, October 31, 1906.

Chief Clerk,
  Seminole Enrollment Division,
  Muskogee, Indian Territory.

Dear Sir:

There is on file in this office an application for the enrollment of Freeman Kernel, born February 28, 1905, to Arretta Kernel, a citizen of the Seminole Nation, and George Kernel, who is identified as a citizen of the Creek Nation, opposite Creek Indian roll number 8942.

You are advised that the name of said child is contained in a partial list of new born citizens by blood of the Creek Nation, approved by the Secretary of the Interior October 15, 1906, opposite roll number 1052.

Respectfully,

Commissioner.

NC 546.

Muskogee, Indian Territory, March 1, 1907.

George Kernel,
  Earlsboro, Oklahoma.

Dear Sir:

You are hereby advised that on February 15, 1907, the Secretary of the Interior approved the enrollment of your minor child, Harry Kernel, as a citizen by blood of the Creek Nation, and that the name of said child appears upon the roll of New Born citizens by blood of the Creek Nation, enrolled under the act of Congress approved March 3rd, 1905, as number 1157.

This child is now entitled to allotment and application therefor should be made without delay at the Creek Land Office, Muskogee, Indian Territory.

Applications for Enrollment of Creek Newborn
Act of 1905   Volume VII

Respectfully,

Commissioner.

BIRTH AFFIDAVIT.

DEPARTMENT OF THE INTERIOR.
COMMISSION TO THE FIVE CIVILIZED TRIBES.

IN RE APPLICATION FOR ENROLLMENT, as a citizen of the CREEK Nation, of Isaiah McIntosh, born on the 28 day of December, 1901

Name of Father: John McIntosh   a citizen of the   Creek   Nation.
Name of Mother: Mary McIntosh   a citizen of the   "   Nation.

Postoffice   Fame

AFFIDAVIT OF MOTHER.

UNITED STATES OF AMERICA, Indian Territory,
  WESTERN DISTRICT.

  I, John McIntosh, on oath state that I am 71 years of age and a citizen by blood, of the Creek Nation; that I am the lawful ~~wife~~ husband of Mary McIntosh, who is a citizen, by blood of the Creek Nation; that a male child was born to me on 28 day of December, 1901, that said child has been named Isaiah McIntosh, and is now living.

          John McIntosh

Witnesses To Mark:
{

  Subscribed and sworn to before me this 30 day of March, 1905.

          Edw C Griesel
           Notary Public.

BIRTH AFFIDAVIT.

DEPARTMENT OF THE INTERIOR.
COMMISSION TO THE FIVE CIVILIZED TRIBES.

IN RE APPLICATION FOR ENROLLMENT, as a citizen of the Creek Nation, of Isaiah J. McIntosh, born on the 28 day of December, 1901

Applications for Enrollment of Creek Newborn
Act of 1905   Volume VII

Name of Father: John McIntosh   a citizen of the   Creek   Nation.
Broken Arrow Town
Name of Mother: Mary McIntosh   a citizen of the   Creek   Nation.
Eufaula Town
                             Postoffice   Fame, Ind. Ter.

AFFIDAVIT OF MOTHER.

UNITED STATES OF AMERICA, Indian Territory, ⎫
    Western   DISTRICT.   ⎭

I, Mary McIntosh , on oath state that I am about 28 years of age and a citizen by blood , of the Creek Nation; that I am the lawful wife of John McIntosh , who is a citizen, by blood of the Creek Nation; that a male child was born to me on 28 day of December , 1901 , that said child has been named Isaiah J. McIntosh , and was living March 4, 1905.

                                              Mary McIntosh
Witnesses To Mark:

Subscribed and sworn to before me this 3 day of April , 1905.

                                              Drennan C Skaggs
                                              Notary Public.

AFFIDAVIT OF ATTENDING PHYSICIAN OR MID-WIFE.

UNITED STATES OF AMERICA, Indian Territory, ⎫
    Western   DISTRICT.   ⎭

I, Mulsie Beaver , a mid-wife , on oath state that I attended on Mrs. May McIntosh , wife of John McIntosh on about the 28 day of December , 1901 ; that there was born to her on said date a male child; that said child was living March 4, 1905, and is said to have been named Isaiah J. McIntosh

                                              Mulsie Beaver
Witnesses To Mark:

Subscribed and sworn to before me this 4 day of April , 1905.

                                              Drennan C Skaggs
                                              Notary Public.

Applications for Enrollment of Creek Newborn
Act of 1905 Volume VII

DEPARTMENT OF THE INTERIOR,
COMMISSION TO THE FIVE CIVILIZED TRIBES.
Holdenville, I. T. March 27, 1905.

In the matter of the application for the enrollment of Wilson Harjo as a citizen of the Creek Nation.

JUDY BRUNER, being duly sworn, testified as follows:

Through Alex Posey Official Interpreter:

BY COMMISSION:
Q What is your name? A Judy Bruner.
Q How old are you? A About twenty.
Q What is your post office address? A Emahaka.
Q Are you a citizen of the Creek Nation? A Yes, Sir.
Q To what town do you belong? A Little River Tulsa.
Q Do you make application for the enrollment of your child, Wilson Harjo, as a citizen of the Creek Nation? A Yes, sir.
Q Who is the father of the child? A Cheparne Harjo.
Q Is he a citizen of the Creek Nation? A No, sir, he is a Seminole.
Q Is Cheparne Harjo your lawfull[sic] husband? A No, sir.
Q Are you married to him according to Indian custom? [sic] No answer.
Q Does Cheparne Harjo acknowledge Wilson as his child? A Yes, sir.
Q Are you and Cheparne Harjo now living together as husband and wife? A We live in the same house.
Q Does he provide for your maintenance? A He provides food.
Q Does he support the child? A No Answer.
Q If it should be found that Wilson Harjo is entitled to be enrolled in either the Creek or Seminole Nations in which nation do you desire to have him enrolled? A In the Creek Nation.

CHEPARNE HARJO, being duly sworn, testified as follows:

Through Alex Posey Official Interpreter:

BY COMMISSION:
Q What is your name? A Cheparne Harjo.
Q How old are you? A About thirty.
Q What is your post office address? A Emahaka.
Q Are you a citizen of the Creek Nation? A Seminole.
Q Are you the husband of Judy Bruner? A I do of know.
Q Are you the father of her child, Wilson Harjo. A Yes, sir, I suppose so.
Q The Commission desires to know positively whether or not you are th[sic] the father of this child? A I can only answer that I suppose I am the father of the child?
Q Were you and Judy Bruner married? A No, sir.
Q Are you now living together as man and wife? A Yes, sir.
Q How long have you been living together as man and wife? A About ten years.

Applications for Enrollment of Creek Newborn
Act of 1905   Volume VII

Q Have you and Judy Bruner ever been separated during that time? A No, sir.
Q Are you married to Judy Bruner according to Indian custom? A Yes, sir.
Q You then regard her as your wife do you? A Yes, sir.
Q Do you know when the child was born? A February 10, 1902.

    I, D. C. Skaggs, on oath state that the above and foregoing is a full and true transcript of my stenographic notes as taken in said cause on said date.   DC Skaggs

    Subscribed and sworn to before me this
18" day of July, 1905.   Edw C Griesel
                                  Notary Public.

NC. 560.

Muskogee, Indian Territory, July 14, 1905.

Commissioner to the Five Civilized Tribes,
    Seminole Enrollment Division,
        Muskogee, Indian Territory.

Gentlemen:

    March 29, 1905, application was made to the Commission to the Five Civilized Tribes for the enrollment of Wilson Harjo, born February 10, 1902, as a citizen by blood of the Creek Nation. It is stated in said application that the father of said child is Cheparney[sic] Harjo, a citizen of the Seminole Nation, and that the mother is Judy Bruner, a citizen of the Creek Nation.

    You are requested to inform the Creek Enrollment Division as to whether application has been made for the enrollment of said Wilson Harjo, as a citizen of the Seminole Nation, and if so, what disposition has been made of the same.

                Respectfully,

                                Commissioner.

DEPARTMENT OF THE INTERIOR.
COMMISSION TO THE FIVE CIVILIZED TRIBES.

Muskogee, Indian Territory, July 19, 1905.

Chief Clerk,
    Creek Enrollment Division.

Applications for Enrollment of Creek Newborn
Act of 1905 Volume VII

Dear Sir:

Receipt is acknowledged of your letter of July 14, 1905 (NC-550) stating that application was made to the Commission to the Five Civilized Tribes for the enrollment of Wilson Harjo, born February 10, 1902, child of Cheparney Harjo, a citizen of the Seminole Nation, and Judy Bruner, a citizen of the Creek Nation, as a citizen by blood of the Creek Nation and requesting to be informed as to whether application was made for the enrollment of said child as a citizen of the Seminole Nation.

In reply to your letter you are advised that it does not appear from an examination of the records of this office that any application was made to the Commission to the Five Civilized Tribes for the enrollment of said Wilson Harjo as a citizen of the Seminole Nation.

Respectfully,

Tams Bixby   Commissioner.

NC 550

Muskogee, Indian Territory, November 12, 1906.

Chief Clerk,
    Seminole Enrollment Division,
        General Office.

Dear Sir:

You are hereby advised that the name of Wilson Harjo, born February 10, 1902, to Cheparney Harjo, an alleged citizen of the Seminole Nation, and Judy Bruner, a citizen of the Creek Nation, is contained in a schedule of New Born citizens of the Creek Nation, approved by the Secretary of the Interior September 27, 1905, opposite Roll No. 522.

Respectfully,

Commissioner.

BIRTH AFFIDAVIT.

Supplemental testimony taken.

DEPARTMENT OF THE INTERIOR.
COMMISSION TO THE FIVE CIVILIZED TRIBES.

IN RE APPLICATION FOR ENROLLMENT, as a citizen of the Creek Nation, of Wilson Harjo, born on the 10 day of February, 1902

Applications for Enrollment of Creek Newborn
Act of 1905 Volume VII

Name of Father: Cheparney Harjo   a citizen of the Seminole Nation.
Name of Mother: Judy Bruner   a citizen of the Creek Nation.
Tulsa Little River Town
         Postoffice   Emahaka, I.T.

AFFIDAVIT OF MOTHER.

UNITED STATES OF AMERICA, Indian Territory,   Child is present
   Western   DISTRICT.

     I, Judy Bruner, on oath state that I am about 20 years of age and a citizen by blood, of the Creek Nation; that I am not the lawful wife of Cheparney Harjo, who is a citizen, by blood of the Seminole Nation; that a male child was born to me on 10 day of February, 1902, that said child has been named Wilson Harjo, and was living March 4, 1905.

                                      her
                              Judy x Bruner
                                 mark

Witnesses To Mark:
   { Alex Posey
     DC Skaggs

    Subscribed and sworn to before me this 27 day of March, 1905.

                              Drennan C Skaggs
                              Notary Public.

AFFIDAVIT OF ATTENDING PHYSICIAN OR MID-WIFE.

UNITED STATES OF AMERICA, Indian Territory,
   Western   DISTRICT.

     I, Lizzie Harjo, a midwife on oath state that I attended on Mrs. Judy Bruner, ~~wife of~~ (blank) on the 10 day of February, 1902; that there was born to her on said date a male child; that said child was living March 4, 1905, and is said to have been named Wilson Harjo
                                   her
                             Lizzie x Harjo

Witnesses To Mark: mark
   { Alex Posey
     DC Skaggs

    Subscribed and sworn to before me this 27 day of March, 1905.

                              Drennan C Skaggs
                              Notary Public.

Applications for Enrollment of Creek Newborn
Act of 1905   Volume VII

HGH

REFER IN REPLY TO THE FOLLOWING:

NC-551.

DEPARTMENT OF THE INTERIOR,
COMMISSIONER TO THE FIVE CIVILIZED TRIBES.

Muskogee, Indian Territory, August 9, 1905.

Taylor Bruner,
    Wetumka, Indian Territory.

Dear Sir:

    In the matter of the application for the enrollment of your minor son Lewis Bruner, born March 5, 1902, as a citizen by blood of the Creek Nation, it will be necessary for you to file with this office the affidavits of two disinterested persons relative to the birth of said child. Said affidavits must set forth said child's name, the date of his birth, the names of his parents and whether or not he was living March 4, 1905.

                  Respectfully,

                            Wm. O. Beall
                            Acting Commissioner.

B. H. MILLS   NAT WILLIAMS

Real Estate Agents
and
Notary Public

                                               Wetumka, Ind. Ter.,   *190*

UNITED STATES OF AMERICA

    INDIAN TERRITORY,   SS:

WESTERN JUDICIAL DISTRICT,

I Washington Lowe, a citizen of the Creek Nation do solumly[sic] swear that I am acquainted with Taylor Bruner and Nancy Bruner, and know them to be husband and Wife, and know that a male child was born to them on the 5th day of March, 1902, and that the said child was named Lewis Bruner, and that it was liveing[sic] on the 4th day of March 1905.   his
                                                            Washington Lowe x
                                                                         mark

Applications for Enrollment of Creek Newborn
Act of 1905 Volume VII

Witness
Dave Barnett
Nat Williams

Subscribed and sworn to before me this the 12th day of Aug 1905.

My Commission Expires Aug 15th 1906.   B.H. Mills
                                                           Notary Public.

B. H. MILLS   NAT WILLIAMS

Real Estate Agents
and
Notary Public

Wetumka, Ind. Ter.,   190

UNITED STATES OF AMERICA

   INDIAN TERRITORY,   SS:

WESTERN JUDICIAL DISTRICT,

I Dave Barnett a citizen of the Creek Nation do solumly[sic] swear that I am acquainted with Taylor Bruner and Nancy Bruner, and know them to be husband and wife, and know that a male child was born to them on the 5th day of March 1902 and that the said child was named Lewis Bruner, and that it was liveing[sic] on the 4th day of March 1905.

                                            Dave Barnett

Subscribed and sworn to before me this the 12th day of Aug 1905.

                                            B.H. Mills
My Commission Expires Aug 15th 1906.   Notary Public.

BIRTH AFFIDAVIT.
                        DEPARTMENT OF THE INTERIOR.
            COMMISSION TO THE FIVE CIVILIZED TRIBES.

    IN RE APPLICATION FOR ENROLLMENT, as a citizen of the Creek Nation, of Lewis Bruner, born on the 5 day of March , 1902

Applications for Enrollment of Creek Newborn
Act of 1905   Volume VII

Name of Father: Taylor Bruner   a citizen of the   Creek   Nation.
(Illegible) Town
Name of Mother: Nancy Bruner (nee *Illegible*)   a citizen of the   Creek   Nation.

Postoffice   Wetumka, Ind. Ter.

AFFIDAVIT OF MOTHER.

UNITED STATES OF AMERICA, Indian Territory,
     Western   DISTRICT.   Child is present

     I, Nancy Bruner , on oath state that I am about 30 years of age and a citizen by blood , of the Creek   Nation; that I am the lawful wife of Taylor Bruner , who is a citizen, by blood of the Creek   Nation; that a male   child was born to me on 5   day of March, 1902 , that said child has been named Lewis Bruner , and was living March 4, 1905.

                                           her
                                Nancy x Bruner
                                   mark

Witnesses To Mark:
{ Alex Posey
{ DC Skaggs

     Subscribed and sworn to before me this 27 day of March , 1905.

                               Drennan C Skaggs
                               Notary Public.

                       Father
AFFIDAVIT OF ~~ATTENDING PHYSICIAN OR MID-WIFE~~.

UNITED STATES OF AMERICA, Indian Territory,
     Western   DISTRICT.

                                                              my wife
     I, Taylor Bruner , ~~a~~ *(blank)* , on oath state that I attended on ^ Mrs. Nancy Bruner , ~~wife of~~ *(blank)* on the 5 day of March , 1902 ; that there was born to her on said date a male child; that said child was living March 4, 1905, and is said to have been named Lewis Bruner

                                   Taylor Bruner
Witnesses To Mark:
{

     Subscribed and sworn to before me this 27 day of March , 1905.

                               Drennan C Skaggs
                               Notary Public.

Applications for Enrollment of Creek Newborn
Act of 1905   Volume VII

BIRTH AFFIDAVIT.

DEPARTMENT OF THE INTERIOR.
COMMISSION TO THE FIVE CIVILIZED TRIBES.

IN RE APPLICATION FOR ENROLLMENT, as a citizen of the CREEK Nation, of Joseph B. Gibson , born on the 17" day of Oct. , 1902

Name of Father: Wm S. Gibson	a citizen of the	Creek	Nation.
Name of Mother: Ethel "	a citizen of the	U.S.	Nation.

Postoffice   Haskell

AFFIDAVIT OF ~~MOTHER~~.
father

UNITED STATES OF AMERICA, Indian Territory, }
     WESTERN   DISTRICT.

I, Wm S. Gibson , on oath state that I am 23 years of age and a citizen by blood , of the Creek Nation; that I am the lawful ~~wife~~ husband of Ethel Gibson, who is a citizen, by ----- of the U.S. Nation; that a male child was born to me on 17" day of October , 1902 , that said child has been named Joseph B. Gibson , and is now living.

William S. Gibson

Witnesses To Mark:
{

Subscribed and sworn to before me this 4 day of April, 1905.

Edw C Griesel
Notary Public.

BIRTH AFFIDAVIT.

DEPARTMENT OF THE INTERIOR.
COMMISSION TO THE FIVE CIVILIZED TRIBES.

IN RE APPLICATION FOR ENROLLMENT, as a citizen of the Creek Nation, of Joseph B. Gibson , born on the 17th day of Oct. , 1902

Name of Father: William S. Gibscn	a citizen of the	Creek	Nation.
Name of Mother: Ethel Gibson	a citizen of the	White	Nation.

Postoffice   Haskell I.T.

Applications for Enrollment of Creek Newborn
Act of 1905   Volume VII

AFFIDAVIT OF MOTHER.

UNITED STATES OF AMERICA, Indian Territory,
Western   DISTRICT.

I, Ethel Gibson , on oath state that I am 21 years of age and a citizen by White, ~~of the~~ *(blank)* Nation; that I am the lawful wife of William S. Gibson , who is a citizen, by blood of the Creek Nation; that a male child was born to me on 17th day of Oct , 1902 , that said child has been named Joseph B. Gibson , and is now living.

Ethel Gibson

Witnesses To Mark:
{

Subscribed and sworn to before me this $3^{\underline{rd}}$ day of April , 1905.

Ralph D. Dresback
Notary Public.

AFFIDAVIT OF ATTENDING PHYSICIAN OR MID-WIFE.

UNITED STATES OF AMERICA, Indian Territory,
Western   DISTRICT.

I, M.T. Smith , a Physician , on oath state that I attended on Mrs. Ethel Gibson, wife of William S. Gibson on the 17th day of Oct , 1902 ; that there was born to her on said date a male child; that said child is now living and is said to have been named Joseph B. Gibson

M. T. Smith

Witnesses To Mark:
{

Subscribed and sworn to before me this $3^{\underline{rd}}$ day of April , 1905.

Ralph D. Dresback
Notary Public.

Applications for Enrollment of Creek Newborn
Act of 1905   Volume VII

BIRTH AFFIDAVIT.

DEPARTMENT OF THE INTERIOR.
COMMISSION TO THE FIVE CIVILIZED TRIBES.

    IN RE APPLICATION FOR ENRCLLMENT, as a citizen of the CREEK Nation, of Joe Watashe, born on the 24" day of March, 1904

Name of Father: Wa ta she	a citizen of the	Creek	Nation.
Name of Mother: Rosa Wa ta she	a citizen of the	"	Nation.

                Postoffice   Kellyville

(Child present.)

AFFIDAVIT OF MOTHER.

UNITED STATES OF AMERICA, Indian Territory, }
    WESTERN   DISTRICT.

    I, Rosa Wa ta she, on oath state that I am 34 years of age and a citizen by blood, of the Creek Nation; that I am the lawful wife of Wa ta she, who is a citizen, by blood of the Creek Nation; that a male child was born to me on 24 day of March, 1904, that said child has been named Joe Watashe, and is now living.

                             her
                      Rosa x Watashe
Witnesses To Mark: mark
  { EC Griesel
    Jesse McDermott
    Subscribed and sworn to before me this 4" day of April, 1905.

                            J McDermott
                                Notary Public.

AFFIDAVIT OF ATTENDING PHYSICIAN OR MID-WIFE.

UNITED STATES OF AMERICA, Indian Territory, }
    WESTERN   DISTRICT.

    I, Alice John, a midwife, on oath state that I attended on Mrs. Rosa Watashe, wife of Wa ta she on the 24" day of March, 1904; that there was born to her on said date a male child; that said child is now living and is said to have been named Joe Watashe

                            Alice John
Witnesses To Mark:
  {

    Subscribed and sworn to before me this 4" day of April, 1905.

Applications for Enrollment of Creek Newborn
Act of 1905 Volume VII

J McDermott
Notary Public.

DEPARTMENT OF THE INTERIOR,
COMMISSION TO THE FIVE CIVILIZED TRIBES.
Holdenville, I T., March 27, 1905.

In the matter of the application for the enrollment of Winnie Harjo as a citizen of the Creek Nation.

Cinda Harjo, being duly sworn, testified as follows:

Through Alex Posey Official Interpreter:

BY COMMISSION:
Q What is your name: Cinda Harjo.
Q How old are you? A About Twenty-three.
Q What is your post office address? A Sasskwa[sic].
Q Are you a citizen of the Creek Nation? A Yes, sir.
Q To what town do you belong? A Little River Tulsa.
Q Do you make application for the enrollment of your child, Winnie, as a citizen of the Creek Nation? A Yes, sir.
Q What is the name of the father of this child? A Bunkey Harjo.
Q Is he a citizen of the Creek Nation? A He is a Seminole.
Q If it should be found that your child, Winnie, is entitled to enrollment in either the Creek or Seminole Nation, in which nation do you desire to have her enrolled? A In the Creek Nation.

---oooOOOooo---

I, D. C. Skaggs, on oath state that the above and foregoing is a full and true transcript of my stenographic notes as taken in said cause on said date.

DC Skaggs

Subscribed and sworn to before me this 18" day of July, 1905.

Edw C Griesel
Notary Public.

Applications for Enrollment of Creek Newborn
Act of 1905   Volume VII

DEPARTMENT OF THE INTERIOR,
COMMISSION TO THE FIVE CIVILIZED TRIBES.
Holdenville, I. T., March 27, 1905.

In the matter of the application for the enrollment of Josie Harjo as a citizen by blood of the Creek Nation.

Cinda Harjo, being duly sworn, testified as follows:

Through Alex Posey Official Interpreter:

BY COMMISSION:
Q What is your name? A Cinda Harjo.
Q How old are you? A About twenty-three.
Q What is your post office address? A Sasakwa.
Q Are you a citizen of the Creek Nation? A Yes, sir.
Q To what town do you belong? A Little River Tulsa.
Q Do you now make application for the enrollment of your child, Josie Harjo as a citizen of the Creek Nation? A Yes, sir.
Q What is the name of the father of Josie? A Bunkey Harjo.
Q Is he a citizen of the Creek Nation? A He is a Seminole.
Q If it should be found that your child, Josie, is entitled to enrollment in either the Creek or Seminole Nation, in which nation do you desire to have her enrolled? A In the Creek Nation.

---oooOOOooo---

I, D. C. Skaggs, on oath state that the above and foregoing is a full and true transcript of my stenographic notes as taken in said cause on said date.

DC Skaggs

Subscribed and sworn to before me this 18" day of July, 1905.

Edw C Griesel
Notary Public.

BIRTH AFFIDAVIT.

DEPARTMENT OF THE INTERIOR.
COMMISSION TO THE FIVE CIVILIZED TRIBES.

IN RE APPLICATION FOR ENROLLMENT, as a citizen of the Creek Nation, of Josie Harjo, born on the 2 day of February, 1902

Applications for Enrollment of Creek Newborn
Act of 1905   Volume VII

Name of Father: Bumkey[sic] Harjo   a citizen of the Seminole   Nation.
Name of Mother: Cinda Harjo (nee Ahnochee) a citizen of the Creek   Nation.
L.R.T.

                        Postoffice   Sasakwa IT

AFFIDAVIT OF MOTHER.

UNITED STATES OF AMERICA, Indian Territory,
    Western   DISTRICT.

                                    23

    I, Cinda Harjo , on oath state that I am about ~~30~~ years of age and a citizen by blood , of the Creek Nation; that I am the lawful wife of Bumkey Harjo , who is a citizen, by blood of the Seminole Nation; that a male child was born to me on 2 day of February , 1902 , that said child has been named Josie Harjo , and ~~was~~ is now living ~~March 4, 1905~~. That no one attended on me as midwife or physician at the birth of the child.

                                      her
                             Cinda x Harjo
Witnesses To Mark: mark
  { Alex Posey
    DC Skaggs

Subscribed and sworn to before me this 27" day of March , 1905.

                              Drennan C Skaggs
    Child not present   Notary Public.

BIRTH AFFIDAVIT.
                     DEPARTMENT OF THE INTERIOR.
            COMMISSION TO THE FIVE CIVILIZED TRIBES.

    IN RE APPLICATION FOR ENROLLMENT, as a citizen of the Creek Nation, of Winnie Harjo , born on the 18 day of January, 1905

Name of Father: Bumkey Harjo   a citizen of the Seminole   Nation.
Name of Mother: Cinda Harjo (nee Ahnochee) a citizen of the Creek   Nation.
L.R.T.

                        Postoffice   Sasakwa Ind Ter

Applications for Enrollment of Creek Newborn
Act of 1905   Volume VII

AFFIDAVIT OF MOTHER.

UNITED STATES OF AMERICA, Indian Territory, ⎫
Western   DISTRICT.   ⎭   Child is present

    I, Cinda Harjo, on oath state that I am about 23 years of age and a citizen by blood, of the Creek Nation; that I am the lawful wife of Bumkey Harjo, who is a citizen, by blood of the Creek[sic] Nation; that a female child was born to me on 18 day of January, 1905, that said child has been named Winnie Harjo, and is now living. That no one attended on me as midwife or physician at the birth of the child.

                                           her
                               Cinda x Harjo
Witnesses To Mark: mark
  { Alex Posey
    DC Skaggs

    Subscribed and sworn to before me this 27" day of March, 1905.

                                   Drennan C Skaggs
                                       Notary Public.

BIRTH AFFIDAVIT.
          Supplemental testimony taken
DEPARTMENT OF THE INTERIOR.
COMMISSION TO THE FIVE CIVILIZED TRIBES.

    IN RE APPLICATION FOR ENROLLMENT, as a citizen of the Creek Nation, of Winnie Harjo, born on the 18 day of January, 1905

Name of Father: Bumkey Harjo   a citizen of the Seminole Nation.
Name of Mother: Cinda Harjo (nee Ahnochee) a citizen of the Creek Nation.
Tulsa Little River Town
                        Postoffice   Sasakwa Ind Ter

AFFIDAVIT OF MOTHER.

UNITED STATES OF AMERICA, Indian Territory, ⎫
Western   DISTRICT.   ⎭   Child is present

    I, Cinda Harjo, on oath state that I am about 23 years of age and a citizen by blood, of the Creek Nation; that I am the lawful wife of Bumkey Harjo, who is a citizen, by blood of the Creek[sic] Nation; that a female child was born to me on 18 day of January, 1905, that said child has been named Winnie Harjo, and is now living. That no one attended on me as midwife or physician at the birth of the child.

Applications for Enrollment of Creek Newborn
Act of 1905   Volume VII

Witnesses To Mark:
{ Alex Posey
  DC Skaggs

                      her
                Cinda x Harjo
                      mark

Subscribed and sworn to before me this 27 day of March, 1905.

                      Drennan C Skaggs
                      Notary Public.

AFFIDAVIT OF DISINTERESTED WITNESS.

UNITED STATES OF AMERICA,
Western DISTRICT,   SS
INDIAN TERRITORY.

    We, the undersigned, on oath state that we are personally acquainted with Cinda Puntka , the wife of Puntka ; that there was born to her a male[sic] child on or about the 18 day of Jan , 1905 ; that the said child has been named Winey Puntka and was living March 4, 1905. and is now living
    We further state that we have no interest in this case.

                      Houston Miller

Witnesses:_____

                      Wallace Cully

Subscribed and sworn to before me this 23 day of October 1906.

                      J McDermott
                      Notary Public.

BIRTH AFFIDAVIT.

                Supplemental testimony taken

DEPARTMENT OF THE INTERIOR.
COMMISSION TO THE FIVE CIVILIZED TRIBES.

    IN RE APPLICATION FOR ENROLLMENT, as a citizen of the Creek Nation, of Josie Harjo , born on the 2 day of February, 1902

Name of Father: Bumkey Harjo   a citizen of the Seminole   Nation.
Name of Mother: Cinda Harjo (nee Ahnochee) a citizen of the   Creek   Nation.
Tulsa Little River Town

                Postoffice   Sasakwa Ind Ter

Applications for Enrollment of Creek Newborn
Act of 1905   Volume VII

AFFIDAVIT OF MOTHER.

UNITED STATES OF AMERICA, Indian Territory, }
    Western   DISTRICT.

    I, Cinda Harjo , on oath state that I am about 23 years of age and a citizen by blood , of the Creek Nation; that I am the lawful wife of Bumkey Harjo , who is a citizen, by blood of the Creek[sic] Nation; that a male child was born to me on 2 day of February , 1902 , that said child has been named Josie Harjo , and is now living. That no one attended on me as midwife or physician at the birth of the child.

                              her
                         Cinda x Harjo
Witnesses To Mark: mark
  { Alex Posey
    DC Skaggs

    Subscribed and sworn to before me this 27 day of March , 1905.

                          Drennan C Skaggs
                            Notary Public.
        Child not present.

AFFIDAVIT CF DISINTERESTED WITNESS.

UNITED STATES OF AMERICA,
Western DISTRICT,   SS
INDIAN TERRITORY.

    We, the undersigned, on oath state that we are personally acquainted with Cinda Puntka , the wife of Puntka ; that there was born to her a male child on or about the 2 day of Feb , 1902 ; that the said child has been named Josie Puntka and was living March 4, 1905. and is now living

    We further state that we have no interest in this case.

                          Houston Miller
Witnesses:_____
                          Wallace Cully

    Subscribed and sworn to before me this 23 day of October 1906.

                          J McDermott
                          Notary Public.

Applications for Enrollment of Creek Newborn
Act of 1905 Volume VII

N.C. 554.

DEPARTMENT OF THE INTERIOR,
COMMISSIONER TO THE FIVE CIVILIZED TRIBES,
Sasakwa, Indian Territory, October 23, 1906.

In the matter of the application for the enrollment of Josie and Winnie (Harjo) Puntka as citizens by blood of the Creek Nation.
CINDA PUNTKA, being duly sworn, testified as follows through Jesse McDermott official interpreter:

BY THE COMMISSIONER:

Q What is your name? A Cindey Puntka.
Q What is your age? A About 34.
Q What is your potsoffice[sic] address? A Sasakwa.
Q Are you a Creek citizen? A Yes.
Q Have you filed on your allotment? A Yes.
Q Have you your deeds to your allotment? A Yes.

The witness presents an allotment certificate issued to Eliz Puntka on Creek Card No. 3785, and states that the land described thereon is an allotment to one of her older children.

There are on file at the office of the Commissioner to the Five Civilized Tribes, two affidavits executed by you on March 27, 1905, in each of which, you state the names of your two children as Josie Harjo and Winnie Harjo respectively.

Q How does it come that your younger children have different names from that one of the older? A When I executed the affidavits at Holdenville, my husband was not with me but a man by the name Alfred Larney was, and he told the Commissioner that my name was Cinda Harjo and the Commissioner made out the papers in that name.
Q So your right name is Puntka instead of Harjo is it not? A yes, all of our mail come to us in that name. My husband is enrolled as Puntka on the Seminole Roll.
Q To which Creek Indian Town do you belong? A Little River Tulsa.
Q Is your husband a fullblood Seminole? A Yes, I think so.
(The husband is present and states that he is).
Q Are both of these children living? A Yes. (The children are present

---oooOOOooo---

I, Jesse McDermott, on oath state that the above and foregoing is a full and true transcript of my notes as taken in said cause on said date.

Jesse McDermott

Applications for Enrollment of Creek Newborn
Act of 1905   Volume VII

Subscribed and sworn to before me this 13th day of December, 1906.

Alex Posey
Notary Public.

BIRTH AFFIDAVIT.

DEPARTMENT OF THE INTERIOR.
COMMISSION TO THE FIVE CIVILIZED TRIBES.

IN RE APPLICATION FOR ENROLLMENT, as a citizen of the Creek Nation, of Josie Puntka, born on the 2 day of Feb, 1902

Name of Father: Puntka   a citizen of the Seminole Nation.
Name of Mother: Cinda Puntka   a citizen of the Creek Nation.
Little River Town
                        Postoffice   Sasakwa IT

AFFIDAVIT OF MOTHER.

UNITED STATES OF AMERICA, Indian Territory, }
    Western   DISTRICT.   }

I, Cinda Puntka, on oath state that I am 34 years of age and a citizen by blood, of the Creek Nation; that I am the lawful wife of Puntka, who is a citizen, by blood of the Seminole Nation; that a male child was born to me on 2 day of February, 1902, that said child has been named Josie Puntka, and was living March 4, 1905.

Cinda x Puntka

Witnesses To Mark:
{ J McDermott
{ S.P. Weedn[sic]
    Subscribed and sworn to before me this 23" day of October, 1906.

My Commission   J McDermott
Expires July 25" 1907   Notary Public.

BIRTH AFFIDAVIT.

DEPARTMENT OF THE INTERIOR.
COMMISSION TO THE FIVE CIVILIZED TRIBES.

IN RE APPLICATION FOR ENROLLMENT, as a citizen of the Creek Nation, of Josie Puntka, born on the 18 day of January, 1905

Applications for Enrollment of Creek Newborn
Act of 1905   Volume VII

Name of Father: Puntka   a citizen of the Seminole   Nation.
Name of Mother: Cinda Puntka   a citizen of the Creek   Nation.

Postoffice   Sasakwa IT

AFFIDAVIT OF MOTHER.

UNITED STATES OF AMERICA, Indian Territory, ⎫
    Western   DISTRICT.   ⎬

I, Cinda Puntka, on oath state that I am 34 years of age and a citizen by blood, of the Creek Nation; that I am the lawful wife of Puntka, who is a citizen, by blood of the Seminole Nation; that a female child was born to me on 18 day of January, 1905, that said child has been named Winey Puntka, and was living March 4, 1905.

her
Cinda x Puntka
mark

Witnesses To Mark:
  { J McDermott
  { S. P. Weedn[sic]

Subscribed and sworn to before me this 23 day of October, 1906.

My Commission   J McDermott
Expires July 25" 1907   Notary Public.

NC. 554.

Muskogee, Indian Territory, July 14, 1904.

Commissioner to the Five Civilized Tribes,
        Seminole Enrollment Division,
                Muskogee, Indian Territory.
Gentlemen:

March 29, 1905, application was made to the Commission to the Five Civilized Tribes for the enrollment of Josie Harjo, born February 2, 1902, and Winnie Harjo, born January 18, 1905, as citizens by blood of the Creek Nation. It is stated in said application that the father of said children is Bumkey Harjo, a citizen of the Seminole Nation, and that the mother is Cinda Harjo, a citizen of the Creek Nation.

You are requested to inform the Creek Enrollment Division as to whether application has been made for the enrollment of said children as citizens of the Seminole Nation, and if so, what disposition has been made of the same.

Applications for Enrollment of Creek Newborn
Act of 1905 Volume VII

Respectfully,

Commissioner.

NC 554.

Muskogee, Indian Territory, July 17, 1905.

Cinda Harjo,
    Sasakwa, Indian Territory.

Dear Madam:

In the matter of the application for the enrollment of your minor children, Josie and Winnie Harjo, as citizens of the Creek Nation, you are advised that without further information it is impossible for this office to identify you on its rolls of citizens of said Nation.

You are requested to furnish this office with your maiden name, the names of your parents, the Creek Indian Town to which you belong, and, if possible, the numbers which appear on your deeds to land in the Creek Nation, and any other information that will help to identify you as a citizen of the Creek Nation.

Respectfully,

Commissioner.

W.F.

DEPARTMENT OF THE INTERIOR.
COMMISSION TO THE FIVE CIVILIZED TRIBES.

Muskogee, Indian Territory, July 18, 1905.

Chief Clerk,
    Creek Enrollment Division.

Dear Sir:

Receipt is acknowledged of your letter of July 14, 1905 (NC-554) stating that application was made to the Commission to the Five Civilized Tribes for the enrollment of Josie Harjo, born February 2, 1902, and Winnie Harjo, born January 18, 1905, children of Bunkey Harjo, a citizen of the Seminole Nation and Cinda Harjo, a citizen of the Creek Nation, as citizens by blood of the Creek Nation and requesting to be informed as to whether application was made for the enrollment of said children as citizens of the Seminole Nation.

Applications for Enrollment of Creek Newborn
Act of 1905   Volume VII

Respectfully,

Tams Bixby   Commissioner.

JWH

N C 554

Muskogee, Indian Territory, March 1, 1907.

Cinda Puntka,
    Sasakwa, Indian Territory.

Dear Madam :--

You are hereby advised that on February 15, 1907, the Secretary of the Interior approved the enrollment of your minor children, Josie and Winey Puntka, as citizens by blood of the Creek Nation, and that the name of said child appears upon the roll of New Born citizens by blood of the Creek Nation, enrolled under the Act of Congress approved March 3, 1905, as numbers 1158 and 1159, respectively.

These children are now entitled to allotment and application therefor should be made without delay at the Creek Land Office, Muskogee, Indian Territory.

Respectfully,

Commissioner.

BIRTH AFFIDAVIT.

DEPARTMENT OF THE INTERIOR.
COMMISSION TO THE FIVE CIVILIZED TRIBES.

IN RE APPLICATION FOR ENROLLMENT, as a citizen of the CREEK Nation, of Lena John, born on the 4" day of Mar , 1904

Name of Father: McCulley John   a citizen of the   Creek   Nation.
Name of Mother: Alice   "   a citizen of the   Creek   Nation.

Postoffice   Mounds I.T.

Applications for Enrollment of Creek Newborn
Act of 1905 Volume VII

Child present

AFFIDAVIT OF MOTHER.

UNITED STATES OF AMERICA, Indian Territory, }
    WESTERN   DISTRICT.

I, Alice John , on oath state that I am 24 years of age and a citizen by blood , of the Creek Nation; that I am the lawful wife of McCully[sic] John , who is a citizen, by blood of the Creek Nation; that a female child was born to me on 4" day of Mar , 1904 , that said child has been named Lena John , and is now living.

Alice John

Witnesses To Mark:
{

Subscribed and sworn to before me this 4" day of April , 1905.

J McDermott
Notary Public.

AFFIDAVIT OF ATTENDING PHYSICIAN OR MID-WIFE.

UNITED STATES OF AMERICA, Indian Territory, }
    WESTERN   DISTRICT.

Rosa

I, ~~Lucy~~ Wattuse , a midwife , on oath state that I attended on Mrs. Alice John , wife of McCully John on the 4 day of Mar , 1904 ; that there was born to her on said date a female child; that said child is now living and is said to have been named Lena John

Rosa her
~~Lucy~~ x Watashe[sic]
mark

Witnesses To Mark:
{ EC Griesel
  Jesse McDermott

Subscribed and sworn to before me this 4" day of April , 1905.

J McDermott
Notary Public.

Applications for Enrollment of Creek Newborn
Act of 1905 Volume VII

BIRTH AFFIDAVIT.

DEPARTMENT OF THE INTERIOR.
COMMISSION TO THE FIVE CIVILIZED TRIBES.

IN RE APPLICATION FOR ENROLLMENT, as a citizen of the Creek Nation, of Hinney Simmer, born on the 19 day of June, 1903

Name of Father: John Simmer   a citizen of the   Creek   Nation.
                                        Simmer
Name of Mother: Jemmima Penter (nee   a citizen of the   Creek   Nation.

Postoffice   Okfuskee Ind Ter

AFFIDAVIT OF MOTHER.

UNITED STATES OF AMERICA, Indian Territory,
  Western   DISTRICT.

I, Jemmima Penter (nee) Simmer, on oath state that I am 30 years of age and a citizen by blood, of the Creek Nation; that I am the lawful wife of John Simmer, who is a citizen, by blood of the Creek Nation; that a female child was born to me on 19 day of June, 1903, that said child has been named Hinney Simmer, and was living March 4, 1905.

                                         her
                            Jemmima x Penter (nee) Simmer
Witnesses To Mark: mark
  { John Simmer
    Thos. H. Dunson

Subscribed and sworn to before me this 25 day of March, 1905.

My Com. Exp. Aug 19-1908   *(No signature given)*
                                          Notary Public.

AFFIDAVIT OF ATTENDING PHYSICIAN OR MID-WIFE.

UNITED STATES OF AMERICA, Indian Territory,
  Western   DISTRICT.

I, Hannah Harjo, a midwife, on oath state that I attended on Mrs. Jemmima Penter (nee) Simmer, wife of John Simmer on the 19 day of June, 1903; that there was born to her on said date a female child; that said child was living March 4, 1905, and is said to have been named Hinney Simmer

Applications for Enrollment of Creek Newborn
Act of 1905 Volume VII

                                            her
                                  Hannah x Harjo

Witnesses To Mark: mark
  { John Simmer
    (Name Illegible)

Subscribed and sworn to before me this 25 day of March, 1905.

My Com. Exp. Aug 19-1908   Tupper Dunn
                                         Notary Public.

NC-556.

                           Muskogee, Indian Territory, August 9, 1905.

Jemmima Simmer,
    c/o John Simmer,
        Okfuskee, Indian Territory.

Dear Madam:

    On April 4, 1905 you filed with this office application for the enrollment of your minor daughter Hinner[sic] Simmer at which time you submitted your affidavit and the affidavit of Hannah Harjo as to the birth of said child. The same are defective inasmuch as the notary publid[sic], Tucker Dunn, neglected to affix his signature to your affidavit and for the further reason that your name appears in said affidavits as Jemmima Penter, nee Simmer, when, apparently, it should appear as Jemmima Simmer, nee Penter.

    For the purpose of making proper proof of the birth of your said dauther[sic] there is inclosed herewith a blank for proof of birth which has been properly filled out. You are requested to have the same executed and when executed to return it to this office in the inclosed envelope. Be careful to see that the notary public before whom the affidavits are acknowledged attaches his name and seal to each affidavit. In case any signature is by mark it must be attested by two disinterested witnesses.

    It appears from your affidavit that you are a citizen by blood of the Creek Nation but this office is unable to identify you upon the final roll of citizens by blood of said nation.
    You are therefore requested to immediately inform this office as to under which you were finally enrolled, the names of your parents and other members of your family, the Creek Indian town to which you belong and your final roll number as the same appears upon your allotment certificate and deeds.

                                    Respectfully,

CTD-36.
Env.   Acting Commissioner.

Applications for Enrollment of Creek Newborn
Act of 1905 Volume VII

Okemah, Ind. Ter.
Town
My Father's name,   Tom Penter   Eufaula ^ Canadian
My Mother's   "   Kogee Penter   Tuckee batchee
"   Town   Tuckee batchee Town

I am not able to furnish you the number of my final rolled[sic].
But will forward the number of my Deeds or certificate of my allotment within early date

Yours
her
Jemmima x Simmer nee Penter
mark

Witness to mark
Tupper Dunn
W.H. Dill

BIRTH AFFIDAVIT.

DEPARTMENT OF THE INTERIOR.
COMMISSION TO THE FIVE CIVILIZED TRIBES.

IN RE APPLICATION FOR ENROLLMENT, as a citizen of the Creek Nation, of Hinney Simmer, born on the 19 day of June, 1903

Name of Father: John Simmer   a citizen of the   Creek   Nation.
                                nee Penter
Name of Mother: Jemmima Simmer   a citizen of the   Creek   Nation.

Postoffice   Okfuskee I. T.

AFFIDAVIT OF MOTHER.

UNITED STATES OF AMERICA, Indian Territory,
Western Judicial   **DISTRICT.**

I, Jemmima Simmer (nee) Penter, on oath state that I am 30 years of age and a citizen by blood, of the Creek Nation; that I am the lawful wife of John Simmer, who is a citizen, by blood of the Creek Nation; that a female child was born to me on 19" day of June, 1903, that said child has been named Hinney Simmer, and was living March 4, 1905.

Applications for Enrollment of Creek Newborn
Act of 1905 Volume VII

her
Jemmima x Simmer (nee) Penter
mark

Witnesses To Mark:
{ L.P. Caldwell
{ Tupper Dunn

Subscribed and sworn to before me this 17 day of Aug, 1905.

My Com. Exp. Aug 19-1908   Tupper Dunn
Notary Public.

AFFIDAVIT OF ATTENDING PHYSICIAN OR MID-WIFE.

UNITED STATES OF AMERICA, Indian Territory, }
Western Judicial   DISTRICT. }

I, Hannah Harjo, a midwife, on oath state that I attended on Mrs. Jemmima Simmer, wife of John Simmer on the 19 day of June, 1903; that there was born to her on said date a female child; that said child was living March 4, 1905, and is said to have been named Hinney Simmer.

her
Hannah x Harjo
mark

Witnesses To Mark:
{ L.P. Caldwell
{ Tupper Dunn

Subscribed and sworn to before me this 17 day of Aug, 1905.

My Com. Exp. Aug 19-1908   Tupper Dunn
Notary Public.

DEPARTMENT OF THE INTERIOR,
COMMISSION TO THE FIVE CIVILIZED TRIBES.
Holdenville, I. T., March 27, 1905.

In the matter of the application for the enrollment of Ida and Sunday Harjo as citizens of the Creek Nation.

LIZA HARJO, being duly sworn, testified as follows:

Through Alex Posey Official Interpreter:

Applications for Enrollment of Creek Newborn
Act of 1905   Volume VII

BY COMMISSION:

Q What is your name? A Lize Harjo.
Q What is your age? A I am over thirty.
Q What is your post office address? A Tidmore.
Q Are you a citizen of the Creek nation? A Yes, sir.
Q Do you make application for the enrollment of your children, Ida and Sunday Harjo, as citizens of the Creek Nation? A Yes, sir.
Q Who is the father of these two children? A Ah Harjo.
Q Is he living? A He is dead.
Q Was he your lawful husband? A Yes, sir.
Q Do you know when Ida was born? A About three years ago. I do not know when she was born, the names of her parents and whether or not she was living on March 4, 1905 but it has been about three years ago. I only know that she was born in the fall when people were pulling corn
Q When was Sunday born? A December 25, year before last.
Q How old was Ida when Sunday was born? A Ida was about two years old at the time Sunday was born.
Q Have you made selection of land for yourself? A The Commission made selection of land for me.
Q Have you received a certificate of allotment or deed to your land? A I have received certificates of allotment.
Q Do you know when they were issued to you? A It was during my husband's lifetime but I do not remember the date.
Q How old was Ida at that time? A The child was old enough to be left at home. Certificates of allotment were mailed to me at Holdenville and I remember that I left her at home when I came for the certificates.
Q Do you know who was Chief of the Creek Nation at the time Ida was born? A I do not know.
Q How long has your husband been dead? A About a year.
Q How old was Ida at the time your husband died? A About two years old.
Q Was there a record made of her birth? A No, sir.
Q Do you know any one who would know when Ida was born? A No, sir.
Q Would not any of your immediate neighbors know? A No, sir, I went among them before coming here and tries to fix the date of her birth but was unable to do so.
Q If it should be found that these children are entitled to enrollment in either the Creek and Seminole Nations in which nation do you desire to have her[sic] enrolled? A In the Creek Nation.

I, D. C. Skaggs, on oath state that the above and foregoing is a full and true transcript of my stenographic notes as taken in said cause on said date.

DC Skaggs

Applications for Enrollment of Creek Newborn
Act of 1905   Volume VII

Subscribed and sworn to before me this 18" day of July, 1905.

                                    Edw C Griesel
                                    Notary Public.

BIRTH AFFIDAVIT.

Supplemental testimony taken
DEPARTMENT OF THE INTERIOR.
COMMISSION TO THE FIVE CIVILIZED TRIBES.

IN RE APPLICATION FOR ENROLLMENT, as a citizen of the Creek Nation, of Ida Harjo, about three years ago
born ~~on the~~ ~~day of~~ , 190

Name of Father: Ah Harjo   a citizen of the   Seminole   Nation.
Name of Mother: Liza Harjo   a citizen of the   Creek   Nation.
Tulsa Little River Town

                  Postoffice   Tidmore, Ind. Ter.

AFFIDAVIT OF MOTHER.

UNITED STATES OF AMERICA, Indian Territory,
    Western   **DISTRICT.**   Child is present

I, Liza Harjo , on oath state that I am over 30 years of age and a citizen by blood , of the Creek   Nation; that I am the lawful wife of Ah Harjo , who is a citizen, by blood of the Seminole Nation. that a female child was born to me ~~on~~ about ~~day of~~ three years ago , ~~4~~ , that said child has been named Ida Harjo , and was living March 4, 1905. That no one attended on me as midwife or physician at the birth of the child.

                                    her
                            Liza x Harjo
Witnesses To Mark: mark
  { Alex Posey
    DC Skaggs
Subscribed and sworn to before me this 27 day of March , 1905.

                                Drennan C Skaggs
                                Notary Public.

(The above Birth Affidavit for Ida Harjo given again)

Applications for Enrollment of Creek Newborn
Act of 1905   Volume VII

Affidavit.

United States of America)
Western District)
Indian Territory)

  Personall[sic] appeared before me a Notary Public in and for the western district Bennie *(Illegible)* a citizen of the Creek Nation and upon oath state that he is well acquainted with Eliza Harjo and that their[sic] was born to her in the fall of 1902, a female child who was named Ida Harjo, and is now dead. And on the 25th day of December 1903 a male child was born to her and was named Sunday Harjo and is now liveing[sic]. Their fathers[sic] name was Ah-Harjo and their mother[sic] name Eliza Harjo, we make this statement only as disinterested parties, and have no claim of any kind whatever in matter.

  They belong to the little river tulsia[sic] band of Creeks.

Bennie *(Illegible)*

Subscribed and sworn to before me this 2nd day od[sic] September 1905

Chas Rider
Notary Public.

My Commission expires July 11th, 1906

Affidavit.

United States of America)
Western District)
Indian Territory)

  Personall[sic] appeared before me a Notary Public in and for the western district Alloway Cain a citizen of the Creek Nation and upon oath state that he is well acquainted with Eliza Harjo and that their[sic] was born to her in the fall of 1902, a female child who was named Ida Harjo, and is now dead. And on the 25th day of December 1903 a male child was born to her and was named Sunday Harjo and is now liveing[sic]. Their fathers[sic] name was Ah-Harjo and their mother[sic] name Eliza Harjo, we make this statement only as disinterested parties, and have no claim of any kind whatever in matter.

  They belong to the little river tulsia[sic] band of Creeks.

his
Alloway Cain x Town King
mark

Applications for Enrollment of Creek Newborn
Act of 1905   Volume VII

Subscribed and sworn to before me this 2nd day od[sic] September 1905

                                       Chas Rider
                                       Notary Public.

My Commission expires July 11th. 1906

BIRTH AFFIDAVIT.

Supplemental testimony taken

DEPARTMENT OF THE INTERIOR.
COMMISSION TO THE FIVE CIVILIZED TRIBES.

IN RE APPLICATION FOR ENROLLMENT, as a citizen of the Creek Nation, of Sunday Harjo, born on the 25 day of December 1903

Name of Father: Ah Harjo   deceased   a citizen of the Seminole Nation.
Name of Mother: Liza Harjo   a citizen of the Creek Nation.
Tulsa Little River Town

                     Postoffice   Tidmore, Ind. Ter.

AFFIDAVIT OF MOTHER.

UNITED STATES OF AMERICA, Indian Territory,
   Western   DISTRICT.   Child is present

I, Liza Harjo , on oath state that I am over 30 years of age and a citizen by blood , of the Creek Nation; that I am the lawful wife of Ah Harjo deceased , who is a citizen, by blood of the Seminole Nation; that a male child was born to me on 25 day of December , 1903 , that said child has been named Sunday Harjo , and was living March 4, 1905. That no one attended on me as midwife or physician at the birth of the child.   her
                                           Liza x Harjo
Witnesses To Mark: mark
    { Alex Posey
    { DC Skaggs

Subscribed and sworn to before me this 27 day of March , 1905.

                                       Drennan C Skaggs
                                       Notary Public.

Applications for Enrollment of Creek Newborn
Act of 1905   Volume VII

NC 557.

Muskogee, Indian Territory, July 14, 1905.

Commissioner to the Five Civilized Tribes,
   Seminole Enrollment Division,
      Muskogee, Indian Territory.

Gentlemen:

    March 30, 1905, application was made to the Commission to the Five Civilized Tribes for the enrollment of Ida Harjo, born about three years ago, and Sunday Harjo, born December 25, 1903, as citizens by blood of the Creek Nation. It is stated in said application that the father of said child is Ah Harjo, deceased, a citizen of the Seminole Nation, and that the mother of[sic] Liza Harjo, a citizen of the Creek Nation.

    You are requested to inform the Creek Enrollment Division as to whether application has been made for the enrollment of said children as citizens of the Seminole Nation, and if so, what disposition has been made of the same.

                Respectfully,

                              Commissioner.

NC 557.

Muskogee, Indian Territory, July 15, 1905.

E liza[sic] Harjo,
   Tidmore, Indian Territory.

Dear Madam:

    In the matter of the application for the enrollment of your minor children, Ida and Sunday Harjo, as citizens of the Creek Nation, you are advised that without further information this office is unable to identify you on its rolls of citizens of said Nation.

    You are requested to state your maiden name, the names of your parents, the Creek Indian Town to which you belong, and, if possible, the numbers which appear on your deeds to land in the Creek Nation, and any other information that will help to identify you as a citizen of the Creek Nation.

                Respectfully,

                              Commissioner.

Applications for Enrollment of Creek Newborn
Act of 1905 Volume VII

DEPARTMENT OF THE INTERIOR.
COMMISSION TO THE FIVE CIVILIZED TRIBES.

Muskogee, Indian Territory, July 19, 1905.

Chief Clerk,
    Creek Enrollment Division,

Dear Sir:

    Receipt is acknowledged of your letter of July 14, 1905 (NC-557) stating that application was made to the Commission to the Five Civilized Tribes for the enrollment of Ida Harjo, born about three years ago, and Sunday Harjo, born December 25, 1903, children of Ah Harjo, deceased, a citizen of the Seminole Nation, and Liza Harjo, a citizen of the Creek Nation, as citizens by blood of the Creek Nation and requesting to be advised as to whether application was made for the enrollment of said children as citizens of the Seminole Nation.

    In reply to your letter you are advised that it does not appear from an examination of the records of this office that any application was made to the Commission to the Five Civilized Tribes for the enrollment of said as a citizen of the Seminole Nation.

    Respectfully,

    Tams Bixby   Commissioner.

NC 557.

Muskogee, Indian Territory, August 9, 1905.

Eliza Harjo,
    Tidmore, Indian Territory.

Dear Madam:

    In the matter of the application for the enrollment of your minor children, Ida Harjo, born in the fall of 1902, and Sunday Harjo, born December 25, 1903, as citizens by blood of the Creek Nation, it will be necessary for you to file with this office the affidavits of two disinterested persons as to the birth of said children. Said affidavits to set forth the names of said children, the dates of their birth, as nearly as possible, the names of their parents and whether or not they were living on March 4, 1905.

    Respectfully,

    Commissioner.

Applications for Enrollment of Creek Newborn
Act of 1905 Volume VII

NC 557.

Muskogee, Indian Territory, September 7, 1905.

Eliza Harjo,
    Tidmore, Indian Territory.

Dear Madam:

    Receipt is acknowledged of affidavits of two disinterested witnesses relative to the birth of your minor children, Ida and Sunday Harjo. It is stated in said affidavit that Ida Harjo is dead.

    There is herewith enclosed a blank form of death affidavit, In having same executed, be careful to see that all blanks are properly filled, all names spelled in full, and in the event that a person signing an affidavit is unable to write, the signature must be witnesses[sic] by two disinterested witnesses who are able to write.

                          Respectfully,

1 DA   Acting Commissioner.

N.C. 557.

Muskogee, Indian Territory, July 5, 1906.

Eliza Harjo,
    Tidmore, Indian Territory.

Dear Madam:

    In the matter of the application for the enrollment of Ida Harjo, born in the autumn of 1902, as a citizen of the Creek Nation, you are advised that in lieu of the affidavit of the midwife you should furnish this office with the affidavits of two disinterested witnesses; and a blank for that purpose is herewith inclosed. Said affidavits should state the name of the child, the names of its parents, the date of its birth, and whether or not it was on living March 4, 1905.
    This matter should receive your prompt attention.

                          Respectfully,

                                        Commissioner.

Dis.
Env.

Applications for Enrollment of Creek Newborn
Act of 1905 Volume VII

NC 557

Muskogee, Indian Territory, November 12, 1906.

Chief Clerk,
    Seminole Enrollment Division,
        General Office.

Dear Sir:

    You are hereby advised that the name of Sunday Harjo born December 25, 1903, to Ah Harjo, deceased, an alleged citizen of the Seminole Nation, and Eliza Harjo, a citizen by blood of the Creek Nation, is contained in a schedule of New Born citizens of the Creek Nation, approved by the Secretary of the Interior January 4, 1906, opposite Roll No. 943.

                Respectfully,

                              Commissioner.

N.C. 557.   COPY

                Earlsboro, Oklahoma, January 10, 1907.

Commissioner to the Five Civilized Tribes,
    Muskogee, Indian Territory.

Sir:

    I have the honor to report that I am unable to secure further evidence in the matter of the application for the enrollment of Ida Harjo as a citizen by blood of the Creek Nation, for the reason that Eliza Harjo, the mother, together with her neighbors state that they do not know the date of the birth and death of said child. Copies of record in the case are herewith enclosed.

                Respectfully,

                          (Signed) Jesse McDermott
                              Clerk in charge.

Applications for Enrollment of Creek Newborn
Act of 1905 Volume VII

NC 557.

Muskogee, Indian Territory, January 14, 1907.

Eliza Harjo,
    Tidmore, Indian Territory.

Dear Madam:

    In the matter of the application for the enrollment of your minor child, Ida Harjo, as a citizen of the Creek Nation, you are advised that this office requires in lieu of the affidavit of the midwife the affidavit of two disinterested witnesses as to her birth, and a blank form for that purpose is herewith enclosed, which you are requested to have properly executed and returned to this office in the enclosed envelope within ten day.

    You are also requested to write this office as to whether said child is living and why nothing has been done relative to its enrollment since the time of the original application for its enrollment March 30, 1905.

                        Respectfully,

                                          Commissioner.

1 Dis. Wit.
Envelope.

N C 557

Muskogee, Indian Territory, March 1, 1907.

Eliza Harjo,
    Tidmore, Indian Territory.

Dear Madam :--

    You are hereby advised that on February 15, 1907, the Secretary of the Interior approved the enrollment of your minor child, Ida Harjo, as a citizen by blood of the Creek Nation, and that the name of said child appears upon the roll of New Born citizens by blood of the Creek Nation, enrolled under the Act of Congress approved March 3, 1905, as number 1160.

    This child is now entitled to allotment and application therefor should be made without delay at the Creek Land Office, Muskogee, Indian Territory.

                        Respectfully,

                                          Commissioner.

Applications for Enrollment of Creek Newborn
Act of 1905   Volume VII

NC-558

Muskogee, Indian Territory, August 22, 1905.

Louis Benden,
    Wewoka, Indian Territory.

Dear Sir:

    In the matter of the application for the enrollment of your minor children, Ida Benden and Louisa Benden, as citizens by blood of the Creek Nation, in the affidavits of your wife, Dicey Benden, and the midwife, Hepsey McGirt, now on file with the records of this Office, your surname and the surname of your said children appears as "Bender."

    For the purpose of correcting this discrepancy as to the surname of your said children, there are enclosed herewith two blanks for proof of birth, which have been filled out. You are requested to have the affidavits therein sworn to before a notary public, and when sworn to, return them to this Office in the enclosed envelope.

    In having the affidavits executed, be careful to see that the notary public before whom same are sworn to, attaches his name and seal to each affidavit. In case the affiants are unable to write and their signatures are by mark, such signatures must be attested by two disinterested witnesses who can write.

    Please give this matter your prompt attention, as nothing further can be done in the matter of your enrollment of your said children as citizens by blood of the Creek Nation, until these affidavits, properly executed, are filed with this Office.

                             Respectfully,

                                           Commissioner.

JYH-22-2
Env

NC-558.

Muskogee, Indian Territory, October 16, 1905.

Louis Bender,
    Wewoka, Indian Territory.

Dear Sir:

Applications for Enrollment of Creek Newborn
Act of 1905   Volume VII

In the matter of the application for the enrollment of your minor children, Ida Bender and Louisa Bender, as citizens by blood of the Creek Nation, in the affidavits of your wife and the midwife, Hepsey McGirt, now on file with the records of this office your surname and the surname of said children appears as Bender. The given name of your wife appears in said affidavits as Tysie and your given name appears as Lewis.

You are identified on the records of this office as Louis Benden and your said wife is identified as Dicey Benden.

For the purpose of correcting these discrepancies there are inclosed herewith two blanks for proof of birth which have been filled out. You are requested to have the affidavits therein sworn to before a notary public, and when sworn to, return them to this Office in the enclosed envelope.

In having the affidavits executed be careful to see that the notary public before whom same are sworn to attaches his name and seal to each affidavit. In case the affiants are unable to write and their signatures are by mark, such signatures must be attested by two disinterested witnesses who can write.

Please give this matter your prompt attention, as nothing further can be done in the matter of your enrollment of your said children as citizens by blood of the Creek Nation, until these affidavits properly executed are filed with this Office.

Respectfully,

Commissioner.

CTD-2
Env.

BIRTH AFFIDAVIT.

DEPARTMENT OF THE INTERIOR.
COMMISSION TO THE FIVE CIVILIZED TRIBES.

IN RE APPLICATION FOR ENROLLMENT, as a citizen of the Creek Nation, of Ida Bender, born on the 13 day of July, 1902

Name of Father: Lewis Bender   a citizen of the   Creek   Nation.
Tuckabatche Town
Name of Mother: Tysie Bender   a citizen of the   Creek   Nation.
Tuckabatche Town
                        Postoffice   Wewoka, Ind. Ter.

Applications for Enrollment of Creek Newborn
Act of 1905   Volume VII

AFFIDAVIT OF MOTHER.

UNITED STATES OF AMERICA, Indian Territory, }
    Western   DISTRICT.   Child is present

    I, Tysie Bender, on oath state that I am about 35 years of age and a citizen by blood, of the Creek Nation; that I am the lawful wife of Lewis Bender, who is a citizen, by blood of the Creek Nation; that a female child was born to me on 13 day of July, 1902, that said child has been named Ida Bender, and was living March 4, 1905.

                                            her
                                     Tysie x Bender
Witnesses To Mark: mark
  { Alex Posey
    DC Skaggs

    Subscribed and sworn to before me this 27 day of March, 1905.

                                     Drennan C Skaggs
                                     Notary Public.

AFFIDAVIT OF ATTENDING PHYSICIAN OR MID-WIFE.

UNITED STATES OF AMERICA, Indian Territory, }
    Western   DISTRICT.

    I, Hepsey McGirt, a midwife, on oath state that I attended on Mrs. Tysie Bender, wife of Lewis Bender on the 13 day of July, 1902; that there was born to her on said date a female child; that said child was living March 4, 1905, and is said to have been named Ida Bender

                                           her
                                   Hepsey x McGirt
                                       mark

Witnesses To Mark:
  { Alex Posey
    DC Skaggs

    Subscribed and sworn to before me this 27 day of March, 1905.

                                     Drennan C Skaggs
                                     Notary Public.

Applications for Enrollment of Creek Newborn
Act of 1905 Volume VII

BIRTH AFFIDAVIT.

DEPARTMENT OF THE INTERIOR.
COMMISSION TO THE FIVE CIVILIZED TRIBES.

IN RE APPLICATION FOR ENROLLMENT, as a citizen of the Creek Nation, of Ida Benden[sic], born on the 13 day of July, 1902

Name of Father: Louis Benden[sic]   a citizen of the   Creek   Nation.
Name of Mother: Dicey Benden[sic]   a citizen of the   Creek   Nation.

Postoffice   Wewoka

AFFIDAVIT OF MOTHER.

UNITED STATES OF AMERICA, Indian Territory,
     Western   DISTRICT.   Child is present

     I, Dicey Benden, on oath state that I am about 35 years of age and a citizen by blood, of the Creek Nation; that I am the lawful wife of Louis Benden, who is a citizen, by blood of the Creek Nation; that a female child was born to me on 13 day of July, 1902, that said child has been named Ida Benden, and was living March 4, 1905.

                                                   her
                                       Dicey x Benden
Witnesses To Mark: mark
    { J.H. Alexander
    { Frank L. Warner
     Subscribed and sworn to before me this 2nd day of December, 1905.

                                       Frank L Warner
                                           Notary Public.
     My Com Exp 3/12/1907

AFFIDAVIT OF ATTENDING PHYSICIAN OR MID-WIFE.

UNITED STATES OF AMERICA, Indian Territory,
     Western   DISTRICT.

     I, Hepsey McGirt, a midwife, on oath state that I attended on Mrs. Dicey Benden, wife of Louis Benden on the 13 day of July, 1902 ; that there was born to her on said date a female child; that said child was living March 4, 1905, and is said to have been named Ida Benden   her
                                       Hepsey x McGirt
Witnesses To Mark: mark
    { J.H. Alexander
    { Frank L. Warner

Applications for Enrollment of Creek Newborn
Act of 1905   Volume VII

Subscribed and sworn to before me this 2nd day of December, 1905.

Frank L Warner
Notary Public.

My Com Exp 3/12/1907

BIRTH AFFIDAVIT.

DEPARTMENT OF THE INTERIOR.
COMMISSION TO THE FIVE CIVILIZED TRIBES.

    IN RE APPLICATION FOR ENROLLMENT, as a citizen of the Creek Nation, of Louisa Benden[sic], born on the 30th day of November, 1904.

Name of Father: Louis Benden[sic]	a citizen of the Creek	Nation.
Name of Mother: Dicey Benden[sic]	a citizen of the Creek	Nation.

                  Postoffice   Wewoka, Ind. Ter

AFFIDAVIT OF MOTHER.

UNITED STATES OF AMERICA, Indian Territory,
    Western   **DISTRICT.**

    I, Dicey Benden, on oath state that I am about 35 years of age and a citizen by blood, of the Creek Nation; that I am the lawful wife of Louis Benden, who is a citizen, by blood of the Creek Nation; that a female child was born to me on 30 day of November, 1904, that said child has been named Louisa Benden, and was living March 4, 1905.

her
Dicey x Benden
mark

Witnesses To Mark:
   { J.H. Alexander
   { Frank L. Warner

    Subscribed and sworn to before me this 2nd day of December, 1905.

Frank L Warner
Notary Public.

My Com Exp 3/12/1907

Applications for Enrollment of Creek Newborn
Act of 1905   Volume VII

AFFIDAVIT OF ATTENDING PHYSICIAN OR MID-WIFE.

UNITED STATES OF AMERICA, Indian Territory,
Western DISTRICT.

I, Hepsey McGirt , a midwife , on oath state that I attended on Mrs. Dicey Benden , wife of Louis Benden on the 30 day of November , 1904 ; that there was born to her on said date a female child; that said child was living March 4, 1905, and is said to have been named Louisa Benden

            her
         Hepsey x McGirt
           mark

Witnesses To Mark:
 J.H. Alexander
 Frank L. Warner

Subscribed and sworn to before me this 2nd day of December , 1905.

          Frank L Warner
           Notary Public.

My Com Exp 3/12/1907

BIRTH AFFIDAVIT.

DEPARTMENT OF THE INTERIOR.
COMMISSION TO THE FIVE CIVILIZED TRIBES.

IN RE APPLICATION FOR ENROLLMENT, as a citizen of the Creek Nation, of Louisa Bender , born on the 30 day of November , 1904

Name of Father: Lewis Bender   a citizen of the   Creek   Nation.
Tuckabatche Town
Name of Mother: Tysie Bender   a citizen of the   Creek   Nation.
Tuckabatche Town

         Postoffice   Wewoka, Ind. Ter.

AFFIDAVIT OF MOTHER.

UNITED STATES OF AMERICA, Indian Territory,
Western DISTRICT.   Child is present

I, Tysie Bender , on oath state that I am about 35 years of age and a citizen by blood , of the Creek Nation; that I am the lawful wife of Lewis Bender , who is a citizen, by blood of the Creek Nation; that a female child was born to me on 30 day of November , 1904 , that said child has been named Louisa Bender , and was living March 4, 1905.

Applications for Enrollment of Creek Newborn
Act of 1905   Volume VII

Witnesses To Mark:
{ DC Skaggs
  Alex Posey

her
Tysie x Bender
mark

Subscribed and sworn to before me this 27 day of March, 1905.

Drennan C Skaggs
Notary Public.

AFFIDAVIT OF ATTENDING PHYSICIAN OR MID-WIFE.

UNITED STATES OF AMERICA, Indian Territory, }
  Western   DISTRICT.

I, Hepsey McGirt, a midwife, on oath state that I attended on Mrs. Tysie Bender, wife of Lewis Bender on the 30 day of November, 1904; that there was born to her on said date a female child; that said child was living March 4, 1905, and is said to have been named Louisa Bender

her
Hepsey x McGirt
mark

Witnesses To Mark:
{ Alex Posey
  DC Skaggs

Subscribed and sworn to before me this 27 day of March, 1905.

Drennan C Skaggs
Notary Public.

BIRTH AFFIDAVIT.

DEPARTMENT OF THE INTERIOR.
COMMISSION TO THE FIVE CIVILIZED TRIBES.

IN RE APPLICATION FOR ENROLLMENT, as a citizen of the Creek Nation, of Alice Narcomey, born on the 1 day of February, 1904

Name of Father: Thomas Narcomey   a citizen of the   Creek   Nation. Tuckabatche Town
Name of Mother: Kizzie Narcomie[sic](nee Lewis) a citizen of the   Creek   Nation. Tuckabatche Town

Postoffice   Holdenville, Ind. Ter.

Applications for Enrollment of Creek Newborn
Act of 1905   Volume VII

AFFIDAVIT OF MOTHER.

UNITED STATES OF AMERICA, Indian Territory,
    Western   DISTRICT.   Child is present

I, Kizzie Narcomey , on oath state that I am 20 years of age and a citizen by blood , of the Creek Nation; that I am the lawful wife of Thomas Narcomey , who is a citizen, by blood of the Creek Nation; that a female child was born to me on 1 day of February , 1904, that said child has been named Alice Narcomey , and was living March 4, 1905.

                                    Kizzie Narcomey

Witnesses To Mark:

    Subscribed and sworn to before me this 27 day of March , 1905.

                                    Drennan C Skaggs
                                    Notary Public.

AFFIDAVIT OF ATTENDING PHYSICIAN OR MID-WIFE.

UNITED STATES OF AMERICA, Indian Territory,
    Western   DISTRICT.

I, Melinda Tiger , a midwife , on oath state that I attended on Mrs. Kizzie Narcomey , wife of Thomas Narcomey on the 1 day of February , 1904 ; that there was born to her on said date a female child; that said child was living March 4, 1905, and is said to have been named Alice Narcomey

                                    her
                                    Melinda x Tiger
                                    mark

Witnesses To Mark:
    Alex Posey
    DC Skaggs

    Subscribed and sworn to before me this 27 day of March, 1905.

                                    Drennan C Skaggs
                                    Notary Public.

Applications for Enrollment of Creek Newborn
Act of 1905   Volume VII

BIRTH AFFIDAVIT.

DEPARTMENT OF THE INTERIOR.
COMMISSION TO THE FIVE CIVILIZED TRIBES.

IN RE APPLICATION FOR ENROLLMENT, as a citizen of the Creek Nation, of Millie Dunson, born on the 12 day of September, 1904

Name of Father: Thos H Dunson   a citizen of the   Creek   Nation.
Name of Mother: Ellen Walker (nee) Dunson   a citizen of the   Creek   Nation.

Postoffice   Fentress Ind. Ter.

AFFIDAVIT OF MOTHER.

UNITED STATES OF AMERICA, Indian Territory,
Western   DISTRICT.

I, Ellen Walker (nee) Dunson, on oath state that I am 23 years of age and a citizen by blood, of the Creek Nation; that I am the lawful wife of Thos H Dunson, who is a citizen, by blood of the Creek Nation; that a female child was born to me on 12 day of September, 1904, that said child has been named Millie Dunson, and was living March 4, 1905.

Ellen Walker nee Dunson

Witnesses To Mark:
{

Subscribed and sworn to before me this 25 day of March, 1905.

My Com Exp Aug 19-1908   Tupper Dunn
                              Notary Public.

AFFIDAVIT OF ATTENDING PHYSICIAN OR MID-WIFE.

UNITED STATES OF AMERICA, Indian Territory,
Western   DISTRICT.

I, Polley Sawyer, a midwife, on oath state that I attended on Mrs. Ellen Walker (nee) Dunson, wife of Thos H Dunson on the 12 day of September, 1904; that there was born to her on said date a female child; that said child was living March 4, 1905, and is said to have been named Millie Dunson

                              her
                     Polley x Sawyer
Witnesses To Mark: mark
{ Thos H Dunson
{ Tupper Dunn

Applications for Enrollment of Creek Newborn
Act of 1905   Volume VII

Subscribed and sworn to before me this 25 day of March, 1905.

My Com Exp Aug 19-1908   Tupper Dunn
                                          Notary Public.

HGH

REFER IN REPLY TO THE FOLLOWING:
NC-561.

DEPARTMENT OF THE INTERIOR,
COMMISSIONER TO THE FIVE CIVILIZED TRIBES.

Muskogee, Indian Territory, August 9, 1905.

Nellie McCosar,
   c/o Burnie McCosar,
      Holdenville, Indian Territory.

Dear Madam:

    In the matter of the application for the enrollment of your son Arthur McCosar as a citizen by blood of the Creek Nation this office is unable to identify you upon the final roll of citizens by blood of said nation.

    You are therefore requested to immediately inform this office as to under which you were finally enrolled, the names of your parents and other members of your family and if possible your roll number as the same appears upon your allotment certificate and deeds.

    It is noted that the date of the birth of your said son is omitted from the affidavit of the attending midwife which is now on file in this office. For the purpose of having said midwife execute another affidavit containing the date of the birth of said child and also for the purpose of securing the affidavit of Bunnie McCosar, the father of said child, relative to his birth there is inclosed herewith a blank for proof of birth which has been filled out. You are requested to have the same properly executed and when so executed return it to this office in the inclosed envelope.

                    Respectfully,

                                Wm. O. Beall
                                Acting Commissioner.

CTD-37.
Env.

Applications for Enrollment of Creek Newborn
Act of 1905 Volume VII

CHAS. RIDER
Farm Loans.

Holdenville, Ind. Ter., August 14th, 1905.

Wm. O. Beall,
Acting Commissioner.

Dear Sir:

My madenname[sic] was Nellie Wallow I am married to Bunny McCosar, my reel[sic] number is 7700, my mothers[sic] name is Sally Wallow, my Fathers[sic] name is Wiley Wallow.

Yours Respt.

(Signed) Nellie McCosar (nee Wallace)
Her x Mark.

Witness to mark,
Chas. Rider
Samego Caser.

BIRTH AFFIDAVIT.

DEPARTMENT OF THE INTERIOR.
COMMISSION TO THE FIVE CIVILIZED TRIBES.

IN RE APPLICATION FOR ENROLLMENT, as a citizen of the Creek Nation, of Arthur McCosar, born on the 9th day of October, 1902

Name of Father: Bunnie McCosar   a citizen of the   Creek   Nation.
Name of Mother: Nellie McCosar   a citizen of the   Creek   Nation.

Postoffice   Holdenville, Ind. Ter.

AFFIDAVIT OF ~~MOTHER~~. Father

UNITED STATES OF AMERICA, Indian Territory, ⎫
    Western   DISTRICT. ⎬

I, Bunnie McCosar, on oath state that I am about 43 years of age and a citizen by blood, of the Nation; that I am the lawful ~~wife of~~ husband of Nellie McCosar, who is a citizen, by blood of the Creek Nation; that a male child was born to ~~me~~ us on 9th

Applications for Enrollment of Creek Newborn
Act of 1905 Volume VII

day of October , 1902 , that said child has been named Arthur McCosar , and is now living.

Bunnie McCosar

Witnesses To Mark:
{ C M Allen
  Chas Rider

Subscribed and sworn to before me this 14th day of August, 1905.

Chas. Rider
Notary Public.

AFFIDAVIT OF ATTENDING PHYSICIAN OR MID-WIFE.

UNITED STATES OF AMERICA, Indian Territory,
    Western   DISTRICT.

I, Sally Wallow , a midwife , on oath state that I attended on Mrs. Nellie McCosar , wife of Bunnie McCosar on the 9th day of October , 1902 ; that there was born to her on said date a male child; that said child was living March 4, 1905, and is said to have been named Arthur McCosar

her
Sally Wallow x
mark

Witnesses To Mark:
{ C M Allen
  Chas Rider

Subscribed and sworn to before me this 14th day of August, 1905.

Chas. Rider
Notary Public.

BIRTH AFFIDAVIT.

DEPARTMENT OF THE INTERIOR.
COMMISSION TO THE FIVE CIVILIZED TRIBES.

IN RE APPLICATION FOR ENROLLMENT, as a citizen of the Creek Nation, of Arthur McCosar, born on the 9 day of October , 1902

Name of Father: Bunnie McCosar   a citizen of the   Creek   Nation.
Tulsa Little River Town
Name of Mother: Nellie McCosar   a citizen of the   Creek   Nation.
Tulsa Little River Town

Postoffice   Holdenville, Ind. Ter.

Applications for Enrollment of Creek Newborn
Act of 1905   Volume VII

AFFIDAVIT OF MOTHER.

UNITED STATES OF AMERICA, Indian Territory, }
    Western   DISTRICT.   Child is present

I, Nellie McCosar, on oath state that I am about 23 years of age and a citizen by blood, of the Creek Nation; that I am the lawful wife of Bunnie McCosar, who is a citizen, by blood of the Creek Nation; that a male child was born to me on 9 day of October, 1902, that said child has been named Arthur McCosar, and was living March 4, 1905.

                                      Nellie x McCosar

Witnesses To Mark:
{ Alex Posey
{ DC Skaggs

Subscribed and sworn to before me this 27 day of March, 1905.

                                      Drennan C Skaggs
                                      Notary Public.

AFFIDAVIT OF ATTENDING PHYSICIAN OR MID-WIFE.

UNITED STATES OF AMERICA, Indian Territory, }
    Western   DISTRICT.

I, Sally Wallow, a midwife, on oath state that I attended on Mrs. Nellie McCosar, wife of Bunnie McCosar ~~on the (blank) day of (blank), 1~~ ; that there was born to her on said date a male child; that said child was living March 4, 1905, and is said to have been named Arthur McCosar
                                     her
                                Sally x Wallow
                                  mark

Witnesses To Mark:
{ Alex Posey
{ DC Skaggs

Subscribed and sworn to before me this 27 day of March, 1905.

                                      Drennan C Skaggs
                                      Notary Public.

Applications for Enrollment of Creek Newborn
Act of 1905   Volume VII

BIRTH AFFIDAVIT.

DEPARTMENT OF THE INTERIOR.
COMMISSION TO THE FIVE CIVILIZED TRIBES.

IN RE APPLICATION FOR ENROLLMENT, as a citizen of the Creek Nation, of Henry McCosar, born on the 8 day of May , 1904

Name of Father: Bunnie McCosar   a citizen of the   Creek   Nation.
Tulsa L. R. Town
Name of Mother: Nellie McCosar   a citizen of the   Creek   Nation.
Tulsa L. R. Town
                              Postoffice   Holdenville, Ind. Ter.

AFFIDAVIT OF MOTHER.

UNITED STATES OF AMERICA, Indian Territory,
       Western   DISTRICT.

I, Bunnie McCosar , on oath state that I am 39 years of age and a citizen by blood, of the Nation; that I am the lawful ~~wife~~ husband of Nellie McCosar , who is a citizen, by blood of the Creek   Nation; that a male   child was born to ~~me~~ her on 8 day of May   , 1904 , that said child has been named   Henry McCosar   , and was not living March 4, 1905.

                                Bunnie McCosar
Witnesses To Mark:
{

  Subscribed and sworn to before me this 28 day of March, 1905.

                          Drennan C Skaggs
                          Notary Public.

DEPARTMENT OF THE INTERIOR.
COMMISSION TO THE FIVE CIVILIZED TRIBES.

In the matter of the death of Henry McCosar   a citizen of the Creek Nation, who formerly resided at or near   Holdenville   , Ind. Ter., and died on the 10 day of July , 1904

Applications for Enrollment of Creek Newborn
Act of 1905 Volume VII

;AFFIDAVIT OF RELATIVE.

UNITED STATES OF AMERICA, Indian Territory, }
Western DISTRICT.

I, Bunnie McCosar, on oath state that I am 29 years of age and a citizen by blood, of the Creek Nation; that my postoffice address is Holdenville, Ind. Ter.; that I am father of Henry McCosar who was a citizen, by blood, of the Creek Nation and that said Henry McCosar died on the 10 day of July, 1904

Bunnie McCosar

Witnesses To Mark:
{

Subscribed and sworn to before me this 28 day of March, 1905.

Drennan C Skaggs
Notary Public.

NC 561 JLD

DEPARTMENT OF THE INTERIOR,
COMMISSIONER TO THE FIVE CIVILIZED TRIBES.

In the matter of the application for the enrollment of Henry McCosar, deceased, as a citizen by blood of the Creek Nation.

. . . .

STATEMENT AND ORDER.

The record in this case shows that on March 30, 1905, application was made, in affidavit form, for the enrollment of Henry McCosar, deceased, as a citizen by blood of the Creek Nation, under the provisions of the act of Congress approved March 3, 1905.

It appears from the affidavit filed in this matter that said Henry McCosar, deceased, was born May 8, 1904, and died July 10, 1904.

The Act of Congress approved March 3, 1905, (33 Stats., 1048), provides:
"That the Commission to the Five Civilized Tribes is authorized for sixty days after the date of the approval of this act to receive and consider applications for enrollment, of children, born subsequent to May twenty-fifth, nineteen hundred and one, and prior to March fourth, nineteen hundred and five, and living on said latter date, to citizens of the Creek tribe of Indians whose enrollment has been approved by the Secretary of the Interior prior to the approval of this act; and to enroll and make allotments to such children."

It is, therefore, ordered that the application for the enrollment of said Henry McCosar, deceased, as a citizen by blood of the Creek Nation, be and the same is hereby dismissed.

Applications for Enrollment of Creek Newborn
Act of 1905   Volume VII

Muskogee, Indian Territory.
JAN 4 – 1907

Tams Bixby Commissioner.

BIRTH AFFIDAVIT.

DEPARTMENT OF THE INTERIOR.
COMMISSION TO THE FIVE CIVILIZED TRIBES.

IN RE APPLICATION FOR ENROLLMENT, as a citizen of the Creek Nation, of Nara Nave, born on the 6th day of October, 1902

Name of Father: John Calvin Nave   a citizen of the United States Nation.
Name of Mother: Alice Nave   a citizen of the   Creek   Nation.

Postoffice   Brokenarrow[sic] I.T.

AFFIDAVIT OF MOTHER.

UNITED STATES OF AMERICA, Indian Territory,
   Western   DISTRICT.

I, Alice Nave, on oath state that I am 24 years of age and a citizen by birth, of the Creek Nation; that I am the lawful wife of John Calvin Nave, who is a citizen, by *(blank)* of the United States ~~Nation~~; that a female child was born to me on 6th day of October, 1902, that said child has been named Nara, and was living March 4, 1905.

                                Alice Nave
Witnesses To Mark:
{

Subscribed and sworn to before me this 30th day of March, 1905.

Com xpires[sic] Jany 9-1906   CW Lumpkin
                                      Notary Public.

AFFIDAVIT OF ATTENDING PHYSICIAN OR MID-WIFE.

UNITED STATES OF AMERICA, Indian Territory,
   Western   DISTRICT.

I, Mattie Emily Ghahan, a midwife, on oath state that I attended on Mrs. Alice Nave, wife of John Calvin Nave on the 6th day of October, 1902 ; that there

Applications for Enrollment of Creek Newborn
Act of 1905 Volume VII

was born to her on said date a female child; that said child was living March 4, 1905, and is said to have been named Nara

                                                         her
                                  Mattie Emily Ghahan x

Witnesses To Mark: mark
{ John Miller
{ Joe Fennell

Subscribed and sworn to before me this 30th day of March, 1905.

Com xpires[sic] Jany 9-1906   CW Lumpkin
                                           Notary Public.

BIRTH AFFIDAVIT.
DEPARTMENT OF THE INTERIOR.
COMMISSION TO THE FIVE CIVILIZED TRIBES.

     IN RE APPLICATION FOR ENROLLMENT, as a citizen of the Creek Nation, of Otha Nave, born on the 6th day of October, 1904

Name of Father: John Calvin Nave   a citizen of the United States Nation.
Name of Mother: Alice Nave   a citizen of the   Creek   Nation.

                          Postoffice   Broken Arrow I.T.

                             AFFIDAVIT OF MOTHER.

UNITED STATES OF AMERICA, Indian Territory }
     Western   DISTRICT.   }

     I, Alice Nave, on oath state that I am 24 years of age and a citizen by Birth, of the Creek Nation; that I am the lawful wife of John Calvin Nave, who is a citizen, by *(blank)* of the United States ~~Nation~~; that a male child was born to me on 6th day of October, 1904, that said child has been named Otha Nave, and was living March 4, 1905.

                                        Alice Nave

Witnesses To Mark:
{
{

     Subscribed and sworn to before me this 30th day of March, 1905.

                                       James S Day
                                        Notary Public.

Applications for Enrollment of Creek Newborn
Act of 1905   Volume VII

AFFIDAVIT OF ATTENDING PHYSICIAN OR MID-WIFE.

UNITED STATES OF AMERICA, Indian Territory,
Western DISTRICT.

I, Nancy Ann Kennedy, a midwife, on oath state that I attended on Mrs. Alice Nave, wife of John Calvin Nave on the 6th day of October, 1904; that there was born to her on said date a male child; that said child was living March 4, 1905, and is said to have been named Otha Nave

her
Nancy Ann x Kennedy
mark

Witnesses To Mark:
{ Thad Jay
{ W J Cooper

Subscribed and sworn to before me this 30th day of March, 1905.

James S Day
My Commission Expires March 10th 1907   Notary Public.

NC-563

Muskogee, Indian Territory, August 9, 1905.

Eliza Long,
   c/o Noah Long,
      Yeager, Indian Territory.

Dear Madam:

In the matter of the application for the enrollment of your minor son Newman Long as a citizen by blood of the Creek Nation this office is unable to identify you upon the final roll of citizens by blood of the Creek Nation.

It will be necessary that you be so identified before the rights of your said son can be finally determined.

You are, therefore, requested to state the name under which you were finally enrolled, the names of your parents and other members of your family, your final roll number as the same appears upon your allotment certificate and deeds and any other information which you think may enable this office to identify you.

Respectfully,

Acting Commissioner.

Applications for Enrollment of Creek Newborn
Act of 1905   Volume VII

Yeager, Ind. Ter.
August 24" 1905

Mr. W. O. Beall
    Acting Commissioner
    Muskogee, I.T.
    Dear Sir
        In reply to your letter #563 of Aug 9" relating to my application for the enrollment of my minor son Newman Long.

    I was enrolled as a citizen of the Creek Nation under the name of Eliza Burt Roll number 3207 as appears on my allotment certificate. Since that time I was married to Noah Long enrolled as a citizen of the Creek Nation No: 4882.

    My father and mother died when I was a child before there was any enrollment and I was taken care of by the mother of Dave Barnett and Jim Barnett who was my aunt.

    I do not know what my fathers[sic] name was though I think he was called Smith. My mother went afterward by the name of Barnett and died in 1883. I have now no brothers or sisters. I had one twin sister who died when she was small.

        Yours Truly
        Eliza Long nee Burt

BIRTH AFFIDAVIT.

DEPARTMENT OF THE INTERIOR.
COMMISSION TO THE FIVE CIVILIZED TRIBES.

    IN RE APPLICATION FOR ENROLLMENT, as a citizen of the Creek Nation, of Newman Long, born on the 29 day of July, 1904

Name of Father: Noah Long Tuckabatche Town	a citizen of the Creek	Nation.
Name of Mother: Eliza Long Tuckabatche Town	a citizen of the Creek	Nation.

        Postoffice   Yeager, Ind. Ter.

        AFFIDAVIT OF MOTHER.   Child present

UNITED STATES OF AMERICA, Indian Territory, ⎫
    Western   **DISTRICT.** ⎭

    I, Eliza Long, on oath state that I am 34 years of age and a citizen by blood, of the Creek Nation; that I am the lawful wife of Noah Long, who is a citizen, by

Applications for Enrollment of Creek Newborn
Act of 1905   Volume VII

blood of the Creek Nation; that a male child was born to me on 29 day of July, 1904, that said child has been named Newman Long, and was living March 4, 1905.

                                  Eliza Long

Witnesses To Mark:
{

Subscribed and sworn to before me this 27 day of March, 1905.

                                Drennan C Skaggs
                                Notary Public.

AFFIDAVIT OF ATTENDING PHYSICIAN OR MID-WIFE.

UNITED STATES OF AMERICA, Indian Territory,
    Western   DISTRICT.

I, Cinda Long, a midwife, on oath state that I attended on Mrs. Eliza Long, wife of Noah Long on the 29 day of July, 1904; that there was born to her on said date a male child; that said child was living March 4, 1905, and is said to have been named Newman Long
                                her
                            Cinda x Long
Witnesses To Mark: mark
 { Alex Posey
  DC Skaggs

Subscribed and sworn to before me this 28 day of March, 1905.

                                Drennan C Skaggs
                                Notary Public.

BIRTH AFFIDAVIT.
DEPARTMENT OF THE INTERIOR.
COMMISSION TO THE FIVE CIVILIZED TRIBES.

IN RE APPLICATION FOR ENROLLMENT, as a citizen of the Creek Nation, of Joseph Tate, born on the 26 day of June, 1903

Name of Father: Deck Tate   a citizen of the United States Nation.
Name of Mother: Mary Tate   a citizen of the Creek Nation.
Eufaula Canadian Town
                      Postoffice   Holdenville, I.T.

Applications for Enrollment of Creek Newborn
Act of 1905   Volume VII

AFFIDAVIT OF MOTHER.

Child present

UNITED STATES OF AMERICA, Indian Territory, }
   Western   DISTRICT.

I, Mary Tate , on oath state that I am 33 years of age and a citizen by blood , of the Creek Nation; that I am the lawful wife of Deck Tate , who is a citizen, ~~by~~ *(blank)* of the United States ~~Nation~~; that a male child was born to me on 26 day of June, 1903 , that said child has been named Joseph Tate , and was living March 4, 1905.

                              Mary Tate

Witnesses To Mark:
{

    Subscribed and sworn to before me this 28 day of March , 1905.

                              Drennan C Skaggs
                              Notary Public.

AFFIDAVIT OF ATTENDING PHYSICIAN OR MID-WIFE.

UNITED STATES OF AMERICA, Indian Territory, }
   Western   DISTRICT.

I, Bettie Walker , a mid-wife , on oath state that I attended on Mrs. Mary Tate , wife of Deck Tate on the 26 day of June , 1903 ; that there was born to her on said date a male child; that said child was living March 4, 1905, and is said to have been named Joseph Tate

                              Bettie Walker

Witnesses To Mark:
{

    Subscribed and sworn to before me this 28 day of March, 1905.

                              Drennan C Skaggs
                              Notary Public.

Applications for Enrollment of Creek Newborn
Act of 1905 Volume VII

N.C. 565										I.D.

DEPARTMENT OF THE INTERIOR,
COMMISSIONER TO THE FIVE CIVILIZED TRIBES.

In the matter of the application for the enrollment of Gertie Taborn as a citizen by blood of the Creek Nation.

......ORDER......

The record in this case shows that on April 4, 1905, Nancy Taborn appeared before the Commission to the Five Civilized Tribes and made application for the enrollment of her minor child, Gertie Taborn, as a citizen by blood of the Creek Nation.

The evidence shows that said Gertie Taborn was born February 22, 1905; that she was living March 4, 1905 at the date of the application herein, and that she is the child of Calvin Taborn and Nancy Taborn.

An examination of the records of this Office shows that the names of said Calvin Taborn and Nancy Taborn, or either of them, are not contained in the lists of citizens of the Creek Nation whose enrollment was approved by the Secretary of the Interior prior to March 3, 1905.

The act of Congress approved March 3rd, 1905 (Public No. 212), provides:

"That the Commission to the Five Civilized Tribes is authorized for sixty days after the date of the approval of this Act to receive and consider applications for enrollments of children born subsequent to May twenty five, nineteen hundred and one, and prior to March fourth, nineteen hundred and five, and living on said latter date, to citizens of the Creek tribe of Indians whose enrollment has been approved by the Secretary of the Interior prior to the approval of this act; and to enroll and make allotments to such children."

It is therefore, ordered that there is no authority of law for the enrollment of said Gertie Taborn as a citizen by blood of the Creek Nation, and that the application for her enrollment as such should be and the same is hereby dismissed.

Commissioner.

Muskogee, Indian Territory,

Applications for Enrollment of Creek Newborn
Act of 1905   Volume VII

HGH

REFER IN REPLY TO THE FOLLOWING:

DEPARTMENT OF THE INTERIOR,
COMMISSIONER TO THE FIVE CIVILIZED TRIBES.

Muskogee, Indian Territory, October 8, 1906.

Calvin Taborn,
    Broken Arrow, Indian Territory.

Dear Sir:

    Receipt is acknowledged of your letter of September 28, 1906, inclosing affidavits in the matter of the application for the enrollment of your minor children, Albert and Gertrude (Gertie) Taborn.

    You are advised that on June 6, 1906, the mother of said children executed an affidavit in which the name of the younger is given as Gertie Taborn, and in her affidavit and the affidavit of Mrs. B. A. Stevenson, midwife, transmitted with your said letter the name of said child is given as Gertrude, and you are requested to have her write this office as to which. if either, of said names is the correct one of said child.

                      Respectfully,
                        Tams Bixby
                          Commissioner.

BIRTH AFFIDAVIT.

DEPARTMENT OF THE INTERIOR.
COMMISSION TO THE FIVE CIVILIZED TRIBES.

    IN RE APPLICATION FOR ENROLLMENT, as a citizen of the Creek Nation, of Gertie Taborn, born on the 22 day of Feb , 1905

Name of Father: Calvin Taborn   a citizen of the United States Nation.
Name of Mother: Nancy (Atkins) Taborn   a citizen of the   Creek   Nation.

                  Postoffice   Catoosa, Ind. Ter'y.

AFFIDAVIT OF MOTHER.

UNITED STATES OF AMERICA, Indian Territory,
~~Western~~ Northern   DISTRICT.

    I, Nancy (Atkins) Taborn , on oath state that I am 28 years of age and a citizen by blood , of the Creek Nation; that I am the lawful wife of Calvin Taborn , who is a

Applications for Enrollment of Creek Newborn
Act of 1905   Volume VII

citizen, by *(blank)* of the United States Nation; that a female child was born to me on 22 day of Feb , 1905 , that said child has been named Gertie Taborn , and is now living.

                                   Nancy Taborn

Witnesses To Mark: His[sic] x mark
{ Calvin Taborn
  W.A. Fletcher

Subscribed and sworn to before me this 31 day of March , 1905.

                                  WW Whitman
My Com Ex Nov 5 1907.   Notary Public.

AFFIDAVIT OF ATTENDING PHYSICIAN OR MID-WIFE.

UNITED STATES OF AMERICA, Indian Territory,
~~Western~~ Northern   DISTRICT.

I, Maggie Stevenson , a midwife , on oath state that I attended on Mrs. Nancy (Atkins) Taborn , wife of Calvin Taborn on the 22 day of Feb , 1905 ; that there was born to her on said date a female child; that said child is now living and is said to have been named Gertie Taborn

                                 Maggie Stevenson

Witnesses To Mark:
{

Subscribed and sworn to before me this 31 day of March , 1905.

                                  WW Whitman
My Com Ex Nov 5 1907.   Notary Public.

(The above Birth Affidavit given again.)

BIRTH AFFIDAVIT.
DEPARTMENT OF THE INTERIOR.
COMMISSION TO THE FIVE CIVILIZED TRIBES.

IN RE APPLICATION FOR ENROLLMENT, as a citizen of the Creek Nation, of Bertha Todd , born on the 15 day of March , 1902

Applications for Enrollment of Creek Newborn
Act of 1905 Volume VII

Name of Father: James Todd a citizen of the United States Nation.
Name of Mother: Katy Todd a citizen of the Creek Nation.
Little River Tulsa Town
                Postoffice Holdenville, I.T.

AFFIDAVIT OF MOTHER.
                                      Child present

UNITED STATES OF AMERICA, Indian Territory, ⎫
    Western   DISTRICT. ⎭

    I, Katy Todd , on oath state that I am about 24 years of age and a citizen by blood , of the Creek Nation; that I am the lawful wife of James Todd , who is a citizen, by *(blank)* of the United States ~~Nation~~; that a female child was born to me on 15 day of March , 1902 , that said child has been named Bertha Todd , and was living March 4, 1905.

                                     Katie Todd

Witnesses To Mark:
{

    Subscribed and sworn to before me this 28 day of March , 1905.

                                  Drennan C Skaggs
                                    Notary Public.

AFFIDAVIT OF ATTENDING PHYSICIAN OR MID-WIFE.

UNITED STATES OF AMERICA, Indian Territory, ⎫
    Western   DISTRICT. ⎭

                                  assisted Pollie Bruner who
    I, James Todd , ~~a *(blank)*~~ , on oath state that I ^ attended on my wife Mrs. Katy Todd , ~~wife of *(blank)*~~ on or about the 15 day of March three years ago the 15 of this month (March) , 1 ; that there was born to her on said date a female child; that said child was living March 4, 1905, and is said to have been named Bertha Todd

                                     James Todd

Witnesses To Mark:
{

    Subscribed and sworn to before me this 28 day of March, 1905.

                                  Drennan C Skaggs
                                  Notary Public.

Applications for Enrollment of Creek Newborn
Act of 1905 Volume VII

HGH

REFER IN REPLY TO THE FOLLOWING:
NC-566.

DEPARTMENT OF THE INTERIOR,
COMMISSIONER TO THE FIVE CIVILIZED TRIBES.

Muskogee, Indian Territory, August 9, 1905.

Katy Todd,
    c/o James Todd,
    Holdenville, Indian Territory.

Dear Madam:

    In the matter of the application for the enrollment of your children Bertha and Arthur Lee Todd as citizens by blood of the Creek Nation there are on file the affidavits of yourself and your husband James Todd only as to the birth of said child stating that no one attended you when he was born of said children. It will be necessary, before the rights of said children as citizens by blood of the Creek Nation can be finally determined for you to furnish this office with the affidavits of the attending physician or midwife at the birth of said children relative to their birth, and for that purpose there are inclosed herewith two blanks for proof of birth, which have been partially filled out.

    You are requested to have the same properly executed and when executed return them to this office in the inclosed envelope. Be careful to see that the notary public before whom the affidavits are acknowledged attaches his name and seal to each affidavit. In case any signature is by mark it must be attested by two disinterested witnesses.

                        Respectfully,

                                  Wm. O. Beall
                                  Acting Commissioner.

CTD-38.
Env.

BIRTH AFFIDAVIT.

DEPARTMENT OF THE INTERIOR.
COMMISSION TO THE FIVE CIVILIZED TRIBES.

    IN RE APPLICATION FOR ENROLLMENT, as a citizen of the Creek Nation, of Bertha Todd , born on the 15 day of March , 1902
Name of Father: James Todd   a citizen of the United States Nation.
Name of Mother: Katy Todd   a citizen of the   Creek   Nation.

                        Postoffice   Holdenville, I.T.

Applications for Enrollment of Creek Newborn
Act of 1905 Volume VII

AFFIDAVIT OF MOTHER.

UNITED STATES OF AMERICA, Indian Territory, ⎫
    Western   DISTRICT. ⎬
                                         ⎭

    I, Katy Todd , on oath state that I am 25 years of age and a citizen by birth , of the Creek Nation; that I am the lawful wife of James Todd , who is a citizen, by birth of the United States Nation; that a Female child was born to me on 15th day of March , 1902 , that said child has been named Bertha Todd , and was living March 4, 1905.

                                                                           her
                                                               Katy Todd x
Witnesses To Mark: mark
  ⎰ C M Allen
  ⎱ Chas Rider

    Subscribed and sworn to before me this 17th day of August , 1905.

                                                Chas Rider
                                                Notary Public.

AFFIDAVIT OF ATTENDING PHYSICIAN OR MID-WIFE.

UNITED STATES OF AMERICA, Indian Territory, ⎫
    Western   DISTRICT. ⎬
                                         ⎭

    I, Pollie Bruner , a midwife , on oath state that I attended on Mrs. Katy Todd , wife of James Todd on the 15th day of March , 1902 ; that there was born to her on said date a female child; that said child was living March 4, 1905, and is said to have been named Bertha Todd

                                                             her
                                                Pollie Bruner x
Witnesses To Mark: mark
  ⎰ C M Allen
  ⎱ Chas Rider

    Subscribed and sworn to before me this 17th day of August , 1905.

                                                Chas Rider
                                                Notary Public.

Applications for Enrollment of Creek Newborn
Act of 1905   Volume VII

BIRTH AFFIDAVIT.

DEPARTMENT OF THE INTERIOR.
COMMISSION TO THE FIVE CIVILIZED TRIBES.

IN RE APPLICATION FOR ENROLLMENT, as a citizen of the Creek Nation, of Arthur Lee Todd , born on the 14 day of October and is now seventeen months old, ~~190~~

Name of Father: James Todd   a citizen of the United States Nation.
Name of Mother: Katy Todd   a citizen of the   Creek   Nation.
Little River Tulsa Town
                    Postoffice   Holdenville, I.T.

AFFIDAVIT OF MOTHER.
                                    Child present

UNITED STATES OF AMERICA, Indian Territory, }
    Western   DISTRICT.

I, Katy Todd , on oath state that I am about 24 years of age and a citizen by blood , of the Creek Nation; that I am the lawful wife of James Todd , who is a citizen, by *(blank)* of the United States ~~Nation~~; that a male child was born to me on 14 day of October ; that said child is seventeen (17) months old, ~~1~~ , that said child has been named Arthur Lee Todd , and was living March 4, 1905.

                                    Katy Todd
Witnesses To Mark:
{

Subscribed and sworn to before me this 28 day of March , 1905.

                            Drennan C Skaggs
                                Notary Public.

AFFIDAVIT OF ATTENDING PHYSICIAN OR MID-WIFE.

UNITED STATES OF AMERICA, Indian Territory, }
    Western   DISTRICT.

                                    assisted the midwife who
I, James Todd , ~~a *(blank)*~~ , on oath state that I ^ attended on my wife Mrs. Katy Todd , ~~wife of *(blank)*~~ on or about the 14 day of October , 1903 ; that there was born to her on said date a male child; that said child was living March 4, 1905, and is said to have been named Arthur Lee Todd
                                    James Todd
Witnesses To Mark:
{

Applications for Enrollment of Creek Newborn
Act of 1905 Volume VII

Subscribed and sworn to before me this 28 day of March, 1905.

Drennan C Skaggs
Notary Public.

BIRTH AFFIDAVIT.

DEPARTMENT OF THE INTERIOR.
COMMISSION TO THE FIVE CIVILIZED TRIBES.

IN RE APPLICATION FOR ENROLLMENT, as a citizen of the Creek Nation, of Arthur Lee Todd, born on the 14th day of October, 1903

Name of Father:	James Todd	a citizen of the United States Nation.
Name of Mother:	Katy Todd	a citizen of the Creek Nation.

Postoffice   Holdenville, I.T.

AFFIDAVIT OF MOTHER.

UNITED STATES OF AMERICA, Indian Territory,
Western   DISTRICT.

I, Katy Todd, on oath state that I am 25 years of age and a citizen by birth, of the Creek Nation; that I am the lawful wife of James Todd, who is a citizen, by birth of the United States Nation; that a male child was born to me on 14th day of October, 1903, that said child has been named Arthur Lee Todd, and was living March 4, 1905.

her
Katy Todd x
mark

Witnesses To Mark:
{ C M Allen
{ Chas Rider

Subscribed and sworn to before me this 17th day of August, 1905.

Chas Rider
Notary Public.

AFFIDAVIT OF ATTENDING PHYSICIAN OR MID-WIFE.

UNITED STATES OF AMERICA, Indian Territory
Western   DISTRICT.

I, Pollie Bruner, a midwife, on oath state that I attended on Mrs. Katy Todd, wife of James Todd on the 14th day of October, 1903; that there was born to her on

Applications for Enrollment of Creek Newborn
Act of 1905   Volume VII

said date a male child; that said child was living March 4, 1905, and is said to have been named   Arthur Lee Todd

her
Pollie Bruner x
mark

Witnesses To Mark:
{ C M Allen
{ Chas Rider

     Subscribed and sworn to before me this   17th day of August , 1905.

Chas Rider
Notary Public.

DEPARTMENT OF THE INTERIOR,
COMMISSION TO THE FIVE CIVILIZED TRIBES.
Holdenville, I. T., March 27, 1905.

    In the matter of the application for the enrollment of Yanah Birdhead as a citizen of the Creek Nation.

        CINDA BIRDHEAD, being duly sworn, testified as follows:

    Through Alex Posey Official Interpreter:

BY COMMISSION:
Q What is your name? A Cinda Birdhead.
Q How old are you? About twenty-eight.
Q What is your post office address? A Spaulding.
Q Are you a citizen of the Creek Nation? A Yes, sir.
Q To what town do ylu[sic] belong? A Little River Tulsa.
Q Do you make application for the enrollment of your child, Yanah Birdhead, as a citizen of the Creek Nation? A Yes, sir.
Q Who is the father of Yanah? A Fuseka or Birdhead.
Q Is he living? A He is dead.
Q Was he a citizen of the Creek Nation? A He was a Seminole.
Q If it should be found that your child, Yanah, is entitled to enrollment in either the Creek or Seminole Nations in which nation do you desire to have her enrolled? A In the Creek Nation.

---oooOOOooo---

    I, D. C. Skaggs, on oath state that the above and foregoing is a full and true transcript of my stenographic notes as taken in said cause on said date.

Applications for Enrollment of Creek Newborn
Act of 1905   Volume VII

D.C. Skaggs

Subscribed and sworn to before me this 17" day of July, 1905.

Edw C Griesel
Notary Public.

NC. 567.

Muskogee, Indian Territory, July 14, 1905.

Commissioner to the Five Civilized Tribes,
      Seminole Enrollment Division,
            Muskogee, Indian Territory.

Gentlemen:

    March 30, 1905, application was made to the Commission to the Five Civilized Tribes for the enrollment of Yanah Birdhead, born November 12, 1901, as a citizen by blood of the Creek Nation. It is stated in said application that the father of said child is Fus-e-ka or Birdhead, a citizen of the Seminole Nation, and that the mother is Cinda Birdhead, a citizen of the Creek Nation.

    You are requested to inform the Creek Enrollment Division as to whether application has been made for the enrollment of said Yanah Birdhead, as a citizen of the Seminole Nation, and if so, what disposition has been made of the same.

Respectfully,

Commissioner.

DEPARTMENT OF THE INTERIOR.
COMMISSION TO THE FIVE CIVILIZED TRIBES.

Muskogee, Indian Territory, July 18, 1905.

Chief Clerk,
    Creek Enrollment Division.

Dear Sir:

    Receipt is acknowledged of your letter of July 14, 1905 (NC-567) stating that application was made to the Commission to the Five Civilized Tribes for the enrollment of Yanah Birdhead, born November 12, 1901, child of Fus-e-ka (or Birdhead), a citizen

Applications for Enrollment of Creek Newborn
Act of 1905   Volume VII

of the Seminole Nation, and Cinda Birdhead, a citizen of the Creek Nation, as a citizen by blood of the Creek Nation and requesting to be advised as to whether application has been made for the enrollment of said child as a citizen of the Seminole Nation.

In reply to your letter you are advised that it does not appear from an examination of the records of this office that any application was made to the Commission to the Five Civilized Tribes for the enrollment of said child as a citizen of the Seminole Nation.

Respectfully,

Tams Bixby   Commissioner.

NC-567.

Muskogee, Indian Territory, August 20, 1905

Sinda[sic] Birdhead,
    Spaulding, Indian Territory.

Dear Madam:

In the matter of the application for the enrollment of your minor daughter Yanah Birdhead, born November 12, 1901, as a citizen by blood of the Creek Nation it will be necessary for you to furnish this office with the affidavits of two disinterested persons relative to the birth of said child. Said affidavits must set forth the name of said child, the date of her birth, the names of her parents and whether or not he was on living March 4, 1905.

You are requested to give this matter your immediate attention.

Respectfully,

Acting Commissioner.

NC 567

Muskogee, Indian Territory, November 12, 1906.

Chief Clerk,
    Seminole Enrollment Division,
        General Office.

Dear Sir:

Applications for Enrollment of Creek Newborn
Act of 1905   Volume VII

You are hereby advised that the name of Yanah Birdhead born November 12, 1902, to Fus-eka or Birdhead, an alleged citizen of the Seminole Nation, and Cinda Birdhead a citizen by blood of the Creek Nation is contained in schedule of minor citizens by blood of the Creek Nation, approved by the Secretary of the Interior, September 27, 1905, opposite Roll Number 546.

Respectfully,

Commissioner.

United States of America   (
Western District   )
                             (
Indian Territory   )

Personall[sic][sic] appeared before me a Notary Public in and for the Western district   Roman Goat   upon oath state that they are personall[sic] acquainted with Sinda Birdhead, and know that their[sic] was born to her on the 12th day of November, 1901, a female child who is named Yanah Birdhead, and that said child is now liveing[sic].

The above Sinda Birdhead is a member of our band and we are personally acquainted with the above facts.

Roman Goat

Subscribed and sworn to before me this 16th day of August, 1905.

(Name Illegible)
Chas Rider
Notary Public.

My Commission Expires July 11th, 1906

United States of America   (
Western District   )
                             (
Indian Territory   )

Personall[sic][sic] appeared before me a Notary Public in and for the Western district   Burnie McCosar   upon oath state that they are personall[sic] acquainted with Sinda Birdhead, and know that their[sic] was born to her on the 12th day of November, 1901, a female child who is named Yanah Birdhead, and that said child is now liveing[sic].

Applications for Enrollment of Creek Newborn
Act of 1905 Volume VII

The above Sinda Birdhead is a member of our band and we are personally acquainted with the above facts.

Burnie McCosar

Subscribed and sworn to before me this 16th day of August, 1905.

Chas Rider
Notary Public.

My Commission Expires July 11th, 1906

BIRTH AFFIDAVIT.

DEPARTMENT OF THE INTERIOR.
COMMISSION TO THE FIVE CIVILIZED TRIBES.

IN RE APPLICATION FOR ENROLLMENT, as a citizen of the Creek Nation, of Yanah Birdhead, born on the 12 day of November, 1901

Name of Father: Fus-eka or Birdhead   a citizen of the Seminole Nation.
Name of Mother: Cinda Birdhead   a citizen of the Creek Nation.
Tulsa Little River Town

Postoffice   Spaulding, Ind. Ter.

AFFIDAVIT OF MOTHER.

UNITED STATES OF AMERICA, Indian Territory, }   Child is present
    Western   DISTRICT.

I, Cinda Birdhead, on oath state that I am 28 years of age and a citizen by blood, of the Creek Nation; that I am the lawful wife of Fus-eka or Birdhead, who is a citizen, by blood of the Seminole Nation; that a female child was born to me on 12 day of November, 1901, that said child has been named Yanah Birdhead, and was living March 4, 1905. That no one attended on me as midwife or physician at the birth of the child.   her

                                           Cinda x Birdhead
Witnesses To Mark: mark
    { Alex Posey
      DC Skaggs

Subscribed and sworn to before me this 27 day of March, 1905.

Drennan C Skaggs
Notary Public.

Applications for Enrollment of Creek Newborn
Act of 1905   Volume VII

C 568

DEPARTMENT OF THE INTERIOR,
COMMISSION TO THE FIVE CIVILIZED TRIBES.
Holdenville, I. T., March 27, 1905.

In the matter of the application for the enrollment of Sarah Buck as a citizen of the Creek Nation.

Rhoda Buck, being duly sworn, testified as follows:

Through Alex Posey Official Interpreter:

BY COMMISSION:
Q What is your name? A Rhoda Buck.
Q How old are you? A Thirty-two
Q What is your post office address? A Wewoka.
Q Are you a citizen of the Creek Nation? A I am a Seminole.
Q Do you make application for the enrollment of your child, Sarah, as a citizen of the Creek Nation? A Yes, sir.
Q What is the name of the father of Sarah A Simpson Buck.
Q Is he a citizen of the Creek Nation? A Yes, sir.
Q In the event that it is found that your child, Sarah, is entitled to be enrolled in either the Creek or Seminole Nations, in which nation do you desire to have her enrolled? A In the Creek Nation.

---OooOOOooOo---

I, D. C. Skaggs, on oath state that the above and foregoing is a full and true transcript of my stenographic notes as taken in said cause on said date.

DC Skaggs

Subscribed and sworn to before me this 18" day of July, 1905.

Edw C Griesel
Notary Public.

Applications for Enrollment of Creek Newborn
Act of 1905 Volume VII

BIRTH AFFIDAVIT.

Supplemental testimony taken.

DEPARTMENT OF THE INTERIOR.
COMMISSION TO THE FIVE CIVILIZED TRIBES.

IN RE APPLICATION FOR ENROLLMENT, as a citizen of the Creek Nation, of Sarah Buck, born on the 17 day of April, 1902

Name of Father: Simpson Buck   a citizen of the Creek Nation.
Tulsa Little River Town
Name of Mother: Rhoda Buck   a citizen of the Seminole Nation.

Postoffice   Wewoka, Ind. Ter.

AFFIDAVIT OF MOTHER.

UNITED STATES OF AMERICA, Indian Territory, }   Child is present
Western   DISTRICT.

I, Rhoda Buck, on oath state that I am 32 years of age and a citizen by blood, of the Seminole Nation; that I am the lawful wife of Simpson Buck, who is a citizen, by blood of the Creek Nation; that a female child was born to me on 17 day of April, 1902, that said child has been named Sarah Buck, and was living March 4, 1905. That no one attended on me as midwife or physician at the birth of the child.

                                        her
                              Rhoda x Buck
Witnesses To Mark: mark
{ Alex Posey
{ DC Skaggs

Subscribed and sworn to before me this 27 day of March, 1905.

                                 Drennan C Skaggs
                                       Notary Public.

Applications for Enrollment of Creek Newborn
Act of 1905 Volume VII

BIRTH AFFIDAVIT.

DEPARTMENT OF THE INTERIOR.
COMMISSION TO THE FIVE CIVILIZED TRIBES.

IN RE APPLICATION FOR ENROLLMENT, as a citizen of the Creek Nation, of Sarah Buck, born on the 17th day of April, 1902

Name of Father: Simpson Buck   a citizen of the   Creek   Nation.
Name of Mother: Rhoda Buck   a citizen of the   Seminole   Nation.

Postoffice   Wewoka, I.T.

AFFIDAVIT OF MOTHER.

UNITED STATES OF AMERICA, Indian Territory,
      Western   DISTRICT.

I, Simpson Buck, on oath state that I am about 30 years of age and a citizen by blood, of the Creek Nation; that I am the lawful ~~wife of~~ husband of Rhoda Buck, who is a citizen, by blood of the Seminole Nation; that a female child was born to me on 17th day of April, 1902, that said child has been named Sarah Buck, and was living March 4, 1905.

                                         Simpson Buck

Witnesses To Mark:

Subscribed and sworn to before me this 22 day of August, 1905.

Com Exp   John W. Willmott
Oct 5-1906   Notary Public.

DEPARTMENT OF THE INTERIOR,
COMMISSION TO THE FIVE CIVILIZED TRIBES.

In the matter of the application for the enrollment of Sarah Buck, born the 17th day of April, 1902, as a citizen ~~by blood~~ of the Creek Nation, Indian Territory.

United States of America, Indian Territory)
) ss.
       Western Judicial District   )
                             Chepon

~~Cheparney~~ Harjo and Lizzie Harjo, being duly sworn, each for himself, depose and say: I am of lawful age, a citizen by blood of the Seminole Nation; that I am personally well acquainted with Simpson Buck and Rhoda Buck, his

Applications for Enrollment of Creek Newborn
Act of 1905   Volume VII

wife, the former being the[sic] a citizen of the Creek Nation, the latter a citizen of the Seminole Nation; that on the 17th day of April, 1902, or about that date, there was born to said Simpson Buck and Rhoda Buck a girl child, which was named Sarah Buck; that said Sarah Buck is personally well known to me; that said Sarah Buck was living on the 4th day of March, 1905, and is still living; that I am entirely disinterested in the matter of the application for the enrollment of said Sarah Buck as a citizen of the Creek Nation of Indians.

And further affiants say not.

Witness: Chepon Harjo
   (Name Illegible)   Lizzie Harjo
   E.A. Wallace

     Subscribed and sworn to before me by said Cheparney[sic] Harjo and Lizzie Harjo, at Wewoka, I.T., this the 22nd day of August, A.D., 1905.

                   John W. Willmott
                   Notary Public.
My com. expires Oct. 5, 1906.

NC. 568.

Muskogee, Indian Territory, July 14, 1905.

Commissioner to the Five Civilized Tribes,
    Seminole Enrollment Division,
        Muskogee, Indian Territory.

Gentlemen:

     March 30, 1905, application was made to the Commission to the Five Civilized Tribes for the enrollment of Sarah Buck, born April 17, 1902, as a citizen of the Creek Nation. It is stated in said application that the father of said child is Simpson Buck, a citizen of the Creek Nation, and that the mother is Rhoda Buck, a citizen of the Seminole Nation.

     It is requested that you inform the Creek Enrollment Division as to whether application has been made for the enrollment of said Sarah Buck as a citizen of the Seminole Nation, and if so, what disposition has been made of the same.

                Respectfully,

                         Commissioner.

Applications for Enrollment of Creek Newborn
Act of 1905 Volume VII

DEPARTMENT OF THE INTERIOR.
COMMISSION TO THE FIVE CIVILIZED TRIBES.

Muskogee, Indian Territory, July 19, 1905.

Chief Clerk,
    Creek Enrollment Division.

Dear Sir:

    Receipt is acknowledged of your letter of July 14, 1905 (NC-568) stating that application was made to the Commission to the Five Civilized Tribes for the enrollment of Sarah Buck, born April 17, 1902, child of Simpson Buck, a citizen of the Creek Nation, and Rhoda Buck, a citizen of the Seminole Nation, as a citizen by blood of the Creek Nation and requesting to be informed as to whether application was made for the enrollment of said child as a citizen of the Seminole Nation.

    In reply to your letter you are advised that it does not appear from an examination of the records of this office that any application was made to the Commission to the Five Civilized Tribes for the enrollment of said Sarah Buck as a citizen of the Seminole Nation.

    Respectfully,

    Tams Bixby   Commissioner.

NC-568.

Muskogee, Indian Territory, August 10, 1905.

Rhoda Buck
    c/o Simpson Buck,
        Wewoka, Indian Territory.

Dear Madam:

    In the matter of the application for the enrollment of your minor daughter Sarah Buck, born April 17, 1902, as a citizen by blood of the Creek Nation, it will be necessary for you to furnish this office with the affidavits of two disinterested persons as to the birth of said child. Said affidavits must set forth the child's name, the date of her birth, the names of her parents and whether or not he was on living March 4, 1905.

    The affidavit of Simpson Buck the father of said child is also required. For the purpose of securing his affidavit there is inclosed a blank for proof of birth which has been filled out. You are requested to have the said Simpson Buck appear before a notary public and swear to the inclosed affidavit; when the same has been executed return it to

Applications for Enrollment of Creek Newborn
Act of 1905 Volume VII

this office in the inclosed envelope together with the affidavits of the two disinterested persons above referred to.

Respectfully,

CTD-39   Env.   Acting Commissioner.

ARCHIBALD S. McKENNON.   JOHN W. WILLMOTT.

LAW OFFICE OF

McKENNON & WILLMOTT,

WEWOKA, I.T.

Aug. 25th, 1905.

Hon. Tams Bixby,
      Commissioner to the Five Civilized Tribes,
          Muskogee, I. T.

Dear Sir:

      Enclosed we beg leave to hand you affidavit of Dianna Dean in the matter of the application for the enrollment of Matilda Thomas as a new born citizen of the Seminole Nation.

      We also enclose affidavits in the matter of the enrollment of Sarah Buck as a citizen of the Creek Nation.

Very truly,

McKennon & Willmott
Attorneys for the Seminoles.

(D)

NC 568

Muskogee, Indian Territory, November 12, 1906.

Chief Clerk,
      Seminole Enrollment Division,
          General Office.

Dear Sir:

Applications for Enrollment of Creek Newborn
Act of 1905   Volume VII

You are hereby advised that the name of Sarah Buck born April 17, 1902 to Simpson Buck, as a citizen by blood of the Creek Nation and Rhoda Buck an alleged citizen of the Seminole Nation, is contained in schedule of minor citizens by blood of the Creek Nation, approved by the Secretary of the Interior, November 27, 1905, opposite Roll Number 707.

              Respectfully,

                          Commissioner.

NC-569.

              Muskogee, Indian Territory, August 10, 1905

Losanna Long,
  c/o Henry Long,
    Yeager, Indian Territory.

Dear Madam:

In the matter of the application for the enrollment of your minor daughter Anna, born July 6, 1904, as a citizen by blood of the Creek Nation, it will be necessary for you to furnish this office with the affidavits of two disinterested persons as to the birth of said child. Said affidavits to set forth the name of the child, the date of her birth, the names of her parents and whether or not he was on living March 4, 1905.

This office has been unable to identify you upon the final roll of citizens by blood of the Creek Nation. It is necessary, before the rights of your said daughter can be determined that you be so identified.

You are, therefore, requested to immediately inform this office of under which you were finally enrolled, the names of your parents and other members of your family, your final roll number as the same appears upon your allotment certificate and deeds and any other information which you think will enable this office to identify you upon the Creek roll.

              Respectfully,

                        Acting Commissioner.

Applications for Enrollment of Creek Newborn
Act of 1905   Volume VII

Dear Sir

    Wish to say that I am a Creek citizen by blood and that my maiden name is Losanna Beaver. Now since then I married Henry Long so you can easly[sic] see the records in the chief office or at the land office in Muskogee

Yours truly,

Losanna Beaver

    his   Now Long
By Henry x Long
    mark
Witness to mark J.R. Dunsey

AFFIDAVIT OF ATTENDING PHYSICIAN OR MID-WIFE.

UNITED STATES OF AMERICA, Indian Territory,
    Western   **DISTRICT.**

    I, Linda McGirt , a midwife , on oath state that I attended on Mrs. Losanna Long , wife of Henry Long on the 6 day of July , 1904 ; that there was born to her on said date a female child; that said child was living March 4, 1905, and is said to have been named Anna Long

                                                                her
                                                           Linda x McGirt
Witnesses To Mark: mark
    W R Clawson
    James Scott

    Subscribed and sworn to before me this 13 day of Sept, 1905.

                                                                    W R Clawson
                                                                     Notary Public.

My Commission Expires June 13 1908 (stamp, inverted)

BIRTH AFFIDAVIT.
DEPARTMENT OF THE INTERIOR.
COMMISSION TO THE FIVE CIVILIZED TRIBES.

    IN RE APPLICATION FOR ENROLLMENT, as a citizen of the Creek Nation, of Anna Long , born on the 6 July day of , 1904

Name of Father: Henry Long   a citizen of the   Creek   Nation.
    Tuckabatche Town
Name of Mother: Losanna Long (nee Beaver)   a citizen of the   Creek   Nation.
    Tuckabatchee Town

Applications for Enrollment of Creek Newborn
Act of 1905   Volume VII

Postoffice   Yeager, Ind. Ter.

AFFIDAVIT OF MOTHER.

UNITED STATES OF AMERICA, Indian Territory, }
   Western   DISTRICT.

Child is present

I, Losanna Long , on oath state that I am about 22 years of age and a citizen by blood , of the Creek Nation; that I am the lawful wife of Henry Long , who is a citizen, by blood of the Creek Nation; that a female child was born to me on 6 day of July , 1904 , that said child has been named Anna Long , and was living March 4, 1905.

                              her
                      Losanna x Long

Witnesses To Mark: mark
 { Alex Posey
   DC Skaggs

Subscribed and sworn to before me this 27 day of March , 1905.

                      Drennan C Skaggs
                      Notary Public.

                 Father
AFFIDAVIT OF ~~ATTENDING PHYSICIAN OR MID WIFE~~.

UNITED STATES OF AMERICA, Indian Territory, }
   Western   DISTRICT.

                              my wife

I, Henry Long , ~~a (blank)~~ , on oath state that I attended on ^ Mrs. Losanna Long , ~~wife of~~ *(blank)* on the 6 day of July , 1904 ; that there was born to her on said date a female child; that said child is now living and is said to have been named Anna Long

                          his
                      Henry x Long

Witnesses To Mark: mark
 { Alex Posey
   DC Skaggs

Subscribed and sworn to before me this 27 day of March , 1905.

                      Drennan C Skaggs
                      Notary Public.

Applications for Enrollment of Creek Newborn
Act of 1905   Volume VII

BIRTH AFFIDAVIT.

DEPARTMENT OF THE INTERIOR.
COMMISSION TO THE FIVE CIVILIZED TRIBES.

IN RE APPLICATION FOR ENROLLMENT, as a citizen of the Creek Nation, of Jennie Leader, born on the 5 day of November, 1901

Name of Father: Barney Leader   a citizen of the   Creek   Nation. Ochiye[sic] Town
Name of Mother: Tilda Leader   a citizen of the   Creek   Nation. *(Illegible)* Town

Postoffice   Calvin, Ind. Ter.

AFFIDAVIT OF MOTHER.

UNITED STATES OF AMERICA, Indian Territory, } Child is present
Western   DISTRICT.

I, Tilda Leader, on oath state that I am 35 years of age and a citizen by blood, of the Creek Nation; that I am the lawful wife of Barney Leader, who is a citizen, by blood of the Creek Nation; that a female child was born to me on 5 day of November, 1901, that said child has been named Jennie Leader, and was living March 4, 1905.

                                                    her
                                          Tilda x Leader

Witnesses To Mark: mark
{ Alex Posey
{ DC Skaggs

Subscribed and sworn to before me this 27 day of March, 1905.

                                      Drennan C Skaggs
                                              Notary Public.

AFFIDAVIT OF ATTENDING PHYSICIAN OR MID-WIFE.

UNITED STATES OF AMERICA, Indian Territory, }
Western   DISTRICT.

I, Emma Williams, a midwife, on oath state that I attended on Mrs. Tilda Leader, wife of Barney Leader on the 5 day of November, 1901; that there was born to her on said date a female child; that said child was living March 4, 1905, and is said to have been named Jennie Leader

                                        Emma Williams

Witnesses To Mark:
{

Applications for Enrollment of Creek Newborn
Act of 1905   Volume VII

Subscribed and sworn to before me this 27 day of March, 1905.

                          Drennan C Skaggs
                          Notary Public.

NC-571.

                      Muskogee, Indian Territory, August 10, 1905.

Chofolop Harjo,
      Morse, Indian Territory.

Dear Sir:

      You are requested to immediately inform this office as to whether or not there was born to your wife on January 29, 1905, two female children one by the name of Fanny Harjo and one by the name of Dana Harjo, or are Fannie Harjo and Dana Harjo one and the same child? If they are one and the same child you are requested to inform this office as to whether or not said child is still living and if dead when she died.

      Please give this matter your prompt attention.

                      Respectfully,

                      Acting Commissioner.

                    Morse, I.T. Aug 21, 1905

Commission to Five Civilized Tribes,
      Muskogee, I T

Gentlemen:

      Replying to your letter of August 10 (NC571) I beg to state that my two children, Fanny and Dana Harjo, were twins born on the 29th day of Jan 1905.
      Fanny Harjo is living and Dana Harjo is dead, and affidavits relative to each child has been sent to your office.
      If this statement is not satisfactory please send necessary blanks and so on and I will execute and return at once.

                very[sic] respectfully
                Chofolop Harjo

Applications for Enrollment of Creek Newborn
Act of 1905   Volume VII

BIRTH AFFIDAVIT.

DEPARTMENT OF THE INTERIOR.
COMMISSION TO THE FIVE CIVILIZED TRIBES.

    IN RE APPLICATION FOR ENROLLMENT, as a citizen of the Creek Nation, of Unasee Harjo , born on the 3 day of May , 1903

Name of Father: Chof o lup Harjo	a citizen of the	Creek	Nation.
Name of Mother: Amey Mikey nee Harjo	a citizen of the	Creek	Nation.

                    Postoffice   Morse I T.

AFFIDAVIT OF MOTHER.

UNITED STATES OF AMERICA, Indian Territory, ⎫
    Western   DISTRICT. ⎭

    I, Amey Mikey (nee) Harjo , on oath state that I am 29 years of age and a citizen by blood , of the Creek Nation; that I am the lawful wife of Chof o lup Harjo , who is a citizen, by blood of the Creek Nation; that a male child was born to me on 3 day of May , 1903 , that said child has been named Una see Harjo , and was living March 4, 1905.

                                          Amy Mikey nee) Harjo

Witnesses To Mark:
{ HG Malot
  Tupper Dunn

    Subscribed and sworn to before me this 29 day of March , 1905.

My Com. Exp. Aug 19-1908   Tupper Dunn
                                                Notary Public.

AFFIDAVIT OF ATTENDING PHYSICIAN OR MID-WIFE.

UNITED STATES OF AMERICA, Indian Territory, ⎫
    Western   DISTRICT. ⎭

    I, Silwar , a midwife , on oath state that I attended on Mrs. Amey Mikey (nee) Harjo , wife of Chof o lup Harjo on the 3 day of May , 1903 ; that there was born to her on said date a male child; that said child was living March 4, 1905, and is said to have been named Una see Harjo   her
                                                  Silwar x
Witnesses To Mark: mark
{ HG Malot
  Tupper Dunn

Applications for Enrollment of Creek Newborn
Act of 1905   Volume VII

Subscribed and sworn to before me this 29 day of March, 1905.

My Com. Exp. Aug 19-1908   Tupper Dunn
                                                                Notary Public.

BIRTH AFFIDAVIT.

DEPARTMENT OF THE INTERIOR.
COMMISSION TO THE FIVE CIVILIZED TRIBES.

IN RE APPLICATION FOR ENROLLMENT, as a citizen of the Creek Nation, of Fanny Harjo, born on the 29 day of January, 1905

Name of Father: Chof o lup Harjo   a citizen of the   Creek   Nation.
Name of Mother: Amey Mikey (nee) Harjo   a citizen of the   Creek   Nation.

Postoffice   Morse Ind Ter.

AFFIDAVIT OF MOTHER.

UNITED STATES OF AMERICA, Indian Territory, }
    Western   DISTRICT.

I, Amey Mikey (nee) Harjo, on oath state that I am 29 years of age and a citizen by blood, of the Creek Nation; that I am the lawful wife of Chof o lup Harjo, who is a citizen, by blood of the Creek Nation; that a female child was born to me on 29 day of January, 1905, that said child has been named Fanny Harjo, and was living March 4, 1905.

                                                Amy Mikey nee) Harjo
Witnesses To Mark:
{ HG Malot
{ Tupper Dunn

Subscribed and sworn to before me this 29 day of March, 1905.

My Com. Exp. Aug 19-1908   Tupper Dunn
                                                                Notary Public.

AFFIDAVIT OF ATTENDING PHYSICIAN OR MID-WIFE.

UNITED STATES OF AMERICA, Indian Territory, }
    Western   DISTRICT.

I, Silwar, a midwife, on oath state that I attended on Mrs. Amey Mikey nee, Harjo, wife of Chof o lup Harjo on the 29 day of January, 1905; that there was born

Applications for Enrollment of Creek Newborn
Act of 1905   Volume VII

to her on said date a female child; that said child was living March 4, 1905, and is said to have been named Fanny Harjo

                                                                         her
                                                                    Silwar x

Witnesses To Mark: mark
  { HG Malot
    Tupper Dunn

Subscribed and sworn to before me this 29 day of March, 1905.

My Com. Exp. Aug 19-1908   Tupper Dunn
                                                                      Notary Public.

BIRTH AFFIDAVIT.

DEPARTMENT OF THE INTERIOR.
COMMISSION TO THE FIVE CIVILIZED TRIBES.

IN RE APPLICATION FOR ENROLLMENT, as a citizen of the Creek Nation, of Amos Harjo, born on the 23 day of December, 1901

Name of Father: Chof o lup Harjo   a citizen of the   Creek   Nation.
Name of Mother: Amey Mikey (nee) Harjo   a citizen of the   Creek   Nation.

                                      Postoffice   Morse Ind. Ter.

AFFIDAVIT OF MOTHER.

UNITED STATES OF AMERICA, Indian Territory,}
    Western   **DISTRICT.**

    I, Amey Mikey (nee) Harjo, on oath state that I am 29 years of age and a citizen by blood, of the Creek Nation; that I am the lawful wife of Chof o lup Harjo, who is a citizen, by blood of the Creek Nation; that a male child was born to me on 23 day of December, 1901, that said child has been named Amos Harjo, and was living March 4, 1905.

                                                     Amy Mikey nee, Harjo

Witnesses To Mark:
  { HG Malot
    Tupper Dunn

    Subscribed and sworn to before me this 29 day of March, 1905.

My Com. Exp. Aug 19-1908   Tupper Dunn
                                                                      Notary Public.

Applications for Enrollment of Creek Newborn
Act of 1905   Volume VII

AFFIDAVIT OF ATTENDING PHYSICIAN OR MID-WIFE.

UNITED STATES OF AMERICA, Indian Territcry, }
    Western   DISTRICT.

I, Silwar , a midwife , on oath state that I attended on Mrs. Amey Mikey (nee) Harjo , wife of Chof o lup Harjo on the 23 day of December , 1901 ; that there was born to her on said date a male child; that said child was living March 4, 1905, and is said to have been named Amos Harjo   her

                                  Silwar x

Witnesses To Mark: mark
  { HG Malot
    Tupper Dunn

Subscribed and sworn to before me this 29 day of March , 1905.

My Com. Exp. Aug 19-1908   Tupper Dunn
                                      Notary Public.

BIRTH AFFIDAVIT.
DEPARTMENT OF THE INTERIOR.
COMMISSION TO THE FIVE CIVILIZED TRIBES.

IN RE APPLICATION FOR ENROLLMENT, as a citizen of the Creek Nation, of Dana Harjo , born on the 29 day of Jan , 1905 and died Feb. 6, 1905.

Name of Father: Chofolup Harjo   a citizen of the   Creek   Nation.
Nuyaka Town
Name of Mother: Emey[sic] Harjo   a citizen of the   Creek   Nation.
Nuyaka Town
                              Postoffice   Morse Ind. Ter.

AFFIDAVIT OF MOTHER.

UNITED STATES OF AMERICA, Indian Territery, }
    Western   DISTRICT.

I, Chofalop Harjo , on oath state that I am 49 years of age and a citizen by blood, of the Creek Nation; that I am the lawful ~~wife~~ husband of Emey Harjo , who is a citizen, by blood of the Creek Nation; that a female child was born to ~~me~~ her on 29 day of January , 1905 , that said child has been named Dana Harjo , and ~~was living March 4, 1905~~. died Feb. 6, 1905   his
                                  Chofalup x Harjo
                                      mark

Applications for Enrollment of Creek Newborn
Act of 1905 Volume VII

Witnesses To Mark:
{ Alex Posey
{ DC Skaggs
Subscribed and sworn to before me this 11 day of April, 1905.

          Drennan C Skaggs
          Notary Public.

NC 571   JLD
     DEPARTMENT OF THE INTERIOR,
  COMMISSIONER TO THE FIVE CIVILIZED TRIBES.
       . . . .

  In the matter of the application for the enrollment of Dana Harjo, deceased, as a citizen by blood of the Creek Nation.
       . . . .

      STATEMENT AND ORDER.

  The record in this case shows that on April 13, 1905, application was made, in affidavit form, for the enrollment of Dana Harjo, deceased, as a citizen by blood of the Creek Nation, under the provisions of the act of Congress approved March 3, 1905.
  It appears from the affidavit filed in this matter that said Dana Harjo, deceased, was born January 29, 1905, and died February 6, 1905.
  The Act of Congress approved March 3, 1905, (33 Stats., 1048), provides:
"That the Commission to the Five Civilized Tribes is authorized for sixty days after the date of the approval of this act to receive and consider applications for enrollment, of children, <u>born subsequent to May twenty-fifth, nineteen hundred and one, and prior to March fourth, nineteen hundred and five, and living on said latter date,</u> to citizens of the Creek tribe of Indians whose enrollment has been approved by the Secretary of the Interior prior to the approval of this act; and to enroll and make allotments to such children."
  It is, therefore, ordered that the application for the enrollment of , deceased, as a citizen by blood of the Creek Nation be, and the same is, hereby dismissed.

         Tams Bixby Commissioner.
Muskogee, Indian Territory.
 JAN 4 – 1907

Applications for Enrollment of Creek Newborn
Act of 1905 Volume VII

HGH

REFER IN REPLY TO THE FOLLOWING:
NC-572.

DEPARTMENT OF THE INTERIOR,
COMMISSIONER TO THE FIVE CIVILIZED TRIBES.

Muskogee, Indian Territory, August 10, 1905.

Samego Caesar,
    Holdenville, Indian Territory.

Dear Sir:

    In the matter of the application for the enrollment of your minor children Hannah and Moser Caesar as citizens by blood of the Creek Nation it will be necessary for you to supply this office with the affidavits of yourself and wife as to the birth of said children and blanks for that purpose, which have been filled out, are inclosed herewith.

    It will also be necessary for you to furnish this office with the affidavits of two disinterested persons as to the birth of said children. Said affidavits must set forth the names of said children, the names of their parents, the dates of their birth, and whether or not they were on living March 4, 1905.

    In having these affidavits executed be careful to see that the notary public, before whom the affidavits are executed, attaches his name and seal to each affidavit. In case any signature is by mark it must be attested by two disinterested witnesses.

                    Respectfully,

                                    Wm. O. Beall,
                                    Acting Commissioner.

CTD-40
Env.

W. P. Langston
Attorney at Law

HOLDENVILLE, IND. TER.

United States of America   (
)
Western District   )
                                                  (
Indian Territory   )

    Personall[sic] appeared before me a Notary Public in and for western district Lewis Curtain   a Creek Citizen and upon oath state that they he are is acquainted with Rachael Caesar and know that a male child was born on the 10th day of June 1901, and a

Applications for Enrollment of Creek Newborn
Act of 1905   Volume VII

Female Child was born to her on the 12th day of August 1903, and both are now liveing[sic].
Their Fathers[sic] name is Samego Caesar, and their Mother is Rachael Caesar.

Lewis Curtain

Sworn and subscribed to before me this the 14th day of August 1905.

Chas Rider
Notary Public.

My Commission Expires July 11th, 1906.

W. P. Langston
Attorney at Law

HOLDENVILLE, IND. TER.

United States of America (
Western District   )
                           (
Indian Territory   )

     Personall[sic] appeared before me a Notary Public in and for western district Burnie McCosar   a Creek Citizen and upon oath state that ~~they~~ he ~~are~~ is acquainted with Rachael Caesar and know that a male child was born on the 10th day of June 1901, and a Female Child was born to her on the 12th day of August 1903, and both are now liveing[sic].
Their Fathers[sic] name is Samego Caesar, and their Mother is Rachael Caesar.

Burnie McCosar

Sworn and subscribed to before me this the 14th day of August 1905.

Chas Rider
Notary Public.

My Commission Expires July 11th, 1906.

Applications for Enrollment of Creek Newborn
Act of 1905   Volume VII

BIRTH AFFIDAVIT.

DEPARTMENT OF THE INTERIOR.
COMMISSION TO THE FIVE CIVILIZED TRIBES.

IN RE APPLICATION FOR ENROLLMENT, as a citizen of the Creek Nation, of Hannah Caesar, born on the 12 day of August, 1903

Name of Father: Samcho[sic] Caesar   a citizen of the   Creek   Nation.
Tulsa Little River
Name of Mother: Rachael Caesar (nee Willmott) a citizen of the   Creek   Nation.
Tulsa Little River

                         Postoffice   Holdenville, Ind. Ter.

AFFIDAVIT OF MOTHER.

UNITED STATES OF AMERICA, Indian Territory,
   Western   DISTRICT.   Child is present

I, Rachael Caesar, on oath state that I am about 26 years of age and a citizen by blood, of the Creek Nation; that I am the lawful wife of Samcho Caesar, who is a citizen, by blood of the Creek Nation; that a female child was born to me on 12 day of August, 1903, that said child has been named Hannah Caesar, and was living March 4, 1905. That no one attended on me as midwife or physician at the birth of the child.

                                      her
                             Racheal[sic] x Caesar
Witnesses To Mark: mark
  { Alex Posey
    DC Skaggs

Subscribed and sworn to before me this   27 day of March, 1905.

                              Drennan C Skaggs
                              Notary Public.

BIRTH AFFIDAVIT.

DEPARTMENT OF THE INTERIOR.
COMMISSION TO THE FIVE CIVILIZED TRIBES.

IN RE APPLICATION FOR ENROLLMENT, as a citizen of the Creek Nation, of Hannah Caesar, born on the 12th day of August, 1903

Name of Father: Samego Caesar   a citizen of the   Creek   Nation.
Name of Mother: Rachael Caesar   a citizen of the   Creek   Nation.

                        Postoffice   Holdenville, I.T.

Applications for Enrollment of Creek Newborn
Act of 1905   Volume VII

AFFIDAVIT OF MOTHER.

UNITED STATES OF AMERICA, Indian Territory, }
   Western   DISTRICT.

   I, Rachael Caesar , on oath state that I am about 26 years of age and a citizen by blood , of the Creek Nation; that I am the lawful wife of Samego Caesar , who is a citizen, by blood of the Creek Nation; that a female child was born to me on 12th day of August , 1903 , that said child has been named Hannah Caesar , and was living March 4, 1905.

                                                                         her

                                         Rachael Caesar x
Witnesses To Mark: mark
{ C M Allen
{ Chas Rider

   Subscribed and sworn to before me this 14th day of August , 1905.

                                         Chas Rider
                                         Notary Public.

AFFIDAVIT OF ~~ATTENDING PHYSICIAN OR MID-WIFE~~. Father

UNITED STATES OF AMERICA, Indian Territory, }
   Western   DISTRICT.

   I, Samego Caesar , ~~a (blank)~~ , on oath state that I attended on Mrs. Rachael Caesar , wife of myself on the 12th day of August , 1903 ; that there was born to her on said date a female child; that said child was living March 4, 1905, and is said to have been named Hannah Caesar

                                         Somyo Caser[sic]
Witnesses To Mark:
{ C M Allen
{ Chas Rider

   Subscribed and sworn to before me this 14th day of August , 1905.

                                         Chas Rider
                                         Notary Public.

Applications for Enrollment of Creek Newborn
Act of 1905 Volume VII

BIRTH AFFIDAVIT.

DEPARTMENT OF THE INTERIOR.
COMMISSION TO THE FIVE CIVILIZED TRIBES.

IN RE APPLICATION FOR ENROLLMENT, as a citizen of the Creek Nation, of Moser Caesar, born on the 10 day of June , 1901

Name of Father: Samcho Caesar   a citizen of the   Creek   Nation.
Tulsa Little River Town
Name of Mother: Rachael Caesar   a citizen of the   Creek   Nation.
Tulsa Little River Town

Postoffice   Holdenville, Ind. Ter.

Father
AFFIDAVIT OF MOTHER.

UNITED STATES OF AMERICA, Indian Territory,
Western   DISTRICT.

I, Samcho Caesar , on oath state that I am about 30 years of age and a citizen by blood , of the Creek Nation; that I am the lawful wife husband of Rachael Caesar , who is a citizen, by blood of the Creek Nation; that a male child was born to me her on 10 day of June , 1901 , that said child has been named Moser Caesar , and was living March 4, 1905.

Samyo Caser[sic]

Witnesses To Mark:

Subscribed and sworn to before me this 27 day of March, 1905.

Drennan C Skaggs
Notary Public.

BIRTH AFFIDAVIT.

DEPARTMENT OF THE INTERIOR.
COMMISSION TO THE FIVE CIVILIZED TRIBES.

IN RE APPLICATION FOR ENROLLMENT, as a citizen of the Creek Nation, of Moser Caesar , born on the 10th day of June , 1901

Name of Father: Samego Caesar   a citizen of the   Creek   Nation.
Name of Mother: Rachael Caesar   a citizen of the   Creek   Nation.

Postoffice   Holdenville, I.T.

Applications for Enrollment of Creek Newborn
Act of 1905   Volume VII

AFFIDAVIT OF MOTHER.

UNITED STATES OF AMERICA, Indian Territory,
Western   DISTRICT.

I, Rachael Caesar , on oath state that I am about 26 years of age and a citizen by blood , of the Creek Nation; that I am the lawful wife of Samego Caesar , who is a citizen, by blood of the Creek Nation; that a male child was born to me on 10th day of June , 1901 , that said child has been named Moser Caesar , and was living March 4, 1905.

                 her
             Rachael Caesar x
Witnesses To Mark: mark
{ C M Allen
 Chas Rider

Subscribed and sworn to before me this 14th day of August , 1905.

           Chas Rider
            Notary Public.

AFFIDAVIT OF ~~ATTENDING PHYSICIAN OR MID-WIFE~~. Father

UNITED STATES OF AMERICA, Indian Territory,
Western   DISTRICT.

I, Samego Caesar , ~~a~~ *(blank)* , on oath state that I attended on Mrs. Rachael Caesar , ~~wife of~~ my wife on the 10th day of June , 1901 ; that there was born to her on said date a male child; that said child was living March 4, 1905, and is said to have been named Moser Caesar

           Somyo Caser[sic]
Witnesses To Mark:
{ C M Allen
 Chas Rider

Subscribed and sworn to before me this 14th day of August , 1905.

           Chas Rider
            Notary Public.

Applications for Enrollment of Creek Newborn
Act of 1905   Volume VII

BIRTH AFFIDAVIT.

DEPARTMENT OF THE INTERIOR.
COMMISSION TO THE FIVE CIVILIZED TRIBES.

IN RE APPLICATION FOR ENROLLMENT, as a citizen of the Creek Nation, of Hulley Barnett, born on the 15 day of November, 1902

Name of Father: Daniel Barnett   a citizen of the   Creek   Nation.
Name of Mother: Lindy Harjo (nee) Barnett   a citizen of the   Creek   Nation.

Postoffice   Weleetka Ind Ter

AFFIDAVIT OF MOTHER.

UNITED STATES OF AMERICA, Indian Territory,
    Western   DISTRICT.

I, Lindy Harjo(nee) Barnett, on oath state that I am 27 years of age and a citizen by blood, of the Creek Nation; that I am the lawful wife of Daniel Barnett, who is a citizen, by blood of the Creek Nation; that a male child was born to me on 15 day of November, 1902, that said child has been named Hulley Barnett, and was living March 4, 1905.

                                    her
                         Lindy x Harjo(nee) Barnett
Witnesses To Mark: mark
   { HG Malot
   { Tupper Dunn

Subscribed and sworn to before me this 24 day of March, 1905.

My Com. Exp. Aug 19-1908   Tupper Dunn
                                       Notary Public.

AFFIDAVIT OF ATTENDING PHYSICIAN OR MID-WIFE.

UNITED STATES OF AMERICA, Indian Territory,
    Western   DISTRICT.

I, Sarfarts cha, a midwife, on oath state that I attended on Mrs. Lindy Harjo(nee) Barnett, wife of Daniel Barnett on the 15 day of November, 1902; that there was born to her on said date a male child; that said child was living March 4, 1905, and is said to have been named Hulley Barnett

                                    her
                           Sarfarts cha x
                                 mark

Applications for Enrollment of Creek Newborn
Act of 1905   Volume VII

Witnesses To Mark:
{ HG Malot
{ Tupper Dunn

Subscribed and sworn to before me this 24 day of March, 1905.

My Com. Exp. Aug 19-1908			Tupper Dunn
						Notary Public.

DEPARTMENT OF THE INTERIOR,
COMMISSION TO THE FIVE CIVILIZED TRIBES.
Holdenville, I. T., March 27, 1905.

In the matter of the application for the enrollment of Emma and Nina Tiger as citizens by blood of the Creek Nation.

Kizzie Tiger, being duly sworn, testified as follows:

Through Alex Posey Official Interpreter:

BY COMMISSION:
Q What is your name? A Kizzie Tiger.
Q How old are you? A About twenty-four.
Q What is your post office address? A Spaulding.
Q Are you a citizen of the Creek nation? A Yes, sir.
Q To what town do you belong? A Little River Tulsa.
Q Do you make application for the enrollment of your children, Emma and Nina Tiger as citizens of the Creek Nation? A Yes, sir.
Q Who is the father of these children? A Ponoska Tiger.
Q Is he a citizen of the Creek Nation? A He is a Seminole.
Q If it should be found that these two children are entitled to be enrolled in either the Creek or Seminole Nations in which nation do you desire to have them enrolled? A In the Creek Nation. in either the Creek or Seminole nations in which nation do you desire to have them enrolled? A In the Creek Nation.

---oooOOOooo---oooOOOooo---

I, D. C. Skaggs, on oath state that the above and foregoing is a full and true transcript of my stenographic notes as taken in said cause on said date.

DC Skaggs

Applications for Enrollment of Creek Newborn
Act of 1905 Volume VII

Subscribed and sworn to before me this 18" day of July, 1905.

> Edw C Griesel
> Notary Public.

N.C. 574

DEPARTMENT OF THE INTERIOR,
COMMISSIONER TO THE FIVE CIVILIZED TRIBES.
Muskogee, Indian Territory, March 2, 1906.

In the matter of the application for the enrollment of Nina Tiger as a citizen by blood of the Creek Nation.

KIZZIE TIGER, being duly sworn, testified as follows through Jesse McDermott official interpreter.

Q What is your name? A Kizzie Tiger.
Q What is your age? A I am not positive but think I am about 24.
Q What is your post office address? A Spaulding.
Q Have you a child named Nina or Nine Tiger? A Yes one named Nina.
Q We have two affidavits executed by you in one you say Nina and in one Nine which is correct? A Nina is correct.
Q Are Nina and Emma Tiger both living? A Yes, sir.
Q What is the name of the father of Nina? A Panosky Tiger.
Q He is not a Creek is he? A No, sir, Seminole.

PANOSKY TIGER, being duly sworn, testified as follows:

Q What is your name? A Panosky Tiger.
Q What is your age? A I am about thirty.
Q What is your post office address? A Spaulding.
Q Have you two children named Nina and Emma Tiger? A Yes
Q If it should be found that these children are entitled to rights in either the Creek or Seminole nation in which nation do you want them enrolled? A I have already filed for one in the Creek Nation and I desire the other one enrolled in the same.

I, Anna Garrigues, on oath state that the above and foregoing is a true and correct copy of my stenographic notes taken in said case on said date.

> Anna Garrigues

Subscribed and sworn to before me
this 8 day of March 1906.

> J McDermott
> Notary Public.

Applications for Enrollment of Creek Newborn
Act of 1905 Volume VII

BIRTH AFFIDAVIT.

DEPARTMENT OF THE INTERIOR.
COMMISSION TO THE FIVE CIVILIZED TRIBES.

IN RE APPLICATION FOR ENROLLMENT, as a citizen of the Creek Nation, of Nina Tiger, born on the 23rd day of January, 1902

Name of Father: Panoska Tiger   a citizen of the Siminole[sic] Nation.
Name of Mother: Kizzie Tiger   a citizen of the Creek Nation.

           Postoffice   Spalding[sic], I.T.

AFFIDAVIT OF MOTHER.

UNITED STATES OF AMERICA, Indian Territory, }
    Western Judicial   DISTRICT.

    I, Kizzie Tiger, on oath state that I am 24 years of age and a citizen by birth, of the Creek Nation[sic] Nation; that I am the lawful wife of Panoska Tiger, who is a citizen, by Birth of the Siminole[sic] Nation; that a Male child was born to me on Twenty Third day of January, 1902, that said child has been named Nine[sic] Tiger, and is now living. and i[sic] further state that i[sic] was all alone when the child was born.   her

                                   Kizzie Tiger x
Witnesses To Mark: mark
{ Thos Sewell
{ S.P. Jennings

    Subscribed and sworn to before me this Eleventh day of September, 1905.

                               Chas Rider
                               Notary Public.

               Supplemental testimony taken

BIRTH AFFIDAVIT.

DEPARTMENT OF THE INTERIOR.
COMMISSION TO THE FIVE CIVILIZED TRIBES.

IN RE APPLICATION FOR ENROLLMENT, as a citizen of the Creek Nation, of Nina Tiger, born on the 23 day of January, 1902

Name of Father: Panosky Tiger   a citizen of the Seminole Nation.
Name of Mother: Kizzie Tiger (nee Birdhead)   a citizen of the Creek Nation.
Tulsa Little River Town

Applications for Enrollment of Creek Newborn
Act of 1905   Volume VII

Postoffice   Spaulding, Ind. Ter.

AFFIDAVIT OF MOTHER.

UNITED STATES OF AMERICA, Indian Territory, }
Western   DISTRICT. }

I, Kizzie Tiger, on oath state that I am about 24 years of age and a citizen by blood, of the Creek Nation; that I am the lawful wife of Panosky Tiger, who is a citizen, by blood of the Semincle Nation; that a male child was born to me on 23 day of January, 1902, that said child has been named Nine[sic] Tiger, and is now living. That no one attended on me as midwife or physician at the birth of the child.

                                                                     her
                                          Kizzie Tiger x
Witnesses To Mark: mark
  { Alex Posey
    DC Skaggs

Subscribed and sworn to before me this 27 day of March, 1905.

                                        Drennan C Skaggs
                                              Notary Public.
                       The child is not present

United States of America   )
)
Indian Territory   ) ss
)
Western Judicial District)

Ottay[sic] Cain being duly sworn on oath, deposes and says that I am a citizen of the Creek Nation by Birth and 44 years of age, that I am well acquainted with Kizzie Tiger and know of my personal knowledge that their[sic] was born to her a male child on the 23 day of January 1902. and is now liveing[sic]. and that on the 23rd day of February 1903 their[sic] was born to this Kizzie Tiger a female child and said child is now liveing[sic], the male child being named Nina Tiger and the Female Child was named Emma Tiger.
The father of these children is Panoska Tiger, Kizzie Tiger is a member of Tulsie band of Creeks.
I further state that I have no interest in this clame[sic], and make this statement as a disinterested party.

Witness to mark.   his
Thos Sewell   Ottaway Cain x Town Chief
S.P. Jennings   mark

Applications for Enrollment of Creek Newborn
Act of 1905 Volume VII

Subscribed and sworn to before me this 11th day of September 1905.

Chas Rider
Notary Public.

My Commission expires July 11th, 1906

BIRTH AFFIDAVIT.

DEPARTMENT OF THE INTERIOR.
COMMISSION TO THE FIVE CIVILIZED TRIBES.

IN RE APPLICATION FOR ENROLLMENT, as a citizen of the Creek Nation, of Emma Tiger, born on the 23 day of February, 1903

Name of Father: Panoska Tiger	a citizen of the Sininole[sic] Nation.
Name of Mother: Kizzie Tiger	a citizen of the Creek Nation.

Postoffice   Spalding[sic], I.T.

AFFIDAVIT OF MOTHER.

UNITED STATES OF AMERICA, Indian Territory,
Western Judicial   DISTRICT.

I, Kizzie Tiger, on oath state that I am 24 years of age and a citizen by Birth, of the Creek Nation; that I am the lawful wife of Panoska Tiger, who is a citizen, by Birth of the Siminole[sic] Nation; that a female child was born to me on Twenty Third day of February, 1903, that said child has been named Emma Tiger, and is now living. and i[sic] further state that i[sic] was all alone when Emma Tiger was born.

her
Kizzie Tiger x
mark

Witnesses To Mark:
 { Thos Sewell
 { S.P. Jennings

Subscribed and sworn to before me this Eleventh day of September, 1905.

Chas Rider
Notary Public.

Applications for Enrollment of Creek Newborn
Act of 1905 Volume VII

BIRTH AFFIDAVIT.

Supplemental testimony taken

DEPARTMENT OF THE INTERIOR.
COMMISSION TO THE FIVE CIVILIZED TRIBES.

IN RE APPLICATION FOR ENROLLMENT, as a citizen of the Creek Nation, of Emma Tiger, born on the 23 day of February, 1903

Name of Father: Panosky Tiger   a citizen of the Seminole Nation.
Name of Mother: Kizzie Tiger (nee Birdhead)   a citizen of the Creek Nation.
Tulsa Little River Town

         Postoffice   Spaulding, Ind. Ter.

AFFIDAVIT OF MOTHER.

UNITED STATES OF AMERICA, Indian Territory, }
    Western   DISTRICT.

Child is present

     I, Kizzie Tiger, on oath state that I am about 24 years of age and a citizen by blood, of the Creek Nation; that I am the lawful wife of Panosky Tiger, who is a citizen, by blood of the Seminole Nation; that a female child was born to me on 23 day of February, 1903, that said child has been named Emma Tiger, and is now living. That no one attended on me as midwife or physician at the birth of this child.

                                           her
                              Kizzie x Tiger
Witnesses To Mark: mark
  { Alex Posey
    DC Skaggs

     Subscribed and sworn to before me this 27 day of March, 1905.

                         Drennan C Skaggs
                             Notary Public.

United States of America   )
)
Indian Territory   ) ss
)
Western Judicial District   )

     Thos Sewell being duly sworn on oath, deposes and says that I am a citizen of the Creek Nation by Birth and 33 years of age, that I am well acquainted with Kizzie Tiger and know of my personal knowledge that their[sic] was born to her a male child on the 23 day of January 1902. and is now liveing[sic]. and that on the 23rd day of

Applications for Enrollment of Creek Newborn
Act of 1905   Volume VII

February 1903 their[sic] was born to this Kizzie Tiger a female child and said child is now liveing[sic], the male child being named Nina Tiger and the Female Child was named Emma Tiger.
The father of these children is Panoska Tiger, Kizzie Tiger is a member of Tulsie band of Creeks.
I further state that I have no interest in this clame[sic], and make this statement as a disinterested party.

Witness to mark.
_____
                                              Thos Sewell
_____

Subscribed and sworn to before me this 11th day of September 1905.

                                              Chas Rider
                                              Notary Public.
My Commission expires July 11th, 1906

_____

NC 574.

                    Muskogee, Indian Territory, July 14, 1905.

Commissioner to the Five Civilized Tribes,
    Seminole Enrollment Division,
        Muskogee, Indian Territory.

Gentlemen:

   March 30, 1905, application was made to the Commission to the Five Civilized Tribes for the enrollment of Nina Tiger, born January 23, 1902, and Emma Tiger, born February 23, 1903, as citizens by blood of the Creek Nation. It is stated in said application that the father of said child is Panosky, a citizen of the Seminole Nation, and that the mother is Kizzie Tiger, a citizen of the Creek Nation.

   You are requested to inform the Creek Enrollment Division as to whether application has been made for the enrollment of said children as citizens of the Seminole Nation, and if so, what disposition has been made of the same.

                          Respectfully,

                                              Commissioner.

_____

(The above affidavit of Thos Sewell given again.)

_____

Applications for Enrollment of Creek Newborn
Act of 1905   Volume VII

(The above affidavit of Ottay Cain given again.)

DEPARTMENT OF THE INTERIOR.
COMMISSION TO THE FIVE CIVILIZED TRIBES.

Muskogee, Indian Territory, July 18, 1905.

Chief Clerk,
    Creek Enrollment Division.

Dear Sir:

    Receipt is acknowledged of your letter of July 14, 1905 (NC-574) stating that application was made to the Commission to the Five Civilized Tribes for the enrollment of Nina Tiger, born January 23, 1902, and Emma Tiger, born February 23, 1903, children of Panosky, a citizen of the Seminole Nation, and Kizzie Tiger, a citizen of the Creek nation, as citizens by blood of the Creek Nation and requesting to be advised as to whether application has been made for the enrollment of said children as citizens of the Seminole Nation.

    In reply to your letter you are advised that it does not appear from an examination of the records of this office that any application was made to the Commission to the Five Civilized Tribes for the enrollment of said Nina Tiger and Emma Tiger as citizens of the Seminole Nation.

Respectfully,

Tams Bixby   Commissioner.

NC-574.

Muskogee, Indian Territory, August 10, 1905.

Kizzie Tiger,
    Spaulding, Indian Territory.

Dear Madam:

    In the matter of the application for the enrollment of your minor children Nina Tiger, born January 23, 1902, and Emma Tiger, born February 23, 1903, as citizens by blood of the Creek Nation, it will be necessary for you to furnish this office the affidavits of two disinterested persons as to the birth of said children. Said affidavits must set forth

Applications for Enrollment of Creek Newborn
Act of 1905 Volume VII

the names of said children, the dates of their birth, the names of their parents and whether or not they were living on March 4, 1905.

Please give this matter your prompt attention.

Respectfully,

Acting Commissioner.

NC-574.

Muskogee, Indian Territory, October 17, 1906.

Kizzie Tiger,
Spaulding, Indian Territory.

Dear Madam:

In the matter of the application for the enrollment of your minor child born January 23, 1902 it appears in your affidavit of March 27, 1905 that the name of said child is Nina Tiger while in your affidavit of September 11, 1905 you state that said child is named Nine Tiger.

You are requested to advise this office as to which of the above names, if either of them is the correct name of said child.

This matter should receive your prompt attention.

Respectfully,

Commissioner.

REFER IN REPLY TO THE FOLLOWING:

**DEPARTMENT OF THE INTERIOR,
COMMISSIONER TO THE FIVE CIVILIZED TRIBES.**

Muskogee, Indian Territory, October 16, 1906.

Kizzie Tiger,
c/o Parnoskey[sic] Tiger,
Holdenville, Indian Territory.

Dear Madam:

Applications for Enrollment of Creek Newborn
Act of 1905   Volume VII

    Replying to your letter of October 5, 1906, you are advised that the matter of the application for the enrollment of your minor child, Nina Tiger, as a citizen of the Creek Nation, is pending before the Secretary of the Interior, and that when this office has been advised of his action in same, you will be duly notified.

                  Respectfully,

                          Tams Bixby   Commissioner.

NC 574.

                  Muskogee, Indian Territory, October 31, 1906.

Chief Clerk,
    Seminole Enrollment Division,
        Muskogee, Indian Territory.

Dear Sir:

    There is on file in this office an application for the enrollment of Emma Tiger, born February 23, 1903, and Nina Tiger, born January 23, 1902, respectively to Parnosky Tiger, a citizen of the Seminole Nation, and Kizzie Tiger, who is identified as a citizen of the Creek Nation, opposite roll number 2472.

    You are advised that the name of Emma Tiger is contained in a partial list of new born citizens by blood of the Creek Nation (enrolled under the act of Congress approved March 3rd, 1905), approved by the Secretary of the Interior November 27, 1905, opposite roll number 709, and that the name of Nina Tiger is contained in a partial list of new born citizens by blood of the Creek Nation, approved by the Secretary of the Interior October 15, 1906, opposite roll number 1053.

                  Respectfully,

                              Commissioner.

Applications for Enrollment of Creek Newborn
Act of 1905   Volume VII

BIRTH AFFIDAVIT.

DEPARTMENT OF THE INTERIOR.
COMMISSION TO THE FIVE CIVILIZED TRIBES.

IN RE APPLICATION FOR ENROLLMENT, as a citizen of the Creek Nation, of Frank Tar yo ley , born on the 25 day of November , 1902

Name of Father: Tar yo ley   a citizen of the   Creek   Nation.
Name of Mother: Marphy Mikey (nee) Taryoley a citizen of the   Creek   Nation.

                             Postoffice   Morse Ind Ter

AFFIDAVIT OF MOTHER.

UNITED STATES OF AMERICA, Indian Territory,
     Western   DISTRICT.

     I, Marphy Mikey (nee) Taryoley , on oath state that I am 27 years of age and a citizen by blood , of the Creek Nation; that I am the lawful wife of Tar to ley , who is a citizen, by blood of the Creek Nation; that a male child was born to me on 25 day of November , 1902 , that said child has been named Frank Tar yo-ley , and was living March 4, 1905.   her

                                Marphy x Mikey (nee) Taryoley
Witnesses To Mark: mark
    { Taryoley
    { Tupper Dunn

     Subscribed and sworn to before me this 29 day of March , 1905.

My Com. Exp Aug 19-1908   Tupper Dunn
                                        Notary Public.

AFFIDAVIT OF ATTENDING PHYSICIAN OR MID-WIFE.

UNITED STATES OF AMERICA, Indian Territory,
     Western   DISTRICT.

     I, Silwar , a midwife , on oath state that I attended on Mrs. Marphy Maggie Taryoley , wife of Tar yo-ley on the 25 day of November , 1902 ; that there was born to her on said date a male child; that said child was living March 4, 1905, and is said to have been named Frank Taryo-ley   her
                                   Silwar x
Witnesses To Mark: mark
    { Taryoley
    { Tupper Dunn

Applications for Enrollment of Creek Newborn
Act of 1905   Volume VII

Subscribed and sworn to before me this 29 day of March , 1905.

My Com. Exp Aug 19-1908   Tupper Dunn
                                  Notary Public.

BIRTH AFFIDAVIT.

DEPARTMENT OF THE INTERIOR.
COMMISSION TO THE FIVE CIVILIZED TRIBES.

IN RE APPLICATION FOR ENROLLMENT, as a citizen of the Creek Nation, of Louina Tayola, born on the 31 day of Oct , 1901

Name of Father: Prince Tayola   a citizen of the   Creek   Nation. Nuyaka Town
Name of Mother: Martha Tayola (nee Mikey)   a citizen of the   Creek   Nation. Nuyaka Town
                           Postoffice   Morse IT

AFFIDAVIT OF MOTHER.

UNITED STATES OF AMERICA, Indian Territory,
     Western   DISTRICT.

I, Prince Tayola , on oath state that I am 27 years of age and a citizen by blood, of the Creek Nation; that I am the lawful ~~wife~~ husband of Martha Tayola , who is a citizen, by blood of the Creek Nation; that a female child was born to me on 31st day of Oct , 1901 , that said child has been named Louina Tayola , and ~~was living March 4, 1905.~~ died Aug 11-1903

                                  Prince Tayola
Witnesses To Mark:

Subscribed and sworn to before me this 13" day of April , 1905.

     (Seal)   J McDermott
                                  Notary Public.

Applications for Enrollment of Creek Newborn
Act of 1905   Volume VII

BIRTH AFFIDAVIT.

DEPARTMENT OF THE INTERIOR.
COMMISSION TO THE FIVE CIVILIZED TRIBES.

  IN RE APPLICATION FOR ENROLLMENT, as a citizen of the Creek Nation, of Lowina Taryoley , born on the 31st day of October , 1901
belong to Nuyaka Town
Name of Father: Taryole is the right name a citizen of the Creek Nation.
Name of Mother: Marsy Mikey (By filing Name a citizen of the Creek Nation.

         Postoffice Morse, Creek Nation, I.T.

AFFIDAVIT OF MOTHER.

UNITED STATES OF AMERICA, Indian Territory,
 Western Judicial DISTRICT.

  I, Marsy Mikey , on oath state that I am 27 years of age and a citizen by Blood, of the Creek Nation; that I am the lawful wife of Taryole, (or Tripole, Taryole) , who is a citizen, by Blood of the Creek Nation; that a Female child was born to me on 31st day of October , 1901 , that said child has been named Louina Taryole is correct name , and was not living March 4, 1905.   her
          Marsy x Mikey
Witnesses To Mark: mark
 { J H Black
  L H McDermott

  Subscribed and sworn to before me this 16 day of August , 1905.

My Commission Expires Sept 6th 1906.   John H. Phillips
           Notary Public.

AFFIDAVIT OF ATTENDING PHYSICIAN OR MID-WIFE.

UNITED STATES OF AMERICA, Indian Territory,
 Western Judicial DISTRICT.

  I, Silwar Mikey , a Mid-Wife , on oath state that I attended on Mrs. Marsy Mikey , wife of Taryole on the 31st day of Oct. , 1901 ; that there was born to her on said date a Female child; that said child was not living March 4, 1905, and is said to have been named Lowine Taryole   her
         Silwar x Mikey
Witnesses To Mark: mark
 { J.H. Black
  J L McDermott

Applications for Enrollment of Creek Newborn
Act of 1905   Volume VII

Subscribed and sworn to before me this 16th day of August, 1905.

My Commission Expires Sept 6th 1906.   John H. Phillips
                                                                        Notary Public.

Department of the Interior,
COMMISSION TO THE FIVE CIVILIZED TRIBES.

In the matter of the death of   Lowine Taryoley   a citizen of the   Creek Nation, who formerly resided at or near   Morse   , Ind. Ter., and died on the 11 day of August   , 1903

AFFIDAVIT OF RELATIVE.

UNITED STATES OF AMERICA,
   INDIAN TERRITORY,
Western Judicial   District.

I, Prince Taryoly   , on oath state that I am   27   years of age and a citizen by blood   , of the   Creek   Nation; that my postoffice address is   Morse   , Ind. Ter.; that I am   Father   of   Lowiney Taryoley   who was a citizen, by blood   , of the Creek   Nation and that said   Lowine[sic] Taryoley   died on the   11 day of August, 1903

                                                                        Prinne[sic] Taryoley
Witnesses To Mark:
   L.P. Caldwell

Subscribed and sworn to before me this 22 day of April, 1905.

My Com. Exp. Aug 19" 19C8   Tupper Dunn
                                                                        Notary Public.

AFFIDAVIT OF ACQUAINTANCE.

UNITED STATES OF AMERICA,
   INDIAN TERRITORY,
Western Judicial   District.

I, Silwar   , on oath state that I am 51   years of age, and a citizen by blood   of the   Creek   Nation; that my postoffice address is   Morse   , Ind. Ter.; that I was personally acquainted with   Lowine Taryoley   who was a citizen, by blood   , of the   Creek   Nation; and that said   Lowine Taryoley   died on the   11   day of August   , 1903.

Applications for Enrollment of Creek Newborn
Act of 1905   Volume VII

Witnesses To Mark:
{ L.P. Caldwell

her
Silwar x
mark

Subscribed and sworn to before me this 22 day of April, 1905.

My Com. Exp. Aug 19- 1908   Tupper Dunn
                                           Notary Public.

Morse I.T.
May 15th 1905
Commission to the Five Tribes
Muskogee
I.T.

In regards to the birth and death of the child Lowiney Taryoley. She was born Oct 31, 1901 and died Aug. 11th 1903. And the mother of the child is on the roll of Creek citizens as Marfy Mikey.

Yours Truely[sic]

Prince Taryoley

NC 575   JLD

DEPARTMENT OF THE INTERIOR,
COMMISSIONER TO THE FIVE CIVILIZED TRIBES.

In the matter of the application for the enrollment of Louina Taryole, deceased, as a citizen by blood of the Creek Nation.
....

STATEMENT AND ORDER.

The record in this case shows that on April 19, 1905, application was made, in affidavit form, for the enrollment of Louina Taryole, deceased, as a citizen by blood of the Creek Nation, under the provisions of the act of Congress approved March 3, 1905.

It appears from the affidavit filed in this matter that said Louina Taryole, deceased, was born October 31, 1901, and died August 11, 1903.

The Act of Congress approved March 3, 1905, (33 Stats., 1048), provides:

"That the Commission to the Five Civilized Tribes is authorized for sixty days after the date of the approval of this act to receive and consider applications for enrollment, of children, <u>born subsequent to May twenty-fifth, nineteen hundred and one, and prior to March fourth, nineteen hundred and five, and living on said latter date,</u> to citizens of the Creek tribe of Indians whose enrollment has been

Applications for Enrollment of Creek Newborn
Act of 1905   Volume VII

approved by the Secretary of the Interior prior to the approval of this act; and to enroll and make allotments to such children."

It is, therefore, ordered that the application for the enrollment of said Louina Taryole, deceased, as a citizen by blood of the Creek Nation, be, and the same is, hereby dismissed.

Tams Bixby   Commissioner.

Muskogee, Indian Territory.

Muskogee, Indian Territory, August 4, 1905.

Prince Taryoley,
    Morse, Indian Territory.

Dear Sir:

April 29, 1905, you filed with this office your affidavit in which it is stated that your child Lowine Taryoley died August 11, 1903.

There is herewith enclosed a blank for proof of birth and you are requested to have the same signed and executed before a notary public; care should be taken that said notary public affixes his signature and official seal to same.

You are requested to state the names of your parents, the Creek Indian town to which you belong, and if possible, the number which appears on your deeds to land in the Creek Nation.

This matter should receive your prompt attention.

Respectfully,

Commissioner.

1 B A
1 env.

NC 575.

Muskogee, Indian Territory, January 16, 1907.

Martha Tayola,
    c/o Prince Tayola,
        Morse, Indian Territory.

Dear Madam:

Applications for Enrollment of Creek Newborn
Act of 1905   Volume VII

There is herewith enclosed one copy of the Statement and Order of the Commissioner to the Five Civilized Tribes, dated January 15, 1907, dismissing the application made by you for the enrollment of your minor child Louina Tayola, deceased, as a citizen of the Creek Nation.

Respectfully,

Commissioner.

LM-58.

N.C. 576.

DEPARTMENT OF THE INTERIOR,
COMMISSIONER TO THE FIVE CIVILIZED TRIBES.
Muskogee, Indian Territory, August 8, 1905.

In the matter of the application for the enrollment of Lewis and Eli Perryman as citizens by blood of the Creek Nation.

McPerryman, being duly sworn, testified as follows partly through Alex Posey Official Interpreter.

By Commissioner.

Q What is your name? A McPerryman.
Q That is the way you are enrolled? A Yes, sir/.[sic]
Q What was your fathers[sic] name? A Lewis Perryman.
Q What is the name of your mother? A Annie

Witness if identified on card No. 2520, roll No. 7489 as McPerryman
Q What is the name of your wife? A Sophia.
Q Did you have two children by her? A Yes, sir
Q What are their names? A Lewis and Eli.
Q Both living? A Yes, sir
Q She made an affidavit and stated that the father of those children was Alex Perryman, did she mean you? A I was always carried on the tribal rolls as McPerryman. My wife in making application for my children designated me as Alex Perryman
Q Can you state how she came to do that? A I am known by both names. When I made selection of land I gave my name in as McPerryman. I belong to Okchiye town.

The witness is advised that along with the affidavit of the mother about these children is found the affidavit of Mickey a midwife, giving the date of the birth of said child and the other is somewhat indefinite giving May or June. Witness is advised that this office requires the affidavit to give the date of the birth. It is advised that in lieu of perfect affidavit of midwife this office will require affidavits of two disinterested witnesses.

Applications for Enrollment of Creek Newborn
Act of 1905   Volume VII

Anna Garrigues on oath states that the above and foregoing is a true and correct transcript of her stenographic notes taken in said cause on said date.

Anna Garrigues

Subscribed and sworn to before me
this 9th day of August 1905.

Henry G Hains
Notary Public.

BIRTH AFFIDAVIT.

DEPARTMENT OF THE INTERIOR.
COMMISSION TO THE FIVE CIVILIZED TRIBES.

IN RE APPLICATION FOR ENROLLMENT, as a citizen of the Creek Nation, of Eli Perryman, born on the 29 day of May, 1904

Name of Father: Alex Perryman   a citizen of the   Creek   Nation. Ochiya[sic] Town
Name of Mother: Sophia Perryman (nee Sewell) a citizen of the   Creek   Nation. Tulsa Little River

Postoffice   Holdenville, Ind. Ter.

AFFIDAVIT OF MOTHER.

UNITED STATES OF AMERICA, Indian Territory, }   Child is present
    Western   DISTRICT.

I, Sophia Perryman, on oath state that I am 19 years of age and a citizen by blood, of the Creek Nation; that I am the lawful wife of Alex Perryman, who is a citizen, by blood of the Creek Nation; that a male child was born to me on 29 day of May, 1904, that said child has been named Eli Perryman, and is now living.

Sophia Perryman

Witnesses To Mark:
{

Subscribed and sworn to before me this 27 day of March, 1905.

Drennan C Skaggs
Notary Public.

Applications for Enrollment of Creek Newborn
Act of 1905 Volume VII

AFFIDAVIT OF ATTENDING PHYSICIAN OR MID-WIFE.

UNITED STATES OF AMERICA, Indian Territory,
    Western   DISTRICT.

    I, Mickey , a midwife , on oath state that I attended on Mrs. Sophia Perryman , wife of Alex Perryman ~~on the (blank) day of~~ May , 1904 ; that there was born to her on said date a male child; that said child is now living and is said to have been named Eli Perryman

                                              her
                                     Mickey x
Witnesses To Mark: mark
  { Alex Posey
    DC Skaggs

    Subscribed and sworn to before me this 27 day of March, 1905.

                                Drennan C Skaggs
                                Notary Public.

United States of America
                          (
Western District   )
                          (
Indian Territory   )

          Personally appeared before me   Burnie McCosar   a citizen of the Creek Nation and upon oath states that he is personally acquainted Alex Perryman (or McPerryman[sic]) and know that a male child was born to his wife Sophia Perryman on the 31st day of August, 1902, that said child has been named Lewis Perryman, and is now living.
I have no interest in this claim and only make this statement as a disinterested party.

                                Burnie McCosar

Sworn and subscribed to before me this the 16th day of August, 1905.

                                Chas Rider
                                Notary Public.
My Commission Expires July 11th, 1906

United States of America
                          (
Western District   )
                          (
Indian Territory   )

Applications for Enrollment of Creek Newborn
Act of 1905 Volume VII

      Personally appeared before me Ottaway[sic] Cain a citizen of the Creek Nation and upon oath states that he is personally acquainted Alex Perryman (or McPerryman[sic]) and know that a male child was born to his wife Sophia Perryman on the 31st day of August, 1902, that said child has been named Lewis Perryman, and is now living.
I have no interest in this claim and only make this statement as a disinterested party.

                                           his
                                Ottawa Cain x
                                      mark

Sworn and subscribed to before me this the 16th day of August, 1905.

                                  Chas Rider
                                  Notary Public.

My Commission Expires July 11th, 1906

Witness to mark
J.W. Todd
Burnie McCosar

BIRTH AFFIDAVIT.

DEPARTMENT OF THE INTERIOR.
COMMISSION TO THE FIVE CIVILIZED TRIBES.

      IN RE APPLICATION FOR ENROLLMENT, as a citizen of the Creek Nation, of Lewis Perryman, born on the 31 day of August, 1902

Name of Father: Alex Perryman   a citizen of the Creek Nation. Ochiya[sic] Town
Name of Mother: Sophia Perryman (nee Sewell) a citizen of the Creek Nation. Tulsa Little River

                                Postoffice   Holdenville, Ind. Ter.

AFFIDAVIT OF MOTHER.

UNITED STATES OF AMERICA, Indian Territory,   Child is present
     Western   DISTRICT.

      I, Sophia Perryman , on oath state that I am 19 years of age and a citizen by blood , of the Creek Nation; that I am the lawful wife of Alex Perryman , who is a citizen, by blood of the Creek Nation; that a male child was born to me on 31 day of August , 1902 , that said child has been named Lewis Perryman , and is now living.

                                Sophia Perryman

Applications for Enrollment of Creek Newborn
Act of 1905   Volume VII

Witnesses To Mark:

{

Subscribed and sworn to before me this 27 day of March, 1905.

Drennan C Skaggs
Notary Public.

AFFIDAVIT OF ATTENDING PHYSICIAN OR MID-WIFE.

UNITED STATES OF AMERICA, Indian Territory, ⎱
  Western   DISTRICT.   ⎰

I, Mickey, a midwife, on oath state that I attended on Mrs. Sophia Perryman, wife of Alex Perryman ~~on the (blank) day of (blank), 1~~ ; that there was born to her on said date a male child; that said child is now living and is said to have been named Lewis Perryman   her
                                                                          Mickey x
Witnesses To Mark: mark
{ Alex Posey
  DC Skaggs

Subscribed and sworn to before me this 27 day of March, 1905.

Drennan C Skaggs
Notary Public.

NC-576

Muskogee, Indian Territory, August 10, 1905

Alex Perryman (or McPerryman),
    Holdenville, Indian Territory.

Dear Sir:

In the matter of the application for the enrollment of your minor son Lewis Perryman, born August 31, 1902, as a citizen by blood of the Creek Nation it will be necessary for you to furnish this office with the affidavit of two disinterested persons as to the birth of said child. Said affidavits must set forth said child's name, the date of his birth, the names of his parents and whether or not he was living on March 4, 1905.

Respectfully,

Acting Commissioner.

Applications for Enrollment of Creek Newborn
Act of 1905 Volume VII

BIRTH AFFIDAVIT.

DEPARTMENT OF THE INTERIOR.
COMMISSION TO THE FIVE CIVILIZED TRIBES.

IN RE APPLICATION FOR ENROLLMENT, as a citizen of the Creek Nation, of Jacob Alex, born on the 30 day of September, 1901

Name of Father: Freeland Alex   a citizen of the   Creek   Nation.
Coweta Town
Name of Mother: Elizabeth Alex (nee Jacobe)   a citizen of the   Creek   Nation.
Tuckabatche Town
                     Postoffice   Wewoka, Ind. Ter.

AFFIDAVIT OF MOTHER.

UNITED STATES OF AMERICA, Indian Territory, }   Child is <u>present</u>
    Western   DISTRICT.

     I, Elizabeth Alex, on oath state that I am 33 years of age and a citizen by blood, of the Creek Nation; that I am the lawful wife of Freeland Alex, who is a citizen, by blood of the Creek Nation; that a male child was born to me on 30 day of September, 1901, that said child has been named Jacob Alex, and was living March 4, 1905.

                                     Elizabeth Alex

Witnesses To Mark:
{

     Subscribed and sworn to before me this 27 day of March, 1905.

                                     Drennan C Skaggs
                                         Notary Public.

AFFIDAVIT OF ATTENDING PHYSICIAN OR MID-WIFE.

UNITED STATES OF AMERICA, Indian Territory, }
    Western   DISTRICT.

     I, C. P. Linn, a physician, on oath state that I attended on Mrs. Elizabeth Alex, wife of Freeland Alex on the 30 day of September, 1901; that there was born to her on said date a male child; that said child was living March 4, 1905, and is said to have been named Jacob Alex

                                     C.P. Linn

Applications for Enrollment of Creek Newborn
Act of 1905   Volume VII

Witnesses To Mark:
{

Subscribed and sworn to before me this 27 day of March, 1905.

                Drennan C Skaggs
                Notary Public.

BIRTH AFFIDAVIT.

DEPARTMENT OF THE INTERIOR.
COMMISSION TO THE FIVE CIVILIZED TRIBES.

IN RE APPLICATION FOR ENROLLMENT, as a citizen of the Creek Nation, of Flora McNevins, born on the 11 day of May, 1902

Name of Father: Lee McNevins   a citizen of the   Creek   Nation.
Tuckabatche Town
Name of Mother: Nancy McNevins   a citizen of the   Creek   Nation.
Tuckabatche Town
                Postoffice   Yeager, I.T.

AFFIDAVIT OF MOTHER.

UNITED STATES OF AMERICA, Indian Territory, }
    Western   DISTRICT.

I, Nancy McNevins, on oath state that I am 28 years of age and a citizen by blood, of the Creek Nation; that I am the lawful wife of Lee McNevins, who is a citizen, by blood of the Creek Nation; that a female child was born to me on 11 day of May, 1902, that said child has been named Flora McNevins, and was living March 4, 1905.

                Nancy McNevins
Witnesses To Mark:
{

Subscribed and sworn to before me this 27 day of March, 1905.

                Drennan C Skaggs
                Notary Public.

Applications for Enrollment of Creek Newborn
Act of 1905   Volume VII

AFFIDAVIT OF ATTENDING PHYSICIAN OR MID-WIFE.

UNITED STATES OF AMERICA, Indian Territory, $\Big\}$
    Western   DISTRICT.

    I, Lucy Stewart , a mid-wife , on oath state that I attended on Mrs. Nancy McNevins , wife of Lee McNevins on the 11 day of May , 1902 ; that there was born to her on said date a female child; that said child was living March 4, 1905, and is said to have been named Flora McNevins

                                             Lucy Stewart

Witnesses To Mark:
$\Big\{$

    Subscribed and sworn to before me this 27 day of March, 1905.

                                              Drennan C Skaggs
                                              Notary Public.

BIRTH AFFIDAVIT.

DEPARTMENT OF THE INTERIOR.
COMMISSION TO THE FIVE CIVILIZED TRIBES.

    IN RE APPLICATION FOR ENROLLMENT, as a citizen of the Creek Nation, of Willie Clay McNevins , born on the 20 day of November , 1905[sic]

Name of Father: Lee McNevins   a citizen of the   Creek   Nation.
Tuckabatche Town
Name of Mother: Nancy McNevins (nee Scott)   a citizen of the   Creek   Nation.
Tuckabatche Town
                              Postoffice   Yeager, I.T.

AFFIDAVIT OF MOTHER.

UNITED STATES OF AMERICA, Indian Territory, $\Big\}$
    Western   DISTRICT.

    I, Nancy McNevins , on oath state that I am 28 years of age and a citizen by blood , of the Creek Nation; that I am the lawful wife of Lee McNevins , who is a citizen, by blood of the Creek Nation; that a male child was born to me on 20 day of November , 1904 , that said child has been named Willie Clay McNevins , and was living March 4, 1905.

                                              Nancy McNevins

Witnesses To Mark:
$\Big\{$

Applications for Enrollment of Creek Newborn
Act of 1905 Volume VII

Subscribed and sworn to before me this 27 day of March, 1905.

Drennan C Skaggs
Notary Public.

AFFIDAVIT OF ATTENDING PHYSICIAN OR MID-WIFE.

UNITED STATES OF AMERICA, Indian Territory, }
    Western   DISTRICT.

I, Lucy Stewart , a mid-wife , on oath state that I attended on Mrs. Nancy McNevins , wife of Lee McNevins on the 20 day of November , 1904 ; that there was born to her on said date a male child; that said child was living March 4, 1905, and is said to have been named Willie Clay McNevins

Lucy Stewart

Witnesses To Mark:
{

Subscribed and sworn to before me this 27 day of March, 1905.

Drennan C Skaggs
Notary Public.

BIRTH AFFIDAVIT.

DEPARTMENT OF THE INTERIOR.
COMMISSION TO THE FIVE CIVILIZED TRIBES.

IN RE APPLICATION FOR ENROLLMENT, as a citizen of the Creek Nation, of McAfee Stublefield[sic] , born on the 5 day of January , 4 this year

Name of Father: Ed. Stublefield   a citizen of the United States Nation.
(nee Hulsey)
Name of Mother: Lousanna Stublefield   a citizen of the   Creek   Nation.
Little River Tulsa
                          Postoffice   Holdenville, I.T.

AFFIDAVIT OF MOTHER.

UNITED STATES OF AMERICA, Indian Territory, }   Child present.
    Western   DISTRICT.

I, Lousanna Stublefield , on oath state that I am 25 years of age and a citizen by blood , of the Creek Nation; that I am the lawful wife of Ed. Stublefield , who is a

Applications for Enrollment of Creek Newborn
Act of 1905   Volume VII

citizen, ~~by~~ *(blank)* of the United States Nation; that a male child was born to me on 5 day of January of the present year, 1, that said child has been named McAfee Stublefield, and was living March 4, 1905.

her
Lousanna x Stublefield
mark

Witnesses To Mark:
{ DC Skaggs
{ Alex Posey

Subscribed and sworn to before me this 27 day of March, 1905.

Drennan C Skaggs
Notary Public.

AFFIDAVIT OF ATTENDING PHYSICIAN OR MID-WIFE.

UNITED STATES OF AMERICA, Indian Territory, }
Central   DISTRICT. }

I, W.B. Bentley, a Physician, on oath state that I attended on Mrs. Lousanna Stubblefield, wife of Ed Stubblefield on the 5th day of Jan., 1905; that there was born to her on said date a Male child; that said child was living March 4, 1905, and is said to have been named McAfee Stubblefield.

Witnesses To Mark:
{
{

Subscribed and sworn to before me this 28 day of March, 1905.

Notary Public.

Applications for Enrollment of Creek Newborn
Act of 1905 Volume VII

NC-580

DEPARTMENT OF THE INTERIOR,
COMMISSIONER TO THE FIVE CIVILIZED TRIBES.
Muskogee, Indian Territory, October 17, 1905

In the matter of the application for the enrollment of James and Sappho Buck as citizens by blood of the Creek Nation.

William Buck, being first duly sworn, testified as follows:

EXAMINATION BY THE COMMISSIONER:
Q What is your name? A William Buck.
Q How old are you? A 28.
Q What is your postoffice? A Wetumka.
Q Are you a citizen of the Creek Nation? A Yes sir.

The witness is identified on Creek Indian card, field No. 1888, opposite Roll No. 5956, and his name is contained in the partial list of citizens by blood of the Creek Nation approved by the Department March 28, 1902.

Q You are the William Buck who previously made application for the enrollment of James and Sappho Buck, are you not? A Yes sir.
Q Who is the mother of these children? A Annie Buck.
Q She is your lawful wife? A Yes sir.
Q What was her name before you married her? A Haney Benson.
Q Who is the father of Haney Benson, do you know? A Jim Benson.
Q And who is her mother? A I don't know.

The mother of these children, Annie Buck, is identified on Creek Indian card, field No. 1428, opposite Roll No. 4538, and her name is contained in the partial list of citizens by blood of the Creek Nation approved by the Department March 13, 1902.

Q The child, James, is now living now? A No sir.
Q When did it die? A I don't kow

The records of this Office examined, and it appears there from that said child, James Buck did January 2, 1903,

Q Sappho Buck is living? A Yes sir.
Q There was no one present at the birth of the child? A No sir.

The witness is notified that this Office desires the affidavits of two disinterested persons as to the birth of said Sappho Buck. Said affidavits must set forth said child'as to the birth of said children. Said affidavits must set forth said child's name, the date of its birth, the names of its parents, and whether or not she was living March 4, 1905.

Applications for Enrollment of Creek Newborn
Act of 1905 Volume VII

INDIAN TERRITORY, Western District.

I, J. Y. Miller, a stenographer to the Commissioner to the Five Civilized Tribes, do hereby certify that the above and foregoing is a true and complete translation of my notes as same appear in my stenographic report of this case.

J.Y. Miller

Sworn to and subscribed before me
this October 18, 1905.

Edw C Griesel
Notary Public.

DEPARTMENT OF THE INTERIOR.
COMMISSION TO THE FIVE CIVILIZED TRIBES.

In the matter of the death of James Buck a citizen of the Creek Nation, who formerly resided at or near Wetumka , Ind. Ter., and died on the 2 day of January, 1903

AFFIDAVIT OF RELATIVE.

UNITED STATES OF AMERICA, Indian Territory,
Western DISTRICT.

I, Annie Buck , on oath state that I am about 22 years of age and a citizen by blood , of the Creek Nation; that my postoffice address is Wetumka , Ind. Ter.; that I am mother of James Buck who was a citizen, by blood , of the Creek Nation and that said James Buck died on the 2 day of January , 1903

Witnesses To Mark:
{ Alex Posey
{ DC Skaggs

her
Annie x Buck
mark

Subscribed and sworn to before me this 28 day of March, 1905.

Drennan C Skaggs
Notary Public.

Applications for Enrollment of Creek Newborn
Act of 1905 Volume VII

BIRTH AFFIDAVIT.

DEPARTMENT OF THE INTERIOR.
COMMISSION TO THE FIVE CIVILIZED TRIBES.

IN RE APPLICATION FOR ENROLLMENT, as a citizen of the Creek Nation, of James Buck, born on the 10 day of October, 1902

Name of Father: William Buck   a citizen of the   Creek   Nation.
Wewoka Town
Name of Mother: Annie Buck   a citizen of the   Creek   Nation.
Hutchechuppa Town

            Postoffice   Wetumka, Ind. Ter.

AFFIDAVIT OF MOTHER.

UNITED STATES OF AMERICA, Indian Territory, }
    Western   DISTRICT.

     I, Annie Buck, on oath state that I am about 22 years of age and a citizen by blood, of the Creek Nation; that I am the lawful wife of William buck, who is a citizen, by blood of the Creek Nation; that a male child was born to me on 10 day of October, 1902, that said child has been named James Buck, and was not living March 4, 1905.
                                            her
                                   Annie x Buck
Witnesses To Mark: mark
{ Alex Posey
{ DC Skaggs

     Subscribed and sworn to before me this 28 day of March, 1905.

                                 Drennan C Skaggs
                                      Notary Public.

NC 580   JLD
DEPARTMENT OF THE INTERIOR,
COMMISSIONER TO THE FIVE CIVILIZED TRIBES.

     In the matter of the application for the enrollment of James Buck, deceased, as a citizen by blood of the Creek Nation.

                 . . . .

STATEMENT AND ORDER.

     The record in this case shows that on March 30, 1905, application was made, in

Applications for Enrollment of Creek Newborn
Act of 1905   Volume VII

affidavit form, supplemented by sworn testimony given on October 17, 1905, for the enrollment of James Buck, deceased, as a citizen by blood of the Creek Nation, under the provisions of the act of Congress approved March 3, 1905.

It appears from the evidence filed in this matter that said James Buck was born October 10, 1902, and died January 2, 1903.

The Act of Congress approved March 3, 1905, (33 Stats., 1048), provides:
"That the Commission to the Five Civilized Tribes is authorized for sixty days after the date of the approval of this act to receive and consider applications for enrollment, of children, born subsequent to May twenty-fifth, nineteen hundred and one, and prior to March fourth, nineteen hundred and five, and living on said latter date, to citizens of the Creek tribe of Indians whose enrollment has been approved by the Secretary of the Interior prior to the approval of this act; and to enroll and make allotments to such children."

It is, therefore, ordered that the application for the enrollment of said James Buck, deceased, as a citizen by blood of the Creek Nation be, and the same is, hereby dismissed.

Tams Bixby   Commissioner.

Muskogee, Indian Territory.
JAN 15 1907

BIRTH AFFIDAVIT.

DEPARTMENT OF THE INTERIOR.
COMMISSION TO THE FIVE CIVILIZED TRIBES.

IN RE APPLICATION FOR ENROLLMENT, as a citizen of the Creek Nation, of Sappho Buck, born on the 28 day of March, 1904

Name of Father: William Buck   a citizen of the   Creek   Nation.
Wewoka Town
Name of Mother: Annie Buck (nee Benson)   a citizen of the   Creek   Nation.
Hutchechuppa Town
             Postoffice   Wetumka, Ind. Ter.

AFFIDAVIT OF MOTHER.

UNITED STATES OF AMERICA, Indian Territory, }   Child is present
     Western   DISTRICT.

I, Annie Buck, on oath state that I am about 23 years of age and a citizen by blood, of the Creek Nation; that I am the lawful wife of William buck, who is a citizen, by blood of the Creek Nation; that a female child was born to me on 28 day of March, 1904, that said child has been named Sappho Buck, and was not living March 4, 1905. That no one attended on me as midwife or physician at the birth of the child.

Applications for Enrollment of Creek Newborn
Act of 1905   Volume VII

Witnesses To Mark:
{ Alex Posey
  DC Skaggs

her
Annie x Buck
mark

Subscribed and sworn to before me this 28 day of March, 1905.

Drennan C Skaggs
Notary Public.

Real Estate Agents
and
Notary Public

UNITED STATES OF AMERICA,

Wetumka, Ind. Ter.,   *190*

INDIAN TERRITORY,   SS:

WESTERN JUDICIAL DISTRICT.

I   Leetchee Harjo   do hereby certify that I am a citizen of the Creek Nation, and that I am personaly[sic] acquainted with Annie Buck, and William Buck, and Know them to be husband and wife, and know that a female child was born to them on the 28th day of March 1904, and that said child was named Sappho Buck, and that said Sappho Buck was liveing[sic] on the 4th of March 1905. I further certify that the said Annie Buck was alloted[sic] under the name of Annie Benson, that her Father's name is James Benson, and her Mother was named Lizzie Benson, they were members of the Hutch-che-chuppel Town and that the said Annie Buck Roll No is _____

Witnesses to mark   her[sic]
Nat Williams   Leetchee Harjo x
Chas Coachman   mark
Subscribed to in my presence and sworn to before me this the 11th day of September 1905.   her[sic]
                                              Lee[sic] B.H. Mills x[sic]
My Commission Expires Aug 15th 1906.   Notary Public.   mark[sic]

Applications for Enrollment of Creek Newborn
Act of 1905 Volume VII

B. H. MILLS   NAT WILLIAMS

Real Estate Agents
and
Notary Public

UNITED STATES OF AMERICA,

Wetumka, Ind. Ter.,   190

INDIAN TERRITORY,

WESTERN JUDICIAL DISTRICT.

I Amanda Harjo do hereby certify that I am a citizen of the Creek Nation, and that I am personaly[sic] acquainted with Annie Buck, and William Buck, and Know them to be husband and wife, and know that a female child was born to them on the 28th day of March 1904, and that said child was named Sappho Buck, and that said Sappho Buck was liveing[sic] on the 4th of March 1905. I further certify that the said Annie Buck was alloted[sic] under the name of Annie Benson, that her Father's name is James Benson, and her Mother was named Lizzie Benson, they were members of the Hutch-che-chup-pel Town and that the said Annie Buck Roll No is _____

Witnesses to mark   her
Nat Williams   Amanda Harjo x
Chas Coachman   mark

Subscribed to in my presence and sworn to before me this the 11th day of September 1905.

                                          B.H. Mills
My Commission Expires Aug 15th 1906.   Notary Public.

BIRTH AFFIDAVIT.

DEPARTMENT OF THE INTERIOR.
COMMISSION TO THE FIVE CIVILIZED TRIBES.

IN RE APPLICATION FOR ENROLLMENT, as a citizen of the Creek Nation, of Sappho Buck , born on the 28 day of March , 1904

Name of Father: William Buck   a citizen of the   Creek   Nation.
Name of Mother: Haney Buck   a citizen of the   Creek   Nation.

                        Postoffice   Wetumka, I.T.

Applications for Enrollment of Creek Newborn
Act of 1905 Volume VII

AFFIDAVIT OF MOTHER.

UNITED STATES OF AMERICA, Indian Territory,
    Western   DISTRICT.

    I, Haney Buck , on oath state that I am 23 years of age and a citizen by blood , of the Creek Nation; that I am the lawful wife of William Buck , who is a citizen, by blood of the Creek Nation; that a female child was born to me on 28 day of March, 1904 , that said child has been named Sappho Buck , and was living March 4, 1905.

                              Haney Buck

Witnesses To Mark:
- B.H. Mills
- Jim Sandrs

    Subscribed and sworn to before me this 30 day of October , 1905.

My Com Exp. July 9-1905   Nat Williams
                                        Notary Public.

NC 580

BIRTH AFFIDAVIT.

DEPARTMENT OF THE INTERIOR.
COMMISSION TO THE FIVE CIVILIZED TRIBES.

    IN RE APPLICATION FOR ENROLLMENT, as a citizen of the Creek Nation, of Sappho Buck, born on the 28 day of March , 1904

Name of Father: William Buck   a citizen of the   Creek   Nation.
Name of Mother: Annie   "   a citizen of the   Creek   Nation.

                      Postoffice   Wetumka I.T.

                            Father
AFFIDAVIT OF ~~MOTHER~~.

UNITED STATES OF AMERICA, Indian Territory,
    Western   DISTRICT.

    I, William Buck , on oath state that I am 29 years of age and a citizen by blood , of the Creek Nation; that I am the lawful ~~wife~~ husband of Annie Buck , who is a citizen, by blood of the Creel Nation; that a female child was born to ~~me~~ her on 28 day of March , 1904 , that said child has been named Sappho Buck , and was living March 4, 1905.

                              William Buck

Applications for Enrollment of Creek Newborn
Act of 1905   Volume VII

Witnesses To Mark:

{

Subscribed and sworn to before me this 17" day of Oct, 1905.

My Commission   J McDermott
Ex July 25" 1907   Notary Public.

NC-580.

Muskogee, Indian Territory, August 10, 1905

Annie Buck,
 c/o William Buck,
  Wetumka, Indian Territory.

Dear Madam:

  In the matter of the application for the enrollment of your minor daughter Sappho Buck, born March 28, 1904, as a citizen by blood of the Creek Nation, it will be necessary for you to file with this office the affidavits of two disinterested persons as to the birth of said child. Said affidavits must set forth said child's name, the date of her birth, the names of her parents, and whether or not she was living on March 4, 1905.

  From the evidence now on file this office is unable to identify you upon the final roll of citizens by blood of the Creek Nation. It is necessary that you be identified before the rights of said child can be finally determined.

  You are, therefore, requested to state the name under which you were finally enrolled, the names of your parents and other members of your family, your roll number as the same appears upon your allotment certificate and deeds and any other information which you think will enable this office to properly identify you.

Respectfully,

Acting Commissioner.

Applications for Enrollment of Creek Newborn
Act of 1905   Volume VII

NC-580.

Muskogee, Indian Territory, October 17, 1905.

Annie Buck,
    c/o William Buck,
        Wetumka, Indian Territory.

Dear Madam:

    In the matter of the application for the enrollment of your minor daughter Sappho Buck, born March 28, 1904, as a citizen by blood of the Creek Nation, it will be necessary for you to file with this office the affidavits of two disinterested persons as to the birth of said child. Said affidavits must set forth said child's name, the date of her birth, the names of her parents and whether or not he was living on March 4, 1905.

    From the evidence now on file this office is unable to identify you upon the final roll of citizens by blood of the Creek Nation. It is necessary that you be identified before the rights of said child can be finally determined. You are, therefore, requested to state the name under which you were finally enrolled, the names of your parents and other members of your family, your roll number as the same appears upon your allotment certificate and deeds and any other information which you think will enable this office to properly identify you.

                Respectfully,

                              Commissioner.

NC-580.

Muskogee, Indian Territory, October 24, 1905.

Annie Buck,
    c/o William Buck,
        Wetumka, Indian Territory.

Dear Madam:

    In the matter of the application for the enrollment of your minor child, Sappho Buck, born March 28, 1904, as a citizen by blood of the Creek Nation, this office is able to identify you, from the information contained in the affidavits of Amanda and Leetchee Harjo, received this day, as Haney Benson. Your name is signed to your affidavit in this case as Annie Buck.

    Inasmuch as your name appears upon the final roll as Haney Benson and you state that you are the lawful wife of William Buck it necessarily follows that your name is Haney Buck and not Annie Buck.

Applications for Enrollment of Creek Newborn
Act of 1905   Volume VII

  For the purpose of correcting the discrepancy as to name there is herewith inclosed a form of birth affidavit properly filled out which you are requested to have executed before a notary public, taking care to sign your name to the affidavit as the same appears in the body thereof. When the affidavit has been sworn to return it to this office in the inclosed envelope.

  This matter should have your immediate attention.

      Respectfully,

              Commissioner.

CTD-20.
Env.

NC 580.

      Muskogee, Indian Territory, January 16, 1907.

Nancy Buck,
  c/o William Buck,
    Wetumka, Indian Territory.

Dear Madam:

  There is herewith enclosed one copy of the Statement and Order of the Commissioner to the Five Civilized Tribes, dated January 15, 1907, dismissing the application made by you for the enrollment of your minor child James Buck, as a citizen by blood of the Creek Nation.

      Respectfully,

              Commissioner.

LM-70.

Applications for Enrollment of Creek Newborn
Act of 1905 Volume VII

DEPARTMENT OF THE INTERIOR,
COMMISSION TO THE FIVE CIVILIZED TRIBES.
Holdenville, I. T., March 27, 1905.

In the matter of the application for the enrollment of Alice Harjo as a citizen of the Creek Nation.

LIZZIE HARJO, being duly sworn, testified as follows:

Through Alex Posey Official Interpreter:

BY COMMISSION:
Q What is your name? A Lizzie Harjo.
Q How old are you? A About forty.
Q What is your post office address? A Emahaka.
Q Are you a citizen of the Creek Nation? A Yes, sir.
Q To what town do you belong? A Little River Tulsa.
Q Do you make application for the enrollment of your child, Alice Harjo, as a citizen of the Creek Nation? A Yes, sir.
Q Who is the father of this child? A Cheparne Harjo.
Q Is he a citizen of the Creek Nation? A He is a Seminole.
Q If it should be found that your child, Alice Harj ,[sic] is entitled to be enrolled in either the Creek or Seminole Nations in which nation do you desire to have her enrolled? A In the Creek Nation.

---oooOOOooo---

I, D. C. Skaggs, on oath state that the above and foregoing is a full and true transcript of my stenographic notes as taken in said cause on said date.

DC Skaggs

Subscribed and sworn to before me this 18" day of July, 1905.

Edw C Griesel
Notary Public.

Applications for Enrollment of Creek Newborn
Act of 1905 Volume VII

BIRTH AFFIDAVIT.

Supplemental testimony taken

DEPARTMENT OF THE INTERIOR.
COMMISSION TO THE FIVE CIVILIZED TRIBES.

IN RE APPLICATION FOR ENROLLMENT, as a citizen of the Creek Nation, of Alice Harjo, born on the 16 day of August, 1904

Name of Father: Cheparney Harjo   a citizen of the Seminole   Nation. Hutka)
Name of Mother: Lizzie Harjo (nee White or   a citizen of the   Creek   Nation. Tulsa Little River Town
                                 Postoffice   Emahaka, I.T.

AFFIDAVIT OF MOTHER.

UNITED STATES OF AMERICA, Indian Territory,   Child is present
    Western   DISTRICT.

I, Lizzie Harjo , on oath state that I am about 40 years of age and a citizen by blood , of the Creek Nation; that I am the lawful wife of Cheparney Harjo , who is a citizen, by blood of the Creek[sic] Nation; that a female child was born to me on 16 day of August , 1904 , that said child has been named Alice Harjo , and was living March 4, 1905.
                                                        her
                                     Lizzie x Harjo
Witnesses To Mark: mark
  { Alex Posey
  { DC Skaggs

Subscribed and sworn to before me this 27 day of March , 1905.

                             Drennan C Skaggs
                                  Notary Public.

AFFIDAVIT OF ATTENDING PHYSICIAN OR MID-WIFE.

UNITED STATES OF AMERICA, Indian Territory,
    Western   DISTRICT.

I, Leah Okfusky , a midwife , on oath state that I attended on Mrs. Lizzie Harjo, wife of Cheparney Harjo on the (blank) day of August , 1904 ; that there was born to her on said date a female child; that said child was living March 4, 1905, and is said to have been named Alice Harjo
                                          her
                                Leah x Okfusky
                                       mark

Applications for Enrollment of Creek Newborn
Act of 1905   Volume VII

Witnesses To Mark:
{ Alex Posey
  DC Skaggs

Subscribed and sworn to before me this 27 day of March, 1905.

                                            Drennan C Skaggs
                                            Notary Public.

BIRTH AFFIDAVIT.

Supplemental testimony taken

DEPARTMENT OF THE INTERIOR.
COMMISSION TO THE FIVE CIVILIZED TRIBES.

IN RE APPLICATION FOR ENROLLMENT, as a citizen of the Creek Nation, of Willie Harjo, born on the 18 day of December, 1901

Name of Father: Cheparney Harjo	a citizen of the Seminole	Nation.
Name of Mother: Lizzie Harjo	a citizen of the Creek	Nation.

                        Postoffice   Emahaka, I.T.

AFFIDAVIT OF MOTHER.

UNITED STATES OF AMERICA, Indian Territory, }   Child is present
    Western   DISTRICT.

I, Lizzie Harjo, on oath state that I am about 40 years of age and a citizen by blood, of the Creek Nation; that I am the lawful wife of Cheparney Harjo, who is a citizen, by blood of the Seminole Nation; that a male child was born to me on 18 day of December, 1901, that said child has been named Willie Harjo, and was living March 4, 1905. That no one attended on me as midwife or physician at the birth of the child.
                                                  her
                                           Lizzie x Harjo
Witnesses To Mark: mark
{ Alex Posey
  DC Skaggs

Subscribed and sworn to before me this 27 day of March, 1905.

                                            Drennan C Skaggs
                                            Notary Public.

Applications for Enrollment of Creek Newborn
Act of 1905   Volume VII

DEPARTMENT OF THE INTERIOR.
COMMISSION TO THE FIVE CIVILIZED TRIBES.

In the matter of the death of Willie Harjo a citizen of the Creek Nation, who formerly resided at or near Emahaka , Ind. Ter., and died on the 26 day of January, 1902

AFFIDAVIT OF RELATIVE.

UNITED STATES OF AMERICA, Indian Territory, } Western DISTRICT.

I, Lizzie Harjo, on oath state that I am about 40 years of age and a citizen by blood , of the Creek Nation; that my postoffice address is Emahaka , Ind. Ter.; that I am the mother of Willie Harjo who was a citizen, by blood , of the Creek Nation and that said Willie Harjo died on the 26 day of January , 1902

                              her
                      Lizzie x Harjo

Witnesses To Mark: mark
{ Alex Posey
{ DC Skaggs

Subscribed and sworn to before me this 27 day of March, 1905.

                          Drennan C Skaggs
                          Notary Public.

AFFIDAVIT OF ACQUAINTANCE.

UNITED STATES OF AMERICA, Indian Territory, } Western DISTRICT.

I, Judy Bruner , on oath state that I am about 20 years of age, and a citizen by blood of the Creek Nation; that my postoffice address is Emahaka , Ind. Ter.; that I was personally acquainted with Willie Harjo who was a citizen, by blood , of the Creek Nation; and that said Willie Harjo died on the 26 day of January , 1902

                            her
                     Judy x Bruner

Witnesses To Mark: mark
{ Alex Posey
{ DC Skaggs

Applications for Enrollment of Creek Newborn
Act of 1905   Volume VII

Subscribed and sworn to before me this 27 day of March, 1905.

Drennan C Skaggs
Notary Public.

NC 581   JLD

DEPARTMENT OF THE INTERIOR,
COMMISSIONER TO THE FIVE CIVILIZED TRIBES.

In the matter of the application for the enrollment of Willie Harjo, deceased, as a citizen by blood of the Creek Nation.

....

STATEMENT AND ORDER.

The record in this case shows that on March 30, 1905, application was made, in affidavit form, for the enrollment of Willie Harjo, deceased, as a citizen by blood of the Creek Nation, under the provisions of the act of Congress approved March 3, 1905.

It appears from the affidavit filed in this matter that said Willie Harjo, deceased, was born December 18, 1901, and died January 26, 1902.

The Act of Congress approved March 3, 1905, (33 Stats., 1048), provides:

"That the Commission to the Five Civilized Tribes is authorized for sixty days after the date of the approval of this act to receive and consider applications for enrollment, of children, born subsequent to May twenty-fifth, nineteen hundred and one, and prior to March fourth, nineteen hundred and five, and living on said latter date, to citizens of the Creek tribe of Indians whose enrollment has been approved by the Secretary of the Interior prior to the approval of this act; and to enroll and make allotments to such children."

It is, therefore, ordered that the application for the enrollment of Willie Harjo, deceased, as a citizen by blood of the Creek Nation be, and the same is, hereby dismissed.

Tams Bixby   Commissioner.

Muskogee, Indian Territory.
JAN 4 – 1907

Applications for Enrollment of Creek Newborn
Act of 1905   Volume VII

NC. 581.

Muskogee, Indian Territory, July 14, 1905.

Commissioner to the Five Civilized Tribes,
   Seminole Enrollment Division,
      Muskogee, Indian Territory.

Gentlemen:

      March 30, 1905, application was made to the Commission to the Five Civilized Tribes for the enrollment of Willie Harjo, born December 18, 1901, and Alice Harjo, born August 16, 1904, as citizens by blood of the Creek Nation. It is stated in said application that the father of said children is Cheparney Harjo, a citizen of the Seminole Nation, and that the mother is Lizzie Harjo, a citizen of the Creek Nation.

      You are requested to inform the Creek Enrollment Division as to whether application has been made for the enrollment of said children as citizens of the Seminole Nation, and if so, what disposition has been made of the same.

      Respectfully,

            Commissioner.

DEPARTMENT OF THE INTERIOR.
COMMISSION TO THE FIVE CIVILIZED TRIBES.

Muskogee, Indian Territory, July 18, 1905.

Chief Clerk,
   Creek Enrollment Division.

Dear Sir:

      Receipt is acknowledged of your letter of July 14, 1905 (NC-581) stating that application was made to the Commission to the Five Civilized Tribes for the enrollment of Willie Harjo, born December 18, 1901, and Alice Harjo, born August 16, 1904, children of Cheparney Harjo, a citizen of the Seminole Nation, and Lizzie Harjo, a citizen of the Creek Nation, as citizens by blood of the Creek Nation and requesting to be informed as to whether application was made for the enrollment of said children as citizens of the Seminole Nation.

      In reply to your letter you are advised that it does not appear from an examination of the records of this office that any application was made to the

Applications for Enrollment of Creek Newborn
Act of 1905   Volume VII

Commission to the Five Civilized Tribes for the enrollment of said Willie Harjo and Alice Harjo as citizens of the Seminole Nation.

Respectfully,

Tams Bixby   Commissioner.

NC 581

Muskogee, Indian Territory, November 12, 1906.

Chief Clerk,
    Seminole Enrollment Division,
        General Office.

Dear Sir:

You are hereby advised that the name of Alice Harjo born August 16, 1904, to Cheparney Harjo, an alleged citizen of the Seminole Nation and Lizzie Harjo, a citizen by blood of the Creek Nation, is contained in schedule of minor citizens by blood of the Creek Nation, approved by the Secretary of the Interior, September 27, 1905, opposite Roll number 560[sic].

Respectfully,

Commissioner.

NC 582.

DEPARTMENT OF THE INTERIOR,
COMMISSIONER TO THE FIVE CIVILIZED TRIBES.
Holdenville, Indian Territory, October 29, 1906.

In the matter of the application for the enrollment of Polly Beaver, deceased, as a citizen by blood of the Creek Nation.

PARTY BEAVER, being duly sworn, testified as follows through Jesse McDermott official interpreter:

BY COMMISSIONER:

Q What is your name? A Party Beaver.
Q What is your age? A About 25.
Q What is your postoffice address? A Holdenville.
Q Are you a Creek citizen? A Yes.
Q To which Creek Indian town do you belong? A Little River Tulsa.

Applications for Enrollment of Creek Newborn
Act of 1905 Volume VII

Q Have you filed on your land? A Yes, I have the deeds here.

The witness presents allotment deeds issued to Party Beaver Creek Roll No. 7538.

Q Have you a child named Polly Beaver? A I did have but she died last Saturday was a week ago.
Q Do you know what date that was? A No, I do not. I am a full-blood Inian and know very little about dates
Q How old was Polly when she died? A I am not sure but I think she a little over three years old when she died.
Q When was she three years old? A Last March.
Q What is the name of Polly's mother? A Lucy Beaver.
Q How long have you and Lucy been married? A We had been married a long while when people began filing on land.

I, Jesse McDermott, being first duly sworn, states, that the above and foregoing is a true and correct transcript of my notes as taken in said cause on said date.

Jesse McDermott

Subscribed and sworn to before me,
this 10 day of December, 1906.

Alex Posey
Notary Public.

DEPARTMENT OF THE INTERIOR.
COMMISSION TO THE FIVE CIVILIZED TRIBES.

In the matter of the death of Polly Beaver a citizen of the Creek Nation, who formerly resided at or near Holdenville , Ind. Ter., and died on the 20" day of October , 1906

AFFIDAVIT OF RELATIVE.

UNITED STATES OF AMERICA, Indian Territory,
Western DISTRICT.

I, Party Beaver , on oath state that I am about 25 years of age and a citizen by blood , of the Creek Nation; that my postoffice address is Holdenville , Ind. Ter.; that I am the father of Polly Beaver who was a citizen, by blood , of the Creek Nation and that said Polly Beaver died on the 20 day of October, 1906

Applications for Enrollment of Creek Newborn
Act of 1905   Volume VII

                                        his
                                Party x Beaver
                                        mark

Witnesses To Mark:
  ⎧ J McDermott
  ⎩ W R Jackson

Subscribed and sworn to before me this 29 day of October, 1906.
My Commission
Expires July 25" 1907   J McDermott
                                                Notary Public.

AFFIDAVIT OF DISINTERESTED WITNESS.

UNITED STATES OF AMERICA,
INDIAN TERRITORY,
Western DISTRICT.   SS

We, the undersigned, on oath state that we are personally acquainted with Lucy Beaver , wife of Party Beaver ; that there was born to her a female child on or about the 10 day of March 1903, that the said child has been named Polly Beaver , and was living March 4, 1905. but died last Saturday was a week ago

We further state that we have no interest in this case.
                                        his
Witnesses: J McDermott   Jackson x Coon
                                        mark
         W R Jackson   her
                                Jennie x Baker
                                        mark

Subscribed and sworn to before me this 29 day of October 1906.

                                J McDermott
My Commission   Notary Public.
Expires July 25" 1907

Applications for Enrollment of Creek Newborn
Act of 1905   Volume VII

BIRTH AFFIDAVIT.
DEPARTMENT OF THE INTERIOR.
COMMISSION TO THE FIVE CIVILIZED TRIBES.

IN RE APPLICATION FOR ENROLLMENT, as a citizen of the Creek Nation, of Polly Beaver, born on the 10 day of March, 1903.

Name of Father: Pahte Beaver   a citizen of the   Creek   Nation.
Tulsa Little River Town
Name of Mother: Lucy Beaver (nee Leader)   a citizen of the   Creek   Nation.
Fishpond Town
                              Postoffice   Calvin, Ind. Ter.

AFFIDAVIT OF MOTHER.

UNITED STATES OF AMERICA, Indian Territory, }   Child is present
    Western   DISTRICT.

    I, Lucy Beaver, on oath state that I am over 30 years of age and a citizen by blood, of the Creek Nation; that I am the lawful wife of Pahte Beaver, who is a citizen, by blood of the Creek Nation; that a female child was born to me on 10 day of March, 1903, that said child has been named Polly Beaver, and was living March 4, 1905. That no one attended on me as midwife or physician at the birth of the child.
                                          her
                                Lucy x Beaver
Witnesses To Mark: mark
 { Alex Posey
   DC Skaggs

    Subscribed and sworn to before me this 28 day of March, 1905.

                                Drennan C Skaggs
                                    Notary Public.

(The above Birth Affidavit given again.)

Applications for Enrollment of Creek Newborn
Act of 1905   Volume VII

NC 582.

Muskogee, Indian Territory, August 10, 1905.

Lucy Beaver,
    c/o Party Beaver,
        Calvin, Indian Territory.

Dear Madam:

    In the matter of the application for the enrollment of your minor daughter, Polly Beaver, born March 10, 1903, as a citizen by blood of the Creek Nation, it will be necessary for you to furnish this office the affidavits of two disinterested witnesses as to the birth of said child. Said affidavits must set forth said child's name, the date of her birth, the names of her parents and whether or not she was living on March 4, 1905.

Respectfully,

Acting   Commissioner.

J D

REFER IN REPLY TO THE FOLLOWING:
NC-582.

DEPARTMENT OF THE INTERIOR,
COMMISSIONER TO THE FIVE CIVILIZED TRIBES.

Muskogee, Indian Territory, October 17, 1905.

Lucy Beaver,
    c/o Party Beaver,
        Calvin, Indian Territory.

Dear Madam:

    In the matter of the application for the enrollment of your minor daughter, Polly Beaver, born March 10, 1903, as a citizen by blood of the Creek Nation, it will be necessary for you to furnish this office the affidavits of two disinterested persons as to the birth of said child. Said affidavits must set forth said child's name, the date of her birth, the names of her parents and whether or not she was living March 4, 1905.

Respectfully,

Tams Bixby
        Commissioner.

Applications for Enrollment of Creek Newborn
Act of 1905 Volume VII

N.C. 582.

Holdenville, Indian Territory, October 30, 1906.

Commissioner to the Five Civilized Tribes,
Muskogee, Indian Territory.

Dear Sir:

There are herewith enclosed affidavits of two disinterested witnesses and a death affidavit all of which are to be considered in the matter of the application for the enrollment of Polly Beaver as a citizen by blood of the Creek Nation. The father of said child is identified as Party Beaver opposite Creek Roll number 7538.

Respectfully,

(No signature given.)

JWH

N C 582

Muskogee, Indian Territory, March 1, 1907.

Lucy Beaver,
    c/o Pahte Beaver,
        Calvin, Indian Territory.

Dear Madam :--

You are hereby advised that on February 15, 1907, the Secretary of the Interior approved the enrollment of your minor child, Polly Beaver, as a citizen by blood of the Creek Nation, and that the name of said child appears upon the roll of New Born citizens by blood of the Creek Nation, enrolled under the Act of Congress approved March 3, 1905, as number 1161.

This child is now entitled to allotment and application therefor should be made without delay at the Creek Land Office, Muskogee, Indian Territory. by the Administrator.

Respectfully,

Commissioner.

Applications for Enrollment of Creek Newborn
Act of 1905 Volume VII

(The below entries typed as given.)

                              Copy

            Explanation

U S Indian Agent

Sir:

      I married a man by the name of Ezra Freeman and you will see my name on the roll Cordelia A. Self When I filed C.C. Doncolis and E.W. Sims made out the application for inrollment[sic] for my minor son and I would like to no[sic] just when I could file for him you will find my name on the application Cordelia Freeman so hoping to here[sic] from you by return mail I remain

                            Yours truly

                            Cordelia Freeman

DEPRTMENT OF THE INTERIOR,
COMMISSION TO THE FIVE CIVILIZED TRIBES.

Inre[sic] application for enrollment, as a citizen of the creek[sic] Nation, of Hovah Monroe Freeman, born on the 19th day of June 1904

name of Father   Ezra Freeman   a citizen of the Creek Nation

name of Mother   Cordelia Freeman   a citizen of the Creek Nation,

                          Postoffice   Bristow I. T.

AFFIDAVIT OF MOTHER

United States of America Indian Territory
Western   District

I   Cordelia Freeman   on oath states that I am   Nineteen   years of age and a citizen by birth of the Creek Nation that I am the law ful wife of Ezra Freeman who is ~~not a~~ CITIZen United States by of the ~~Creek~~ Nation that a   male   child was born to me on   19th   day of June   1904/ that said child has been named   Hovah Monroe Freeman   and was living Mar 4, 1905

                          Cordelia Freeman

Applications for Enrollment of Creek Newborn
Act of 1905 Volume VII

Must be two   EW Sims

witnesses   C C *(Illegible)*

Subscribed and sworn to before me this   27th   day of   March   1905

                                                   EW Sims
                                                   Notary Public.

Affidavit of attending phician of Mid Wife,

United XXXXXXXXX States of America Indian Territory

    Western   District

I   Martha A Self   a   *(blcnk)*   on oath statebthat I attended on Mrs   Codela Freeman   wife of   Ezra Freeman   on the   19th   day of   June   1904   ; that there was born to her on said date a   male   Child that said child was living Mar 4th 1905 and is said to have been named   Hovah Monroe Freeman

Witness to Mark   Martha A Self

   must be two   EW Sims

witnesses   C C *(Illegible)*

Subscribed and sworn to before me this   27th   day of   March   1905

                                                   EW Sims
                                                   Notary Public.

                                    Copy

                            Bristow, Ind Terr
                            August 18, 1905

Hon Indian Agent Kelsey
       Muskogee, I T

Sir

       I would like to know when I can file for my minor child I have been told that they filed just like they was inrolled I would like to no if they come like this the first one that was put on roll file first and so ontell they all file and if I will have to wait tell the Secretary approves the application for inrollment[sic] if I can file for my minor child Hovah Monroe Freeman I would like to hear from you by return mail I am waitin your reply at once

                Cordelia A Freeman nee Self

Index

ADELHELM
    Charlie Antion 36,37
    Chester.................... 37,38
    Jennie................... 36,37,38
    William................... 36,37,38
AHNOCHEE
    Cinda 197,198,199
ALEX
    Elizabeth............................... 298
    Freeland............................. 298
    Jacob.................... 298
ALEXANDER
    J H 223,224,225
ALLEN
    C M......231,246,248,249,273,275
ANDER
    Amos 11
ANDERSON
    Amos 11,12,13
    Jennie........................... 11,12,13
    Jimmie 12
    Jinnie.. 13
    Viol... 12
    Viola........................... 11,13
ATKINS
    Nancy 242,243
ATKINS & HICKS.................... 109

BAKER
    Jennie... 321
BARBER
    Carnie 52
    Carrie................................. 52,53
    Mary E................................... 52,53
    Robert T 52,53
BARNARD
    D C 5
    Lillie 117
BARNETT
    Austin 47
    Cheparne.................................. 125
    Cheparney...123,124,125,126,127
    Daniel 276

    Dave 190,238
    Hulley.................................276
    Jim....................................238
    Jimmie 123,124,125,126,127
    Lindy 276
    Liza.......................................47
    Mahaly 123,124,125,126,127
    Millie 127
BEALL
    W O 42,238
    William O..............................109
    Wm O..34,73,74,85,109,181,189,
    229,230,245,270
BEAR
    Kizzie 117,119,120
    Lillie 119,120
    Polar................................117,119
    Poley................................119,120
    Wisey 119
BEAVER
    Lindy 87
    Losanna 261
    Lucy 68,320,321,322,323,324
    Mulsie......................................184
    Pahte................................322,324
    Party 68,319,320,321,323,324
    Polly 319,320,321,322,323,324
    Sally 111
BENDEN
    Dicey 220,221,223,224,225
    Ida.................................220,223
    Louis...........220,221,223,224,225
    Louisa.......................220,224,225
BENDER
    Ida...................................221,222
    Lewis.......................221,222,225
    Louis...220
    Louisa.......................221,225,226
    Tysie.................221,222,225,226
BENSON
    Annie.......................306,307,308
    Haney 303,311
    James...............................307,308

Index

Jim 303
Lizzie 307,308
BENTLEY
  W B 302
BENTON
  Nancy 91,93
BEWLEY
  Elizabeth 41,43
  Elizabeth Yargee 42
  Eugene L 42,43
  Lawrence W 42,43
BIGHEAD
  George ...65,66,67,68,69,70,71,74
  Jennie.....65,67,68,69,70,72,73,75
  Pa-tham-ka 69,71,72
  Pathlumka.............65,66,68,70,73
  Pa-thlum-ka 64,65,66,67,68,
69,70,72,73,74,75
BIRDHEAD...........249,250,252,253
  Cinda 249,250,251,252,253
  Kizzie 279,282
  Sinda........................251,252,253
  Yanah 249,250,251,252,253
BIXBY
  Jason Best 121
  Tams............4,11,15,16,34,36,50,
59,62,67,72,82,94,105,114,124,
135,139,141,142,157,168,178,180,
  182,187,205,216,235,242,251,258
,259,269,284,286,292,306,317,
319,323
BLACK
  J H 289
BOLEY 118,119
BONNER
  H R 54
BRENNAN
  Francis R 121
BRUNER
  Addie 160,161,162,163
  Ida.. 163
  Judy 185,186,187,188,316
  Katie 161

Leah.........................160,162,163
Lewis................................189,190
Liza...152
Losanna 161,162
Mary 161
Nancy 189,190,191
Pollie 244,246,248,249
Sadie......................................161
Susie 161,162
Taylor 189,190,191
William....................160,162,163
Willie...............................161,162
BUCK
  Annie 303,304,305,306,307,
308,310,311
  Hanes..................................312
  Haney 308,309,311
  James 303,304,305,306
  Nancy 312
  Rhoda ..254,255,256,257,258,260
  Sappho
    ... 303,306,307,308,309,310,311
  Sarah..........254,255,256,257,258,
259,260
  Simpson............254,255,256,257,
258,260
  William......303,305,306,307,308,
309,310,311,312
BURT
  Eliza 238
BUTLER
  D M 46

CAESAR
  Hannah 270,272,273
  Moser 270,274,275
  Rachael.............270,271,272,273,
274,275
  Racheal..................................272
  Samcho...........................272,274
  Samego.............270,271,272,273,
274,275
CAIN

Alloway 213
Mary 96,97
Ottawa 96,97,296
Ottaway 280,296
Ottay 280,284
CALDWELL
L P 210,290,291
CARR
Bettie 158,159,160
Ida 158,159
CARSON
Usher 53
CASER
Samego 230
Samyo 274
Somyo 275
CATHLOCCO
George 66
CHAPMAN
J C 5
CHARLIE
Addie 162
Little 160,162,163
CHILDERS
Lydia 57
Lydie 54
Pratt 54,55,56,57,58
Richard 55
Virgie 54,55,56,57,58,59
CLARK
Rev T B 144
CLAWSON
L L 19
W R 14,16,17,18,19,31,33, 86,261
CLINE
H R 46
COACHMAN
Charles 105,106,108
Chas 307,308
COKER
Hettie 172
COLE

Clara 166
COLONEL
Arra 180
Freeman 180
George 180
Harry 180
Retta 180
COMPIER
Mitchel 31
Mitchell 30,33
COOK
Mattie 144
Mrs H E 148,151
COON
Jackson 321
COOPER
W J 237
COWEE
Sarty 102
CULLER
Leah 14,15,17,18
Mary 13,14,15,16,18
Millie 13,14,15,16,17
Thomas 13,14,15,17,18
Tom 16
CULLY
Wallace 199,200
CUMSEH
Manie 155,157
CURTAIN
Lewis 270,271
Louis 146,149

DAVIDSON
Charles A 40
Chas A 39,40,144
DAVIS
Jim 86
DAY
James S 236,237
DEAN
Dianna 259
Kate 20

329

DILL
  W H 209
DOLYE
  Wallace 22
DONCOLIS
  C C 325
DOWNING
  Ambrose 128,129
  Jesse 127,128,129
  Jessie 128
  Katie 127,128
  Katy 129
DOYLE
  Clarinda 19,20,23,24,25
  David 19
  Maud 22,23,24,25,26
  Maud S 20,21,23,25,26
  Maude 19
  Minnie May 19,20,21,22,25,26
  Susie 19,20
  Susie L 26
  Susie Lee 20,21,27
  Wallace 19,20,21,22,23,24,25, 26,27
DOYLE, ... 28
DRESBACK
  Ralph D 193
DUNCAN
  H S 46
DUNN
  Tucker 208
  Tupper 208,209,210,228,229, 265,266,267,268,276,277,287,288, 290,291
DUNSEY
  J R 261
DUNSON
  Ellen 228
  Millie 228
  Thos H 207,228
DUNZY
  J R 107,113,115,116,120

ELLIS
  D D 121,122
  D D, MD 122
  David D, MD 121
FACTOR
  Cinda 80
  Cogee 90,91,92,94,95
  George 88,89,93,95
  Nancy 88,89,90,91,92,93,94,95
  Sissy 138
  Willaim 89
  William 88,90,91,92,93,94,95
FENNEL
  Joe 236
FIFE
  James 131,132
  Jesey 131,132
  Lucy 131,132
FISH
  Jimsey 47,48,49,50,51
  Jinsey 47,48,49
  Lizzie 47,48,51
  Suckey 47,48
  Sucky 47,48,49,51
  Susie 49,50
FIXICO
  Watty 140
FLEET
  Alice J 130
  James H 130
  John J 130
FLETCHER
  W A 243
FOWLER
  J W 76,77,131,132,166
FRANK
  Albert 137,138,139
  Alfred 80,140,141,142
  Jane 134,136
  Johnson 137,138,139,140, 141,142
  Sissie 137,139,140,142

Sissy 138,141,142
FREEMAN
   Codela 326
   Cordelia 325
   Cordelia A 326
   Ezra 325,326
   Hovah Monroe 325,326
FUSEKA 249
FUS-EKA 252,253
FUS-E-KA 250

GARRIGUES
   Anna 27,31,103,278,294
GAUDEN
   N L 58
GHAHAN
   Mattie Emily 235,236
GIBSON
   Ethel 192,193
   Joseph B 192,193
   N Z 5
   William S 192,193
   Wm S 192
GOAT
   Alfred 97
   A F 140
   John R 135
   Roman 252
   W A 140
   Wardley 97
GRAT
   W R 80
GRAY
   Walter 105,106,108
GREEN
   Mandy 60
GRIESEL
   E C 48,129,194,206
   E D 49
   Edw 186
   Edw C 1,20,30,40,44,45,48,49,50, 52,55,57,65,77,78,91,118,126,129, 137,154,161,169,183,192,195,196 ,212,250,254,278,304,313

HAILEY
   Maude 28
HAINS
   H G 47
   Henry G 40,118,164,294
HALE
   N A 39
HALEY
   Mrs 19,20
   R L 21
HARJO
   Ah 211,212,213,214,215, 216,218
   Alice 313,314,318,319
   Amanda 308,311
   Amey 265,266,267,268
   Amos 267,268
   Amy 265
   Bumkey 197,198,199,200,203
   Bunkey 196,204
   Cheparne 185,313
   Cheparney . 186,187,188,256,257, 314,315,318,319
   Chepon 256,257
   Chof o lup 265,266,267,268
   Chofalop 268
   Chofalup 268
   Chofolop 264
   Chofolup 268
   Cinda .. 195,196,197,198,199,200, 201,203,204
   Dana 264,268,269
   E liza 215
   Eliza 213,216,217,218,219
   Emey 268
   Fannie 264
   Fanny 264,266,267
   Hannah 207,208,210
   Hepsey 32
   Ida 211,212,213,215,216,217,218,219

Index

Josie...........196,197,199,200,201, 203,204
Leetchee 307,311
Lilla 31
Lindy 276
Liza......210,211,212,214,215,216
Lizzie..154,155,188,256,257,313, 314,315,316,318,319
Nokos 67
Sunday.......210,211,213,214,215, 216,217,218
Tarkosar................................. 5
Una see 265
Unasee 265
Willie..........315,316,317,318,319
Wilson 185,186,187,188
Winnie.......195,197,198,201,203, 204
Wysenda 173

HARLAN
  John 145
HARRISON
  Bettie 95,96,97,98
  Lena 151
  Peter....................95,96,97,98
  R P 144,145
  Rhoda 95,96,97,98
HASTON
  W S 5
HERD
  Maria 61
HERROD
  Cilla 59,60
  Maria 60,61,62,63,64
HICKS
  B N 109
HILL
  George 152
  Hilly 152
  Mitchell 152
HINES
  Will S 122,123
HIPICO
  Watty 80
HOWELL
  H A 112
  H A, MD 112
HULLIE
  Dave 118
  Eliza 118
  Tarpie 118
HULSEY
  Lousanna 301
HUNTER
  R C 39
HUTKA
  Lizzie 314

INTIE 8

JACK
  Allice 42
JACKSON
  Annie R 7
  Anton 111,112
  Diamond 111,112
  R 321
  Sallie 112
  Sally 111,112
  Susie 89,93
  W R 155
JACOBE
  Elizabeth 298
JACOBS
  John A 69
JAY
  Thad 237
JENNINGS
  S P 279,280,281
JOBE
  G W 41,53
  G W, MD 41
JOHN
  Alice 194,205,206
  Eliza 118
  Hotulke 118

Lena 205,206
McCulley 205
McCully 206
Wesley 118
JOHNSON
Caesar 118
JONES
Goliah 106,107,113,115,120
Goliath 116
S F 128
JORDAN
Lula A 54,56,58
Lula A Perryman 56,58

KELSEY
Agent 326
KENDRICK
Mrs M E 145
KENERL
George 179
KENNEDY
Nancy Ann 237
KERNAL
Freeman 181
George 181
KERNEL
Arra 172,176,177
Arreta 174,175
Arretta 169,172,173,175,176,
179,182
Freeman 169,172,179,182
George 169,172,173,174,175,
176,179,180,182
Harry ... 174,175,176,177,179,182
KERNELL
George 175
KERNELLS 180
Arretta 168,170,171,172,175,
176,177,179,181
Erretta 178
Freeman 168,170,178,179,181
George 168,170,171,172,176,
177,178,179,181

Harry ... 168,171,172,176,177,178
KING
R F 46
KIZZIE 118,119

LACY
A J 22,24
LAMB
F E 128
N P 128
LANGSTON
W Y 270,271
LARNEY
Alfred 201
LEADER
Allice 114,115
Barney 263
Dave 114,115,116
Jennie 263
Lizzie 115,116
Lucy 322
Nancy 99,100,107,110,113,
114,115,116
Nannie 102
Sosee 112,113,114
Tilda 263
LEE
David A 22,24,25
LEWIS
Kizzie 226
LIKOWSKI
Senora E 166
Simon 76
LINN
C P 298
LONE
Cendey 109
LONG
Anna 260,261,262
Cinda 239
Eliza 237,238,239
Henry 86,260,261,262
Losanna 260,261,262

Index

Newman 237,238,239
Noah 237,238
LOSELUSE 109
LOTT
  Jennie........................ 117
  Lucy........................ 117
  Tena........................ 117
  Tommie 117
LOWE
  Andy........................ 101
  Columbus 100,110
  Jennie......98,99,100,101,102,104, 105,106,107,108,109,110,111
  Jno W 37
  Jno W, MD 37
  Joe 99
  Joseph........................ 101
  Mary 103,115,120
  Mille 101
  Millie 99
  Salle........................ 108
  Sallie.....99,100,101,102,103,104, 105,106,107,108,109,110,113,116
  Tobeler 106,107,111
  Tobler...99,100,101,102,103,104, 105,106,107,108,109,110
  Washington........................ 189
LOWERY
  Lucy Taylor 5
LOWRY
  Amos 1,2,3,4,5,6
  John 1,2,3,4,6
  Lucy........................ 1,2,3,4,6
LUMPKIN
  C W 235,236
LUMSEY 8
LYNCH
  Robert E 43,44

MCADOO
  W C 23,24,26
MCBRIDE
  Veldoni 13
Wm D 13
MCCOSAR
  Arthur 229,230,231,232
  Bunnie 230,231,232,233,234
  Bunny 230
  Burnie..........67,135,229,252,253, 271,295,296
  Henry........................ 233,234
  Nellie..........229,230,231,232,233
MCCOY
  Ida........................ 158,159
  Nettie 158
  Robert Elihu 159,160
  W A 147,149
  William A 158,159
MCDANIEL
  Henry A 128
MCDERMOTT
  J ....8,28,31,48,49,59,61,80,89, 104,155,164,165,167,174,194,195, 199,200,202,203,206,278,288,310 ,321
  Jesse 7,60,77,78,101,110,129, 194,201,206,218,278,320
  L H 289
MCFARLAN
  R M 5
MCGASLIN
  Jennie 36
MCGEE
  George 32,34,35
  Hepsey................30,31,32,34,35
  John 30,32,34,35
MCGERT
  Daniel 99
MCGIRT
  Buckner 86,87
  Hepsey...13,15,16,17,18,220,221, 222,223,225,226
  John 86,87,101
  Linda 86,261
  Lindy 87
  Mongie 101

Index

MCINTOSH
  Isaiah 183
  Isaiah J 183,184
  John 183,184
  Marry 184
  Mary 183,184
MCKAN
  George 30,31,32,36
  Georger 33
  Hepsey 30,31,33,35
  John 30,31,33,35
  William 30
MCKANE
  Epsey 29
  Hepsey 33
  John 29
  William 29,33
MCKENNON
  Archibald S 259
MCKENNON & WILLMOTT .. 180
MCNEVINS
  Flora 299,300
  Lee 299,300,301
  Nancy 299,300,301
  Willie Blay 301
  Willie Clay 300
MCPERRYMAN ... 293,295,296,297
MCPHERSON
  Dr J M 130
MALOT
  H G 265,266,267,268,276,277
MANES
  William H 43
  William H, MD 43
MANVILLE
  M T 144
MARKS
  George 6,7
  John 6,7
  Martha 6,7
MARS
  H L 56,58
MARSEY 8

Katie 8
MARTIN
  William T 102,105,106,108
MERRICK
  Lona 47
MICKEY 293,295,297
MIKEY
  Amey 265,266,267,268
  Amy 265
  Marfy 291
  Marphy 287
  Marsy 289
  Martha 288
  Silwar 289
MILLER
  Daisy 54,58
  Daisy Childers 55,56,57,58,59
  H W 13
  Houston 199,200
  J Y 8,55,118,304
  James 58
  Jennie 11,12
  John 236
  L M 5
  Savil H 130,131
  Virgie 56
MILLS
  B H 145,146,147,189,190,307,
  308,309
MOORE
  Edward L 41
MORTON
  Joseph C 21
MYERS
  James B 162

NARCOMEY
  Alice 226,227
  Kizzie 226,227
  Thomas 226,227
NARCOMIE
  Kizzie 226
NAVE

335

Index

Alice 235,236,237
John Calvin...............235,236,237
Nara............................... 235,236
Otha............................. 236,237
OKFUSKY
  Leah............................... 314
OSBORN
  C M............................. 131,132

PARRISH
  Zera Ellen 20
PENTER
  Jemmima 207,208,209,210
  Kogee 209
  Tom 209
PERRYMAN
  Alex 293,294,295,296,297
  Annie 293
  Eli 293,294,295
  Lewis 293,295,296,297
  Sophia.........293,294,295,296,297
PETER
  Jennie....64,65,66,67,69,70,71,72,
  73,74,75
PHELPS
  R 147
PHILLIPS
  John H 289,290
POLEMAN
  Young................................... 28
POSEY.. 40
  Alex 2,3,9,17,29,30,32,64,65,
  66,68,70,71,73,79,81,87,88,91,92,
  93,96,97,98,99,100,101,111,117,
  119,126,127,134,138,148,151,152,
  153,154,158,160,161,162,163,171
  ,172,177,185,188,191,195,196,
  197,198,199,200,202,210,212,214,
  222,226,227,232,239,249,253,254
  ,255,262,263,269,272,277,280,
  282,293,295,297,302,304,305,307,
  313,314,315,316,320,322

Henry...39
Henry A........................38,40,41
Mary E...............................40,41
May 38
William Edward............38,40,41
PUNTKA........199,200,201,202,203
  Cinda...199,200,201,202,203,205
  Eliz...201
  Josie.................200,201,202,205
  Winey......................199,203,205
  Winnie..................................201

RED
  D J..121
RENFRO
  Tillie..38
RIDER
  Chas..........68,69,80,135,136,140,
  213,214,230,231,246,248,249,253,
  271,273,275,279,281,283,295,296
RILEY
  Claud...142,145,146,149,150,151
  Claud A 143
  Henry E 142,143,147,148
  Henry Earl 145,146,147
  Horace 142,143,144,145,146,
  148,150,151
  Horace R 146,147,148,149
  Mattie 142,143,145,146,147,
  148,149,150,151
ROBBINS
  Mrs 60
ROBISON
  Hilly 152
RUDER
  Chas.....................................252

SANDERS
  Jim..309
  N L 56
SARFARTS CHA....................276
SAWYER
  Polley 228

336

SCOTT
- James 261
- Lola 10
- Mahoye 10
- Nancy 300
- William 10

SELF
- Cordelia A 325,326
- Martha A 326

SEWELL
- Louisa 151
- Sophia 294,296
- Thos 279,280,281,282,283

SHANK
- W H 39

SHIELDS
- Charles J 23,24,25,26

SHIPLEY
- Coejagie 13,15,16,17,18,19

SHUDER
- Robert 31

SILWAR 265,266,267,268, 287,290,291

SIMMER
- Hinner 208
- Hinney 207,209,210
- Jemmima 207,208,209,210
- John 207,208,209,210

SIMON
- Cheparne 153
- Cheparney 154,155,156,157

SIMPSON
- Mary Emiline 149

SIMS
- E W 325,326

SIMSON
- Mary Emiline 146

SKAGGS
- D C ..... 1,2,3,9,17,30,32,65,66,68, 70,79,81,87,89,91,92,93,97,98,99, 101,119,125,126,127,137,138,148, 151,152,153,154,158,160,161,163 ,169,171,172,177,186,188,191, 195,196,197,198,199,200,211,212, 214,222,226,227,232,239,249,250 ,253,254,255,262,263,269,272, 277,280,282,295,297,302,304,305, 307,313,314,315,316,322
- Drennan C ....2,3,7,9,17,32,36,37, 38,70,81,87,88,92,93,94,98,112, 118,126,127,133,134,138,148,150, 151,152,153,154,158,159,160,163 ,170,171,172,177,184,188,191, 197,198,199,200,212,214,222,226, 227,232,233,234,239,240,244,247 ,248,253,255,262,263,264,269, 272,274,280,282,294,295,297,298, 299,300,301,302,304,305,307,314 ,315,316,317,322

SMITH 238
- Lou 170,172,177
- M T 193
- O D 69

SNAKE 160

SPANIARD
- James 117

SPRINGER
- J D 61

STEEN
- Samantha 20,22,23,24,25,26

STEVENSON
- Maggie 243
- Mrs B A 242

STEWART
- Lucy 300,301
- M E 147

STIDHAM
- Liza 118
- Mattie 118
- Timmie 106,107,113,115,116, 118,120

STOUT
- Mattie 46
- Mrs Mattie 45

STUBBLEFIELD
- Ed 302

Index

Lousanna 302
McAfee 302
STUBLEFIELD
  Ed 301
  Lousanna 301,302
  McAfee 301,302
STUCKEY 40
  Mary 39

TABORN
  Albert 242
  Calvin 241,242,243
  Gertie 241,242,243
  Gertrude 242
  Nancy 241,242,243
TAR YO LEY 287
  Frank 287
TAR YO-LEY 287
TARMOCHEE 8
TARYOLE 289
  Louina 289
  Lowine 289
TARYOLEY 287,289
TARYO-LEY
  Frank 287
TARYOLEY
  Louina 291,292
  Lowina 289
  Lowine 290,292
  Lowiney 291
  Marphy 287
  Marphy Maggie 287
  Prince 291,292
  Prinne 290
TARYOLY
  Prince 290
TATE
  Deck 239,240
  Joseph 239,240
  Mary 239,240
TAYLOR
  Eli 77,78
  Ely 76

Liza 77,78
Lucy 5
Sarpecy 78
Sarpsey 77,78
Serpsy 76
Sorply 76
TAYOLA
  Louina 288,293
  Martha 288,292
  Prince 288,292
THOMAS
  Eliza 76
  Katie 76
  Malind 76
  Malinda 76
  Matilda 259
THORN
  E M 173
TIGER
  Cinda 79,80,81,82,83,84,85
  Cindy 84,85
  Cogee 91,92
  Emma 277,278,280,281,282,
283,284,286
  John 79,80,81,82,83,84,85,140
  Josiah 2
  Kizzie 277,278,279,280,281,
282,283,284,285,286
  Lizzie 5
  Lucy 2
  Melinda 227
  Minnie 153,154,156,157
  Nina 277,278,279,280,283,
284,285,286
  Nine 279,280,285
  Panoska 279,280,281,283
  Panosky 278,279,280,282,
283,284
  Parnoskey 285
  Parnosky 286
  Ponoska 277
  Roman 153,154,155,156,157
  Selanie 79,80,81,82,83,84,85

Index

TODD
- Arthur Lee 245,247,248,249
- Bertha 243,244,245,246
- J W 296
- James 244,245,246,247,248
- Katie 244
- Katy 244,245,246,247,248

TRIPOLE 289

VARION
- Sarah 13

WA TA SHE 194
- Rosa 194

WALKER
- Bettie 240
- Ellen 228

WALLACE
- E A 257
- Nellie 230

WALLOW
- Nellie 230
- Sally 230,231,232
- Wiley 230

WARNER
- Frank L 223,224,225

WASHINGTON
- Alfred 60,61,63,64
- Ralph 59,60,61,62,63
- Wallace 60

WATASHE
- Joe 194
- Lucy 206
- Rosa 194,206

WATTUSE
- Lucy 206
- Rosa 206

WEEDN
- S P 202,203

WHITE
- Lizzie 314

WHITMAN
- W W 243

WILLHITE
- J N 131,132,166

WILLIAMS
- Benjamin Franklin 133,134
- Charley 132,135,136
- Emma 132,133,135,136,263
- John Randolph 132,135,136
- Nat 146,147,149,150,189,190, 307,308,309

WILLMOTT
- Jno W 173
- John W 169,173,176,256,257, 259
- Rachael 272

WILLS
- Hazel I 122
- Hazel Irene 121
- Henry F 121,122
- Joseph 164,165,166,167
- Lillie 164,165
- Lilly 164,166
- Mary A 121,122
- Nancy 165,166,167
- Sandy 167,168

WILSON
- Bettie 118
- H C 44,45,46
- Lucy 44,45,46
- Minnie 118
- Robert Henry 44,45,46
- Thomas 118
- Wisey 118

WINSTON
- J A 27,28
- James A 27

WISEY 8
- E D C 86

WOOD
- Wilford E 23,24,26

WPPD
- Wilford E 25

YAHOLA

Rhoda 98
YARGE
   Amos 8
YARGEE
   Allice 42
   Amos 7,8,9
   Anna 9
   Annie 8
   Cully 7,8,9
   Elizabeth 42
   George 17
   George Washington 42
   Katie 8
   Katy 9
YARHOLA
   Maula 132
YORGEE
   Amos 10
   Culley 10
   Katie 10

www.ingramcontent.com/pod-product-compliance
Lightning Source LLC
Chambersburg PA
CBHW020243030426
42336CB00010B/588